POETS AND THE

C000155672

On January 18 1914, seven male poets gathered to eat a peacock. W. B. Yeats and Ezra Pound, the celebrities of the group, led four lesser-known poets to the Sussex manor house of the man they were honouring, Wilfrid Scawen Blunt, the poet, horse-breeder, Arabist, and anti-imperialist married to Byron's only granddaughter. In this story of the curious occasion that came to be known as the "peacock dinner," immortalized in the famous photograph of the poets standing in a row, Lucy McDiarmid writes a literary history derived from intimacies rather than "isms." The dinner evolved from three close literary friendships, those between Pound and Yeats, Yeats and Lady Gregory, and Lady Gregory and Blunt, whose romantic affair thirty years earlier was unknown to the others. Through close readings of unpublished letters, diaries, memoirs, and poems, in an argument at all times theoretically informed, McDiarmid reveals the way marriage and adultery, as well as friendship, offer ways of transmitting the professional culture of poetry. Like the women who are absent from the photograph, the poets at its edges (F.S. Flint, Richard Aldington, Sturge Moore, and Victor Plarr) are also brought into the discussion, adding interest by their very marginality. This is literary history told with considerable style and brio, often comically aware of the extraordinary alliances and rivalries of the "seven male poets" but attuned to significant issues in coterie formation, literary homosociality, and the development of modernist poetics from late-Victorian and Georgian beginnings. *Poets and the Peacock Dinner* is written with critical sophistication and a wit and lightness that never compromise on the rich texture of event and personality.

Lucy McDiarmid is Marie Frazee-Baldassarre Professor of English at Montclair State University. The recipient of fellowships from the Guggenheim Foundation, the Cullman Center for Scholars and Writers at the New York Public Library, and the National Endowment for the Humanities, she is the author or editor of seven books. Her scholarly interest in cultural politics, especially quirky, colorful, suggestive episodes, is exemplified by *The Irish Art of Controversy* as well as by *Poets and the Peacock Dinner*. She is also a former president of the American Conference for Irish Studies. Her most recent book is *At Home in the Revolution: what women said and did in 1916*.

'This fascinating and original book explores the complex dynamics of friendship, mentoring, rivalry, and professionalization among a group of men and illuminates the central but often invisible role that women played in mediating those dynamics. Wide-ranging and meticulously observed, rigorous and imaginative, *Poets and the Peacock Dinner* is a masterful combination of literary history, biography, and cultural theory.'

Marjorie Howes, Boston College

'This captivating book confers its rightful importance on the event commemorated in the title. From the event itself, the author conjures up a cast of characters, real men and women involved collectively as cultural participants and individually as collaborators, friends, and lovers.'

Marie Boroff, Yale University

'A splendid book in every respect . . . truly grown-up feminist criticism.'

Adrian Frazier, National University of Ireland, Galway

'[A]n excellent book which deserves to be widely-read . . . . with a strong narrative construction and with much fascinating biographical and historical material which is nevertheless critically sophisticated and at all times theoretically aware.'

Matthew Campbell, University of York

'An absorbing work of rigorous scholarship consistently enlivened by a sharp and delightful wit . . . Few indeed are the books which so substantially vindicate the most ambitious claims of literary-historical scholarship.'

Edward Larrissy, Queen's University, Belfast

'McDiarmid's book is a highly original work of literary sociology . . . McDiarmid has cast her net widely for the published and unpublished sources that provide the details of her story, and she hauls it in with a sure hand and a lively and lucid prose style that bear her considerable learning lightly.'

Matthew Sperling, *Literary Review*

'a lively, engaging account of the dinner, its varied significances, and its participants. Highly recommended.'

G. Grieve-Carlson, *Choice*

'There is a strong Irish element to the background of this story, and no one is better placed or qualified than McDiarmid, with her deep knowledge of Irish cultural history, to unravel and clarify the details and complexities . . . scholarly and engaging.'

Michael Copp, *New Canterbury Literary Society News*

'The occasion in January 1914 when seven poets headed by Yeats and Pound sat down to a dinner of peacock in honour of the ageing poet and public agitator Wilfrid Scawen Blunt is a key moment in literary history. Or so it emerges in Lucy McDiarmid's brilliant exploration of the event. With her extraordinary flair for imaginative scholarship, she illuminates the origins and precedents for the peacock dinner, the offstage role of Lady Gregory, Yeats's close friend and Blunt's former lover, in organising this all-male gathering, the rivalries and alliances in those invited and excluded, and its long-term significance in terms of the genealogies of poetic modernism. Whatever the roast peacock tasted like, this is a book to be savoured and enjoyed.'

Nicholas Grene, Trinity College Dublin

'From a minor incident, one lunch eaten by seven male poets, Lucy McDiarmid serves up a literary historical analysis of major importance. The pivotal role played by a woman who wasn't one of the diners sustains this sophisticated reading of sexual intimacies, cultural transmission, modernist poetics, and literary professionalism. *Poets and The Peacock Dinner* is also utterly delicious: only McDiarmid can deliver a concoction at once this erudite and sexy, offering page-turning consumption in the time it takes to eat a long lunch but lingering satisfaction for much longer.'

Margaret Mills Harper, University of Limerick

'The book grapples with the complexities of art, politics, and the "male homosocial friendships" that permeate literary history . . . McDiarmid brings into focus a world on the brink of change and an event that managed to connect the pre- and post-Victorian world by traditionally paying homage to the literary past while making way for the poets of tomorrow.'

Matthew Skwiat, *Irish America*

POETS & THE PEACOCK DINNER

The Literary History of a Meal

LUCY McDIARMID

OXFORD
UNIVERSITY PRESS

Great Clarendon Street, Oxford, OX2 6DP,
United Kingdom

Oxford University Press is a department of the University of Oxford.
It furthers the University's objective of excellence in research, scholarship,
and education by publishing worldwide. Oxford is a registered trade mark of
Oxford University Press in the UK and in certain other countries

First published 2014
First published in paperback 2016

Impression: 1

Published in the United States of America by Oxford University Press
198 Madison Avenue, New York, NY 10016, United States of America

British Library Cataloguing in Publication Data
Data available

Library of Congress Cataloging in Publication Data
Data available

ISBN 978–0–19–872278–6 (Hbk.)
ISBN 978–0–19–878833–1 (Pbk.)

Printed in Great Britain by
Ashford Colour Press Ltd, Gosport, Hampshire

For Frank

Acknowledgments

The Dorothy and Lewis B. Cullman Center for Scholars and Writers at the New York Public Library granted me a fellowship in 2005–2006 that gave me access to all the Library's research collections, and I am ever grateful for the year I spent in those marble halls. Most of the unpublished letters by Wilfrid Blunt, Lady Gregory, and W. B. Yeats that I cite in this book were transcribed that year from the originals in the Berg Collection. I would like to thank Jean Strouse, Pamela Leo, and Adriana Nova for their help and support, and all the other fellows for their lively conversation, good ideas, and a few stories that I continue to dine out on.

The Marie Frazee-Baldassarre Chair has provided financial support for all aspects of my work on this book since 2009. As the first person to hold this generous professorship, I am grateful to the Department of English at Montclair State University for honoring me with it.

Although I wasn't present for the peacock dinner, I got close: in 1995 I shared a taxi with Anne Yeats; I have a letter from Catherine Aldington Guillaume (in 2004) giving me permission to quote a poem of her father's; Frank Flint's grandson Oliver Flint and granddaughter Siddhimala (Linda Flint) have written giving me permission to quote from unpublished letters written by their grandfather; Mary de Rachewiltz, Ezra Pound's daughter, sent me a lovely message, saying that she still had "a copy of the famous photograph" and offering to "sacrifice a peacock" when I visit Brunnenburg; Leonie Sturge-Moore and Charmian O'Neil, executors for their grandfather Thomas Sturge Moore, have blessed this book; and in 1995 I spent a day with Lady Gregory's granddaughters, the late Anne Gregory de Winton and the late Catherine Kennedy. Closest of all was my visit to Newbuildings Place: on a bright, crisp spring day in 2009, Wilfrid Blunt's great-grandson, the fifth Earl of Lytton, and the Countess of Lytton generously entertained me in their house, showing me the room in which the peacock dinner was eaten, the wall against which the famous photograph was taken, and Blunt's grave.

Only Victor Plarr of the seven poets at the dinner has left no heirs or executors, but I have unearthed both books written by his daughter Marion Plarr (Barwell) and comment on them in Chapter 5.

For taking the time to read and critique the entire manuscript at an early stage, I would like to thank three friends, Maria DiBattista, Adrian Frazier, and Nicholas Grene. In their different ways, each recognized what I was after in this book and offered suggestions accordingly.

I am grateful to my hosts on the occasions when I gave talks based on material in this book, beginning in 2001: Rebecca Beasley at the London Modernism Seminar, Christy Burns at the College of William and Mary (Sara and Jess Cloud Professorship lecture), the members of the Columbia Irish Studies Seminar, Claire Connolly at University College Cork, Declan Foley at the Third John Butler Yeats Seminar, Adrian Frazier at the Synge Summer School, Geraldine Higgins at Emory University and the Yeats International Summer School, Emily Isaacs and Naomi Liebler at the inaugural Marie Frazee-Baldassarre Lecture at Montclair State University, Andy McGowan of the W. B. Yeats Society of New York, Ronnie O'Gorman and Marion Cox at the Lady Gregory Autumn Gathering, Jean Strouse and Pamela Leo at the Cullman Center for Scholars and Writers, and Mary Helen Thuente at North Carolina State University.

Without the many kinds of support offered by my assistant Janet Dengel (research and accounting, among others) I couldn't have managed anything, and I am eternally grateful to her. For wise and careful help with the proofs of this book, and for years of friendship, I am also grateful to Nancy Pepper. I would also like to thank Michael Copp for sending me much useful information about Frank Flint, James Kelly for reviewing my transcriptions of Blunt's diaries, and Alec Marsh for answering many questions about Ezra Pound. James Longenbach's excellent *Stone Cottage: Pound, Yeats, and Modernism* has been of great help, and I feel lucky that I've had it to refer to. I was also lucky to have met Geoffrey O'Byrne White, who generously offered me an image of his grand-aunt Lady Gregory's painting of Galway Gaol.

For other help of various kinds, thanks are due to Lauren Arrington, Lee Behlman, Veronica Crolius Boswell, Angela Bourke, Helen Carr, Rimi B. Chatterjee, Patricia Coughlan, Jared Curtis, Julie Dalley, Mia Foster, Jonathan Franzen, Christine Froula, Peter Gay, David Getsy, Arin Gilbert, Jonathan Greenberg, Saskia Hamilton, Margaret Mills Harper, Samuel Hynes, Alice Kelly, Declan Kiberd, Declan Kiely, Harold Koda, Maureen Lees, Ann Lesch, Wendy Lesser, Ed Maggs, Tricia Matthew, Sarah McKibben, Deirdre McMahon, Mount Mansfield Maple Products, Wendy Nielsen, Eunan O'Halpin, Tina O'Toole, James Pethica, William Pratt, Yopie Prins, Suzanne Raitt, Robert Rubin, Ann Saddlemyer, Nicole Scimone, Sharon Setzer, Lauren Shohet, Bonnie Slotnick, Colin Smythe, Judith Walkowitz, and Maureen Waters. My dearly missed friend Pat Sheeran, who died in 2001, would have loved hearing about the peacock dinner. His essay "Wilfrid Scawen Blunt: A Tourist of the Revolutions" remains as a sign of his interest in Blunt, as well as a comment he once made to me about Blunt's play *Fand*: "It's a curious thing. You ought to take a look at it." I hadn't then, but I have since.

Here and there in this book I have drawn on earlier work of my own: "The Demotic Lady Gregory" (*High and Low Moderns: Literature and Culture 1889–1939*, 1996); "Lady Gregory, Wilfrid Blunt, and London Table Talk" (*Irish University Review*, 2004); "A Box for Wilfrid Blunt" (*PMLA*, 2005); and, most recently, "Resentment on the Menu: Poets of the Peacock Dinner" (*The Times Literary Supplement*, 2014). Thanks to Anne Fogarty, Judy Goulding, Alan Jenkins, and Eric Worth for their editorial expertise. Thanks also to the many librarians and archivists who have helped my work on this book: Isaac Gewirtz, Curator, Anne Garner, and Philip Milito at the Berg Collection of the New York Public Library; Stella Panayotova and Emma Darbyshire at the Fitzwilliam Museum, Cambridge; Justine E. Sundaram at the John J. Burns Library, Boston College; Declan Kiely, Robert H. Taylor Curator and Department Head, Literary and Historical Manuscripts, The Morgan Library & Museum; Richard Watson at the Harry Ransom Center, The University of Texas at Austin; Timothy Murray, University of Delaware Library; and Frances Lansley, West Sussex Record Office.

I am grateful to the staff at Oxford University Press (UK), especially Jacqueline Baker and Rachel Platt, who answered emails with admirable speed and watched over my manuscript with kind attention. I also thank them for choosing Fiona Barry to help me with the proofs in the final stages.

And finally: I couldn't have written this book without Frank Miata's loving companionship and close reading. Even when I woke him up at two in the morning to ask questions like "What would Adorno have thought of Lady Gregory?" he was polite, though not always loquacious. He has certainly earned the dedication.

For permission to quote from unpublished or copyright texts, grateful acknowledgment is made to the Henry W. and Albert A. Berg Collection of English and American Literature, The New York Public Library, Astor, Lenox, and Tilden Foundations, for quotations from unpublished letters by W. S. Blunt, Lady Gregory, and W. B. Yeats; the Harry Ransom Center, The University of Texas at Austin, Oliver Flint, and Siddhimala (Linda Flint) for quotations from the Flint Papers; University of Delaware Library, Newark, Delaware for quotation from Victor Plarr's inscription in Ezra Pound's *A Quinzaine for This Yule*; Fitzwilliam Museum, University of Cambridge, for quotations from W. S. Blunt's unpublished diaries; the National Library of Ireland for quotations from W. S. Blunt's poem on Roger Casement in the McGarrity Papers; Leonie Sturge-Moore and Charmian O'Neil for permission to quote from the poetry of Thomas Sturge Moore; New Directions Publishing Corporation and Faber and Faber Ltd for permission to quote "Homage to Wilfrid Blunt" and "The Return" by Ezra Pound, from *Collected Early Poems*, copyright 1976 by The Ezra Pound Literary Property Trust; for permission to quote lines from "Hugh Selwyn Mauberley" by Ezra Pound, from *Personae*, copyright 1926 by Ezra Pound, and for permission to quote lines from Canto LXXXI by Ezra Pound, from *The Cantos of Ezra Pound*, copyright 1948 by Ezra Pound; West Sussex Record Office, for quotations from WSRO Blunt Mss Box 21. Quotations from Lady Gregory's letters and poems are made with the kind permission of Colin Smythe Ltd. "In the Via Sestina" by Richard Aldington is reproduced by kind permission of the Estate of Richard Aldington, care of Rosica Colin Limited, London.

For permission to reproduce images, acknowledgment is made to the Earl and Countess of Lytton; Geoffrey O'Byrne White; Syndics of the Fitzwilliam Museum, Cambridge; The New York Public Library/ Art Resource, New York; the Dorset County Museum, Dorchester; the Henry W. and Albert A. Berg Collection, The New York Public Library, Astor, Lenox, and Tilden Foundations; Freer Gallery of Art, Smithsonian Institution, Washington, D.C.; the British Library Board; Oliver Flint and Siddhimala (Linda Flint); Colin P. Smythe; West Sussex Record Office.

Every effort has been made to trace copyright holders and to obtain their permission for the use of copyright material. I apologize for any errors or omissions and would be grateful to be notified of corrections that should be incorporated in future reprints or editions of this book.

Contents

List of Illustrations

List of Abbreviations

AG	Augusta Gregory (Lady Gregory)
CL	*The Collected Letters*
DW	Dorothy Wellesley
EP	Ezra Pound
FSF	F. S. (Frank) Flint
HB	Hilaire Belloc
NYPL	The New York Public Library
OBMV	*The Oxford Book of Modern Verse*
OED	*The Oxford English Dictionary*
TLS	*The Times Literary Supplement*
WBY	William Butler Yeats
WSB	Wilfrid Scawen Blunt

Prologue
Seven Poets and a Peacock

I

On 18 January 1914, seven poets gathered to eat a peacock.

The meal was organized as a tribute to the handsome man with the impressive white beard in the center of the photograph: Wilfrid Scawen Blunt, the Sussex landowner, horse-breeder, and poet married to Byron's only granddaughter, Lady Anne Isabella King-Noel. He was also an Arabist and anti-imperialist, proud to have saved the life of the Egyptian nationalist Urabi and to have been the first Englishman who "suffered even the shortest imprisonment for

Figure 1. Wilfred Scawen Blunt's personal copy of the photograph from the dinner honoring him. Private collection.

Ireland's sake." The six other poets (from left to right) were Victor Plarr (1863–1929), Thomas Sturge Moore (1870–1944), W. B. Yeats, Ezra Pound, Richard Aldington (1892–1962), and F. S. (Frank) Flint (1885–1960). They rented a car from Harrods for £5 and drove from London to Newbuildings Place, Blunt's manor house in Horsham, West Sussex, arriving at 12:30 p.m. Blunt served them roast peacock and roast beef; the poets gave him a marble box designed by Henri Gaudier-Brzeska containing samples of their poems and engraved "Homage to W. S. BLVNT."

John Masefield and Frederic Manning were also invited and contributed poems but did not attend the dinner. Blunt's neighbor Lord Osborne de Vere Beauclerk joined the company for dinner, and Hilaire Belloc arrived at tea time, drinking claret from "a large crystal goblet." The day was cloudy and cold, with temperatures in the thirties, but after the meal the sun came out briefly, and the poets stood against the old stone wall to be photographed (Figure 1). They left at 5:00 p.m.[1]

Accounts of the afternoon were published in five periodicals, and Blunt was surprised to see one in *The Times* several days later. Its placement on page five made it "look like a really important event," he wrote in his diary. His comment suggests that he had not until then seen the dinner as "important." To Lady Gregory, who helped arrange the event, Blunt had written gratefully, "I found all of them interesting and hope they will come down again separately that I may make their acquaintance better. I feel that I owe this most agreeable little fete to you." To his friend Sydney Cockerell at the Fitzwilliam Museum, he wrote, "I can't make out what brought them down to *me* or who suggested the idea." But, he continued, "they all meant it most kindly and were really capital fellows, with wit and intelligence, and I feel they will be an addition to my weekend life here."[2]

Why was this friendly Sunday afternoon visit of "capital fellows," this "little fete," worthy of an article in *The Times*? Or for that matter, why is it worthy of a book? Its main organizers, Pound and Yeats, obviously thought it was important, because they saw to it that the dinner was publicized and photographed. It was a "really important event" to Pound especially, who liked the photograph so much that he requested extra copies and sent one back to America for the office of *Poetry* magazine. One of the accounts of the tribute to Blunt was planted in the *Boston Evening Transcript*, so the news was out on both sides of the Atlantic.[3]

It was the photograph that first drew me in, the odd symmetry, the serious faces, the formal poses, against a beautiful wall with each stone visible in separate relief. And who were those men at the edges, whose names I could never seem to remember? For years, off and on, I came across the picture in one book or another on modern poetry, and as I gradually accumulated bits of information about the story behind it, I was drawn further in by its quirkiness. And the more I learned about Wilfrid Scawen Blunt—his arrest in Galway, his prison sonnets, his philandering and romances, his passion for Egypt and Byron and Arab horses—the more I wanted to understand how he came to be in a picture with these particular poets, and why they ate a peacock together. Blunt seemed a character out of opera, bigger even than Falstaff, perhaps an heir to Don Giovanni, but a comic one, who wrote that he wished to "live now for myself a sober life / Loving my neighbour and my neighbour's wife."[4] Unlike Don Giovanni, Blunt died quietly in bed at home and was buried, wrapped in his favorite scorpion carpet, in the woods behind his house.

II

Blunt's beard makes obvious the generational difference between his visitors and himself. He was a Victorian, born in 1840; even the oldest of the poets, Victor Plarr, was twenty-three years younger than Blunt, and the younger poets to his left were Imagists, the newest thing in poetry. The peacock dinner took place at precisely the moment when modernism in all the arts was bursting forth: the International Exhibition of Modern Art (also known as the New York Armory Show) opened in February 1913; Stravinsky's *Sacre du Printemps* was performed by Diaghilev's Ballets Russes in May; two Imagist manifestos, "Imagisme" (by F. S. Flint) and "A Few Don'ts by an Imagist" (by Pound), had been published in *Poetry* in March 1913, and the anthology *Des Imagistes* came out in 1914, as did the first issue of *Blast*, the English Vorticist magazine. In 1913 *Du côté de chez Swann*, the first volume of Proust's *À la recherche du temps perdu*, was published, as was D. H. Lawrence's *Sons and Lovers*. Joyce's *Dubliners* and parts of *A Portrait of the Artist as a Young Man* were published the next year, as were Gertrude Stein's *Tender Buttons*, Yeats's *Responsibilities*, and Clive Bell's *Art*. Also in 1914, Vanessa Bell painted *Still Life on Corner of a Mantelpiece*, and Kafka was writing, but had not yet published, *Der Prozess*.

Blunt's taste had been formed in another era. Masefield was his favorite contemporary poet. When, after the poets left, Blunt opened the marble box and read the poems he had been given, he didn't understand them; they were "word puzzles," he wrote. Using that phrase, he sounded like the art critics who had condemned as "picture puzzles" the paintings by Picasso, Duchamp, Gleizes, Delaunay, and others at the New York Armory Show the previous year.[5] Two years earlier, in 1912, Nellie Hozier had taken Blunt to see the Futurist Exhibition at the Sackville Gallery, to which he responded (privately, in his diaries) with distaste:

These, as art, are mere nonsense, the sort of things a child might make . . . They have neither design nor drawing . . . One cannot assign a meaning to any of them, or even the suggestion of a meaning. Degeneracy cannot go further than this . . .[6]

The marble box itself, Blunt wrote Cockerell, had a "terribly paulo-post-futurist bas-relief engraved on it which I have been obliged to turn with its face to the wall." Fortunately, however, the six poets who had dined at Newbuildings "all meant it most kindly . . ."[7]

So much for the older generation; Blunt was not interested in the new styles of art. But the younger generation, especially Pound, was eager to look back, to participate in what he called the "Apostolic Succession" of poets. "Besides knowing living artists I have come in touch with the tradition of the dead," he wrote in the 1913 essay "How I Began." "[P]eople whose minds have been enriched by contact with men of genius," he continued, "retain the effects of it. I have enjoyed meeting Victorians and Pre-Raphaelites and men of the nineties through their friends. I have seen Keats'[s] proof sheets. I have had personal tradition [sic] of his time at secondhand."[8] Through his friendship with Plarr, a "man of the nineties," Pound had got to hear stories of the Rhymer Ernest Dowson, who had died in 1900, eight years before Pound arrived in London. He had also wanted "to meet certain men whose work I admired . . . I have done this. I have had good talk in plenty."

The visit to Blunt was part of this impulse, to be "enriched by contact with men of genius," to absorb the tradition of poetry by coming "in touch," literally, with living poets. Proximity was fundamental, as were the material traces of the dead, such as "Keats'[s] proof sheets." The "Apostolic Succession" was created by touch. Pound's famous description of the peacock dinner in Canto LXXXI implies that the visit was successful in this respect: he "gathered from the air a live tradition / or from a fine old eye the unconquered flame."

III

I couldn't meet Blunt, or Yeats, or Pound, or any of the others, but I could at least "come in touch" with the peacock dinner by standing in the room where it was eaten. In the spring of 2009 I visited Newbuildings Place, the seventeenth-century stone house where the dinner took place and where Blunt's great-grandson and his family live. I saw the oak-panelled room with its beamed ceiling, stone floor, and large fireplace. It was not a grand room; the scale (8.131 m long × 5.288 m wide × 3.425 m high) was such that with eight people around a table, the men must have been sitting fairly close to one another. No wonder Pound could see the "fine old eye."

It was "entirely a men's dinner," in the words of the letter broaching the idea, and the peacock dinner finds some of its significance as part of a tradition of dinners celebrating masculine achievement. Although, like the "banquet Rousseau" given in Picasso's studio in 1908, it was organized by younger artists in homage to an older one, it was not so large or so rowdy as that long evening party with its drinks, song, music, and "spontaneous display of high spirits."[9] In its formality and its emphasis on conversation, the peacock dinner was closer to Plato's feast in the Symposium; in its professional focus, it was closer to the famous "immortal dinner" of Wordsworth and Keats at the house of Benjamin Robert Haydon; and in its main symbol, it was similar to the "Peacock Feast" given in May 1914, only months after the tribute to Blunt, by Louis Comfort Tiffany in honor of "men of genius."[10] The peacock dinner was constructed collectively by Pound, Lady Gregory, Yeats, and Blunt, taking shape gradually in correspondence during December 1913 and January 1914, created without a thought of these predecessors, but it nevertheless belongs to this tradition and is illuminated by this context.

Although it may be outrageous to draw comparisons between a dinner with Socrates and one with Wilfrid Blunt, it is nevertheless the case that their formations are similar. The guests gathered at Plato's imagined feast in the Symposium, set in Athens in 416 B.C., are upper-class men of different generations, leaders of their city in politics, art, and philosophy. At the Symposium, as at the peacock dinner, the serious business of conversation does not involve women. Even the woman musician is sent out of the room so the men's talk can begin: "I next propose that the flute-girl who came in just now be dismissed: let her pipe to herself or, if she likes, to the women-folk within, but let us seek our entertainment today in conversation."[11] Like Blunt, Socrates is the oldest man present, one to whom a younger man delivers a speech of praise—Alcibiades to Socrates, Pound and Yeats to Blunt— as a culmination of the ritual. In a form of "turn-taking" not unlike the post-prandial remarks at Newbuildings Place, the speeches about love by Phaedrus, Pausanias, Eryximachus, Aristophanes, Agathon, and Socrates, and the speech of Alcibiades about Socrates, are rhetorical displays offered by men to men.[12] Central to the Symposium, as to the peacock dinner, was the transmission of knowledge from older, wiser men to younger ones through conversation.

The microtransmissions of culture that take place on such an occasion, or whenever friends are gathered intimately around a table, were especially notable at the "immortal dinner," when Keats, Charles Lamb, Wordsworth, and a few others met at the house of the painter Benjamin Robert Haydon on 28 December 1817. The original purpose was to introduce the emerging young poet John Keats to the senior, established poet William Wordsworth. A year earlier, when Haydon had volunteered to send a sonnet by Keats to Wordsworth, Keats (who had not then met Wordsworth), wrote Haydon, "The idea of your sending it to Wordsworth puts me out of breath; you know with what reverence I should send my well-wishes to him." Keats met Wordsworth two weeks before the immortal dinner at the house of Thomas Monkhouse, but the acquaintance was of course still new when they met at Haydon's. The joyful hilarity of the immortal dinner was inspired in large part by the charming, tipsy remarks of Lamb, who addressed the serious Wordsworth affectionately as "you rascally Lake poet," and the intellectual innocence of the "Comptroller of Stamps" who asked Wordsworth if he thought Milton a "great genius." It was one thing for Keats to read Wordsworth on the page and quite another to observe and hear him in real time at a dinner party. Although the conversation at the immortal dinner was less systematic and deliberate than that at the Symposium, there was nevertheless an intense and intimate conversational dynamic, recorded precisely by Haydon. On display in the room where the great Romantics ate was Haydon's monumental historical painting *Christ's Entry into*

Jerusalem. The exhibition of the painting was as much the purpose of the dinner as the introduction of the two poets.

Like Haydon, the American artist Louis Comfort Tiffany (1848–1933) gave a dinner in large part to show off his artistic work, in this case the entire domestic site, Laurelton Hall in Cold Spring Harbor, Long Island: the gardens, the enormous house, and its magnificent decoration. Like Blunt, Tiffany kept a flock of peacocks, but his interest in them was more aesthetic than agricultural: he "had them brought from the farm buildings so he could watch them walk around the grounds."[13] One of many such grand parties Tiffany gave, the dinner was all about spectacle: it featured among other theatrical effects a parade of young girls in "gauzy" gowns wearing peacock headdresses and carrying peacocks, a sight designed no doubt to please the "men of genius" being honored (Figure 2). This procession was followed by one of younger girls "also in pale

MISS PHYLLIS DE KAY AS JUNO
(Photos by Bachlitz.)

Figure 2. Phyllis de Kay entering at Louis Comfort Tiffany's "Peacock Feast," 1914. Reproduced by permission of the New York Public Library/ Art Resource, New York.

gowns with gauzelike headscarves, each carrying a torch and a bas-
ket of rose petals," and the second procession was followed by children from the same families "carrying platters of suckling pig."[14]
Peacock was not on the menu; it was part of the decoration.

There were in 1914 enough women poets to honor at a meal,
had anyone wanted to organize a peahen dinner. Such an occasion
might have included the women poets of the time who lived and
worked on the periphery of the seven poets' professional lives, all
in relationships defined by male patronage.[15] They are so numerous and so respected today, years after their deaths—many of them
certainly read more widely than Plarr, Sturge Moore, Aldington,
and Flint—that it is possible to imagine a gathering of modern
British, Irish, and American women poets: Katharine Tynan (1859–
1931), Charlotte Mew (1869–1928), Amy Lowell (1874–1925), Mina
Loy (1882–1966), Anna Wickham (1884–1947), H.D. (1886–1961),
Marianne Moore (1887–1972), Elizabeth Daryush (1887–1977), and
Sylvia Townsend Warner (1893–1978). Why didn't the peahen dinner happen? Because cultural power was in the hands of men.
Although some of these women knew one another, their networks
were not yet developed enough to provide the means, the impulse,
or the inspiration for such an occasion. Their day came, but not
in 1914.[16]

IV

Lacking the high philosophical discourse of the Symposium,
the hilarity of the immortal dinner, and the lavish theatricality
of the Tiffany event, the peacock dinner might appear to have
more in common with Georgian literary networking, especially
as imagined by Max Beerbohm in "Hilary Maltby and Stephen
Braxton" (1917). Their rivalry over an invitation to Keeb Hall, the
country house of the Duke and Duchess of Hertfordshire, reflects
all too accurately the status sought by writers through connection
to aristocratic households, as well as the cultural capital sought by
aristocrats.[17] "I want to create for myself an unpopular theatre and
an audience like a secret society where admission is by favour and
never to many," Yeats wrote in 1919; "I need a hostess."[18] Yeats's

Noh play *At the Hawk's Well* was performed in 1916, first at Lady Cunard's London house and then at Lady Islington's before an audience that included "Queen Alexandra, Princess Victoria, the Grand Duchess George of Russia, the Princess of Monaco, the Ranee of Sarawak, the Spanish ambassador, Margot Asquith, the duchess of Marlborough . . . and Lady Randolph Churchill."[19] In 1912, Pound's "Three Lectures on Medieval Poetry" were delivered in the "private gallery" of Lord and Lady Glenconner's house at Queen Anne's Gate.[20]

Lady Glenconner, the former Pamela Wyndham, was Blunt's cousin; her brother George was his close friend. Although Blunt had no title, he had many titled relations, most notably his wife Lady Anne Blunt, and most notoriously his cousin Lord Alfred Douglas. He purported to be surprised that the dinner might be considered "a really important event," but the "importance" had been mutually conferred. His was a name, however iconoclastic, to conjure with.

But there was more than status and networks animating the peacock dinner. At its heart were three intimate friendships, those between Blunt and Lady Gregory, between Lady Gregory and Yeats, and between Yeats and Pound. These intimacies spanned several generations, and all combined close physical proximity with literary partnership. Blunt and Lady Gregory had an affair for a year, beginning in the summer of 1882; he was the muse for her first published work, a feature in *The Times* on Urabi, and for a secret sonnet sequence she handed him after their last night together. Beginning in 1897, Lady Gregory and Yeats worked together over many summers in her house at Coole Park, collaborating on manifestos, essays, plays, and folklore; and of course, they founded and administered the Abbey Theatre together. Yeats and Pound lived together for three winters in Stone Cottage, Sussex, reading one another's new poems and closely involved in one another's professional lives.

These overlapping friendships made possible the peacock dinner, which originated in Pound's desire to meet Blunt. The cross-generational, transnational "men's dinner" required a woman to bring it about: the first letter about the dinner was written from Stone Cottage to Lady Gregory in Coole Park. She provided access to the great Victorian that the young American wanted to meet. The story of the peacock dinner is the story of small transmissions of poetic culture from person to person in domestic spaces. And so this book does not see literary history in terms of the traditional *isms* but in terms of intimacies.

In the pages that follow, I sketch the emerging collective sense of professionalism among poets at the time by considering the male homosocial friendships central to the Georgians and the Dymock poets ("Male Poets in Proximity"). When, in November 1913, Lady Gregory was enlisted to contact her old friend Wilfrid Blunt, she waited to invite him in person during her visit to Newbuildings after Christmas, thereby giving herself more authority as the invitation issued from her mouth ("Lady Gregory's Ideas"). Before looking at the dinner in detail, I introduce its backstory, the secret romance between Blunt and Lady Gregory that, as I see it, helped her become a writer and mellowed into the attachment that made the peacock dinner possible ("Victorian Adultery" and "A Woman's Sonnets").

With all the manuscripts, diaries, and letters now available, the dinner itself appears a more complex occasion than its published accounts implied. Its antagonisms are conveyed obliquely in the speeches delivered by its three principal participants and suggested by their arrangement in the photograph ("Alliances and Rivalries"). Lady Gregory was not the only woman present by her absence at the tribute to Blunt. The men—four of them, at any rate—were linked in an intricate pattern through the women who introduced them, those they married, and those they loved. The marble box made by Gaudier-Brzeska, with its bas-relief that Blunt didn't like, a nude woman, introduced the erotic female element otherwise missing from the dinner, as did some of the poems the poets placed inside the box ("The Naked Muse").

Anyone who has worked off and on for over ten years on a four-and-a-half-hour literary occasion is bound to see it as central to literary history, and of course I do see it that way. The peacock dinner survived not only in post-prandial correspondence but in major works by Blunt, Yeats, and Pound that reconfigure the history of poetry and implicitly define the peacock dinner as a turning point in that history ("a really important event"). Pound's *Hugh Selwyn Mauberly*, one of those texts, continues the attacks on Victor Plarr that he had voiced earlier in other contexts. Unbeknownst to Pound, however, Plarr had already attacked him in a very private poem not available until recently. By a stroke of luck, hoping to find some new scrap of information about Victor Plarr, I happened in August 2011 to google his name on one of the few days that Maggs Rare Books was advertising for sale Plarr's personal copy of Pound's 1908 book *A Quinzaine for this Yule* ("printed for Elkin Mathews by W. Pollock and Co."). On the back of the final page was a handwritten poem that could only have been by Plarr, because of its phrase "I, once Victor Plarr."

The appearance of these lines did not create much of a stir; Plarr's is not a name to conjure with. But the two quatrains, an attack on Pound's poetry, find their significance in the larger pattern of professional rivalries expressed at the peacock dinner. The only passage of poetry explicitly about the dinner is the most famous part of Pound's Canto LXXXI, "to have knocked that a Blunt should open," lines Pound wrote in 1945 when he, like Blunt, had become a prison poet ("A Live Tradition").

V

"The Great War came as a surprise," Pound observed in his *Paris Review* interview with Donald Hall, and it is worth remembering that the "storm clouds of war" were not hanging over Sussex on 18 January 1914, though it was a cloudy day. As Elizabeth Day has pointed out, ". . . in January 1914 Europe seemed to be enjoying a period of relative calm . . . The Peace Palace had recently opened in The Hague 'for the peaceful settlement of differences between peoples' and Kaiser Wilhelm of Germany was being hailed as a glorious peacemaker with 25 conflict-free years of rule behind him."[21]

Not that, of course, the peacock poets were unaffected by the war. Writing Sydney Cockerell on 8 August about his "pessimistic" view of things, Blunt added a final unhopeful note about his forthcoming *Poetical Works*, whose publication was one result of the dinner: "I am sending you . . . the corrected first proofs of my new volumes of poems—the Macmillan ones. I suppose they will not be published now till the war is over, if ever."[22] Pound wrote Harriet Monroe in November that Blunt "has barred his front door and put up a sign 'BELLIGERENTS WILL PLEASE GO ROUND TO THE KITCHEN.'"[23]

Aldington enlisted and served with the Third Royal Sussex Regiment in France but, according to one account, kept his gun unloaded at the front, "refusing . . . to participate in that massacre . . ."[24] His war novel *Death of a Hero* was published in 1929. Flint was not called up till 1918 and did not go to the front; during his postings in England and Scotland he taught French to the other soldiers and worked at "menial tasks" such as gardening and clerking.[25] Frederick Manning (who had a poem in the marble box but did not show up for dinner) served in the King's Shropshire Light Infantry, managing to survive the Battle of the Somme. Under the military pseudonym Private 19022 he published a war memoir originally titled *The Middle Parts of Fortune*. Even Pound, who did not enlist, was affected. Living in Stone Cottage in Sussex with Yeats during the early years of the war, Pound and his wife Dorothy were summoned to the police station because they were in "a prohibited area," Yeats wrote George Mair, adding, "I have cross questioned the two aliens carefully and they seem[s] to be generally observing the laws."[26]

Henri Gaudier-Brzeska, who had made the marble box, was killed at Neuville St Vaast in June 1915.[27] He was 23 years old. Pound wrote in Canto XVI:

> the lake of bodies, aqua morta,
> of limbs fluid, and mingled, like fish heaped in a bin,
> and here an arm upward, clutching a fragment of marble
>
>   .   .   .   .   .
>
> And Henri Gaudier went to it,
>   and they killed him
> And killed a good deal of sculpture . . .

In prose at the time, he wrote, "The arts will incur no worse loss from the war than this is."[28]

The date 1914 will inevitably suggest the Great War, but the poets did not have prophetic powers. If they spoke of war at the dinner, the conversation was not recorded. They were talking about poetry. In Blunt's words,

A peacock, by Yeats's request, was served up in full plumage on the table, and they all ate two helpings of it and some a helping of roast beef besides, and there was good discussion of the arts of versification afterwards on a plane very much above my comprehension; for several of the young men are futurists and believe that verse should be written without metre rhyme or scansion, a region where I am unable to follow.[29]

So Blunt, too, gathered from the air a live tradition. His *Poetical Works* followed soon, in spite of the war, as a result of the peacock dinner: the "really important event" gave him, temporarily, the professional literary status it had praised him for having.

I

Male Poets in Proximity

so that I recalled the noise in the chimney
as it were the wind in the chimney
but was in reality Uncle William
downstairs composing

Ezra Pound, Canto LXXXIII

B efore the peacock dinner, there was the cat dinner. No one ate a cat, but two cats sat peacefully on the table during a formal dinner given by an aging poet for younger poets who had come to honor him. The cats belonged to Mrs. Thomas Hardy, "two very fine cats," and they "sat to right and left of her plate on the table itself."

At the dinner in question, on 1 June 1912, Henry Newbolt, poet of public schools, cricket, and the British navy, and W. B. Yeats, sworn member of the Irish Republican Brotherhood, traveled together to Max Gate to honor Hardy on his 72nd birthday. This peculiar occasion looks like a rehearsal for the peacock dinner: a party of poets leaves London to visit a Victorian poet in his country house, to eat dinner at his table, and to bestow an honor on him at an all-male gathering before returning to London the same day. Speeches are given and responded to, an object symbolizing the honor is bestowed on the poet, and the event is recorded in *The Times*.[1]

These poetic award dinners are so similar in morphology that it is worth considering the cat dinner in order to appreciate the idiosyncrasies of the peacock dinner. Yeats participated in both, but he left no account of the visit to Hardy. With the Celtic twilight behind him, Yeats was now better known as a manager of the Abbey Theatre.

As a member of the Academic Committee of the Royal Society of Literature, Yeats joined his fellow committee member Newbolt in presenting to Hardy the Society's gold medal. Fortunately, Henry Newbolt recorded the event in his memoirs.[2]

The two poets arrived at Dorchester by train "on the appointed day" and were surprised to find a "deserted platform and a town without any sign of public interest" in Hardy's 72nd birthday. They were further surprised to discover that Mr. and Mrs. Hardy had "asked no other guests to meet us." There was a hasty and furtive consultation before dinner: Newbolt asked Yeats what on earth they should do. Yeats ("with Irish good sense") suggested that Newbolt speak first, and then Yeats himself, who would "produce the medal from his pocket." Hardy, they assumed, would thank them, and "the whole thing would be done."

The occasion was not that simple. There was a meal to be got through first. The four diners sat at a long table, with Mr. and Mrs.

Figure 3. Mrs. Emma Hardy with one of her cats. Reproduced by permission of the Dorset County Museum.

Hardy facing one another "the longer way." Hardy questioned Newbolt formally about "the architecture of Rome and Venice," from which cities Newbolt had just returned.

Through this conversation I could hear and see Mrs. Hardy giving Yeats much curious information about two very fine cats, who sat to right and left of her plate on the table itself. In this situation Yeats looked like an Eastern Magician overpowered by a Northern Witch—and I too felt myself spellbound by the famous pair of Blue Eyes . . .

When they had finished eating,

. . . Hardy rose from his seat and looked toward his wife: she made no movement, and he walked to the door. She was still silent and unmoved: he invited her to leave us for a few minutes for a ceremony which in accordance with his wish was to be performed without witnesses. She at once remonstrated, and Yeats and I begged that she should not be asked to leave us. But Hardy insisted and she made no further appeal but gathered up her cats and her train with perfect simplicity and left the room.

With the room cleared of women and cats, the ceremony could begin (Figure 3).

Hardy asked the poets to commence, but he seemed anxious. "I was not surprised," writes Newbolt, "that he listened uneasily to my little lecture on the Novels of Thomas Hardy." But then Yeats "began his much longer and more remarkable oration" on Hardy's poetry. While Yeats spoke "in his happiest and most serious manner," Hardy appeared to grow more apprehensive. Finally Yeats completed his speech and gave Hardy the medal. But, Newbolt continues, Hardy's face was still full of "dismay." He took a "roll of paper" from his pocket and began a speech of his own. The two visiting poets protested that Hardy need not cause himself more anxiety by giving such a formal reply. Nevertheless, he said

. . . he was bound to give us his speech aloud . . . because he had already given a copy of it to the reporters from London. The world would read next morning that he had addressed the Deputation in such and such words and phrases—he could not allow himself to make the falsehood theirs instead of his.

Behind that anxious face, however, Hardy was listening carefully. In his diary he remarked, "Newbolt wasted on the nearly empty room the best speech he ever made in his life, and Yeats wasted a very good one: mine in returning thanks was as usual a bad one, and the audience was quite properly limited."[3] And so it was printed, Hardy's five paragraphs of classic *oldfartisme*, a complaint about the "appalling increase every day in slipshod writing that would not have been tolerated for one moment a hundred years ago" and closing with a quotation from George Sand to the effect that (nonetheless) "Poesy cannot die."

It would be amusing to see a photograph of the expressions on the faces of Yeats and Newbolt as they listened to Hardy's effusion, but the cat dinner, unlike the peacock dinner, was never photographed. In the map of Georgian literary culture, the two dinners occupied different places. The cat dinner had institutional backing; the medal from the Royal Society of Literature signified official support of the arts. Newbolt and Yeats were emissaries of the state. The peacock dinner had no such formal backing; it emerged solely from Pound's desire to meet Wilfrid Blunt. Pound referred to the group of poets involved as "the committee," but the term creates the false impression of an established group, something more stable than simply the mixed bag of London poets that Yeats and Pound were able to round up.

However, with their mixture of formal praise and table talk and their improvised small-group rituals, the two poets' dinners were kin to one another, and the "cat" helps create a context in which the "peacock" may be understood. Both occasions should be seen as aspects of the emergent professionalism of poets. The remarkable burst of energy among poets at the time of the cat and peacock dinners, the founding of bookstores, poetry readings, societies, and journals, the creation of an infrastructure for poetry, all this was poets' idiosyncratic, unorganized way of organizing themselves to make the profession of poetry more visible and more "important."[4] The Poetry Society was founded in London in 1909, and its American counterpart in 1910. Although the Poetry Society never sought to organize poets, it did help to promote "a more general recognition and appreciation of poetry."[5] In 1912, Harold Monro started the *Poetry Review*, later to be followed by *Poetry and Drama* (1913–1914) and opened the Poetry Bookshop, where he instituted a bi-weekly series of poetry readings.

Pound's idealistic term for the larger collective entity of which the poets at the dinner were a "committee" was "the world of letters."

"It concerns only the world of letters," he insisted to Yeats, rejecting the idea of a photograph of the poets for newspapers.[6] Unlike the
Royal Society of Literature, this realm was abstract, de-centered,
transnational; and unlike the organization of other professions, it was
less a guild than a loosely associated group of kindred spirits devoted
to art. It was a virtual world.

The virtual world of letters was actualized in the peacock dinner
and other dinners as male poets gathered in small groups, gravi-
tating to one another in friendship, admiration, and professional
need.

Male Friendships and Professional Poets

In organizing such an event as the dinner, Pound was constructing
(though he never used the word) a poets' society of a very exclusive
kind. If he and Yeats had summoned all the poets in England, Ireland,
Scotland, and Wales to a large, inclusive meeting, had constituted
those present an association, written by-laws, articulated professional standards, collected dues, made a membership list, and sched-
uled annual meetings, they might have resembled the dentists, who
defined their professional qualifications in the British Dentists Act of
1878; or the doctors, who founded the British Medical Association of
1856; or the architects, who met as the Architects Association in 1847;
or any number of professional groups organized in the nineteenth
century.[7]

But the poets did not resemble the dentists and doctors; nor did
they resemble sculptors, painters, and musicians, whose arts were
taught in classes at the Royal College of Arts, the Slade, and the
Royal Academy of Music. There was no Royal Academy of Poetry.
The Royal Society of Literature did not in 1914 (as it does now)
run master classes in writing: it elected members, who elected other
members, who read papers to one another and distributed prizes.

English poets had no institutional procedure so formal as compul-
sory licensing, nor were modern poets trained in anything resem-
bling the ancient Irish bardic colleges, with their systematic learning,
strict curricula, and formal tutelage; nor had the making of poetry
and fiction found an identity as "creative writing" and an institutional home in universities. Pound invented such a system, his own

bardic college, in Part Two of "Patria Mia" (1912–1913), where he urged the establishment of a "respectable school of the arts,"

> . . . a college of one hundred members, chosen from all the arts, sculptors, painters, dramatists, musical composers, architects, scholars of the art of verse, engravers, etc., and they should be fed there during the impossible years of the artists' life—i.e., the beginning of the creative period.[8]

To encourage the "propagation and preservation of the arts" within existing universities, Pound argues, practitioners of poetry, for example, should teach alongside professors of literature. Listening to a debate between these two, students would be inspired and enlightened: "New life would be infused into the study of letters. Literature would come to be regarded as something living, something capable of constant transformation, and rebirth."[9]

The kind of program Pound envisioned did not come into being at the time. Yet in other ways poets participated in what Harold Perkin calls "the growing collective organization of the professions." Poets' "organization" emerged in a less systematic way.[10] It appeared in fits and starts from poets functioning in small, fragmented groups, their populations overlapping and constantly shifting according to the vagaries of friendships and book reviews. The Rhymers of the Nineties functioned as such a group for Yeats: *"Poets with whom I learned my trade,"* he wrote in "The Grey Rock," acknowledging them as a kind of school; *"Companions of the Cheshire Cheese,"* he added affectionately. But most of the Rhymers were too enervated and self-destructive to do more than leave behind a handful of beautiful lyrics and provide material for Yeats. As Yeats famously wrote of the Rhymers, some "went mad, some drank, drinking not as happy men drink but in solitude . . . Some turned Catholic . . ." The alcoholic Lionel Johnson, author of the brilliant opening lines "Dark Angel, with thine aching lust / To rid the world of penitence," died of a stroke in 1902 at the age of 35. Ernest Dowson, to whom we owe the phrases "gone with the wind" and "days of wine and roses," hopelessly in love with the 11-year-old Soho waitress Adelaide Foltinowicz, died of alcoholism at the age of 32 (in 1900). And the amazing Count Erik Stenbock, memorably characterized by Yeats as "scholar, connoisseur, drunkard, poet, pervert, most charming of men," also died at 35, though not from alcoholism (legend says that he was attacking "someone in the house" in Estonia with a poker but fell backwards, striking his head on a grate in the fireplace). But "Before burial his heart was placed in a jar and sent to the family church in Estonia."[11]

These, at any rate, in their short lives, met over many a beverage and dinner, talked poetry, and in some ways formed the spectral antecedents of the peacock dinner: Pound was drawn to London in large part to meet the few surviving former Rhymers such as Selwyn Image (who lived to be 81), Ernest Rhys, and Victor Plarr, not to mention Yeats himself. But at the turn of the century there was a dramatic change:

> Then in 1900 everybody got down off his stilts; henceforth nobody drank absinthe with his black coffee; nobody went mad; nobody committed suicide; nobody joined the Catholic church; or if they did I have forgotten.[12]

With a typically sweeping gesture, Yeats conveys the change in a metaphor of physical activity—"everybody got down off his stilts"—without assigning a cause other than the numerological: "Then in 1900 . . ." In 1913, the two founders of the Rhymers, Yeats and Ernest Rhys, were still alive and healthy, still functioning professionally, still active in poetic groups, and connected (one directly, one indirectly) with the peacock dinner.

Examples of this professionalizing energy can best be seen in vignettes, moments in which poets were asserting and publicizing their expertise. Some of these are now famous, such as the conversation in which Pound named Hilda Doolittle "H.D. Imagiste," an historic moment that took place either in the British Museum tea-room or the Fuller tea-shop in Kensington, depending on whose account you accept; or the regular Thursday meetings of the "Poets' Club," organized by Frank Flint and including Pound and T. E. Hulme among the regulars, at the Tour Eiffel, for discussions of poetics.[13] Other such conversations began in less deliberately professional mode, emerging not in the crossover public/private spaces of cafés and restaurants but in domestic spaces, especially the intimacy of homosocial friendships à deux. Edward Marsh's memoir offers a vignette of the intimate moments from which the anthology *Georgian Poetry* emerged. (Marsh, later to become Sir Edward Marsh KCVO CB CMG, was at that time Winston Churchill's private secretary.) Rupert Brooke was sitting "half-undressed" on his bed in Edward Marsh's rooms at Raymond Buildings, Gray's Inn. It was 19

September 1912—within weeks of the announcement of Imagism—
and Marsh had returned late from his job at the Admiralty:

> Rupert announced one evening, sitting half-undressed on his bed, that he
> had conceived a brilliant scheme. He would write a book of poetry, and
> publish it as a selection from the works of twelve writers, six men and six
> women, all with the most convincing pseudonyms. That, he thought, *must*
> make them sit up. It occurred to me that as we both believed there were at
> least twelve flesh-and-blood poets whose work, if properly thrust under
> the public's nose, had a good chance of producing the effect he desired, it
> would be simpler to use the material which was ready to hand. Next day . . .
> we lunched in my rooms with Gibson and Drinkwater, and Harold Monro
> and Arundel del Re (editor and sub-editor of the *Poetry Review*), and started
> the plan of the book which was published in December under the name of
> *Georgian Poetry, 1911–1912* . . .[14]

Soon Marsh came up with "my proud ambiguous adjective—Georgian."
The collection was put together quickly; by the first week of December
Marsh was sending off review copies. Although the names James Elroy
Flecker, Lascelles Abercrombie, and Wilfrid Wilson Gibson are not now
ones to conjure with, Marsh's claim in his introduction that "English
poetry is now once again putting on a new strength and beauty" reveals
the new assertiveness of poets that Yeats had observed and the professional self-consciousness noted in other vocational groups in the same
period.[15] Organizing a power lunch with editors within hours of gen-
erating their grand idea, Marsh and Brooke were certainly not on stilts.

Robert Frost and Edward Thomas were another such pair. Frost
stumbled into the poetry scene in London, going uninvited to the
formal opening of Monro's Poetry Bookshop in January 1913.[16] The
gathering of "over three hundred people . . . a mixture of writers, artists, critics, book editors, bohemians, and literary hangers-on" signified the emergence of precisely the kind of expert who would define
the profession. There Frost met Frank Flint, who soon introduced
him to Pound, but his deeper professional friendships came into being
with the "Dymock" poets Abercrombie, Brooke, John Drinkwater,
Gibson, and Edward Thomas, who spent time in rural Gloucestershire
between 1911 and 1914. (Brooke didn't live in Dymock but visited
Gibson and Abercrombie there.) The most significant friendship was
between Frost and Thomas: as Frost's biographer Jay Parini puts it,
"Thomas was stimulated by Frost, who beckoned him toward writing poems, while Frost basked in the warm attention of a strong,

critical mind." Of his "new vocation," poetry, Thomas wrote Frost, "I am in it & make no mistake," and again, "I won't begin thanking you just yet, tho if you like I will put it down now that you are the only begetter right enough."

The two men took "botanizing walks" together, during which Thomas always "regretted the particular path he had taken." Frost said to him, "No matter which road you take, you'll always sigh, and wish you'd taken another."[17] From these long, rambling, poetic walks—Thomas regretting the choice of direction, Frost mocking Thomas's indecision, yet each man reinforcing the other's poetic vocation—came Frost's most famous poem, "The Road Not Taken":

> I shall be telling this with a sigh
> Somewhere ages and ages hence
> Two roads diverged in a wood, and I –
> I took the one less traveled by,
> And that has made all the difference.

Frost may have been Thomas's "only begetter," but in this instance at least Thomas was Frost's muse, as Brooke was the inspiration for *Georgian Poetry*.

Gibson's nostalgic poem "The Golden Room," written in 1926 after the deaths of Brooke and Thomas in the Great War, describes what in memory appeared a hallowed gathering of the Dymock poets in June 1914, their own equivalent of the peacock dinner:

> Do you remember that still summer evening
> When, in the cosy cream washed living room
> Of the Old Nailshop, we all talked and laughed—
> Our neighbours from The Gallows, Catherine
> And Lascelles Abercrombie; Rupert Brooke;
> Elinor and Robert Frost, living awhile
> At Little Iddens, who'd brought over with them
> Helen and Edward Thomas?

Whatever these lines lack in genius and beauty, they make up in literary and social history, as they show a professional group coalescing around a dinner table. As at the peacock dinner, the one American was a strong presence:

> We talked and laughed; but, for the most part, listened
> While Robert Frost kept on and on and on,
> . . . Holding us with shrewd turns and racy quips . . .

In retrospect, the meal that evening came to embody the Dymock poets' "capture of the idyllic English pastoral dream."[18] Unlike the poets gathered at Blunt's in January of the same year, these poets already formed a group; and they evidently had no objection to "literary men's wives" dining at the same table.

In August of the same year they even enjoyed a second such meal at the house where Thomas's friend Eleanor Farjeon was staying. As Farjeon writes, "a covey of poets had gathered on the border of Gloucestershire," and even the owners of the house where she was staying felt that "Literary fame was in the air." Mr. and Mrs. Farmer wanted to participate in the professionalization they were witnessing: "the ebb and flow of poets suddenly went to Mrs. Farmer's head." The Farmers decided they wanted to give a party in their house for all the poets. This dinner was not so exotic or international or artsy as the dinner *chez* Blunt: it was in Olde Englishe style. Farjeon wore her "nicest cotton frock" for the occasion, and when the poets arrived—the Frosts, the Thomases, the Gibsons, the Abercrombies—they were welcomed into the best parlor and invited to "look at the photograph albums."[19] They dined on "a ham, a great joint of beef, a raised pie and birds" (no mention of peacock) and for dessert "fruit-tarts and trifles and cheesecakes."[20] No claret here, but the Farmers were especially generous with the cider; at the end of the meal the poets were too drunk to stand up. Finally, clinging to one another, "two brace of poets staggered out into the moonlight and went hilariously homeward." Farjeon writes, "I have boasted ever since of the night when I drank all the poets in Gloucestershire under the table."[21] (It is amazing to realize that one of the poets present at both those jolly old-fashioned occasions was also present live on television on 20 January 1961, at John F. Kennedy's inauguration.)

Frost's and Thomas's Gloucestershire friendship, with its walks, talks, and poems, seems to some extent like a later version of Wordsworth's and Coleridge's in Somerset during the magic years that generated *Lyrical Ballads*, a friendship that was also part of an emergent poetic professionalism.[22] But Frost and Thomas formed part of a network: they were connected to literary impresarios Marsh and Pound in London, to Harold Monro and the poetic infrastructure he was building, to a metropolitan center where poets were in a continual state of collaboration and competition. Beginning in the late autumn of 1913, two of the busiest of those poets, Yeats (age 48) and Pound (age 28), were sharing domestic space and talking shop in Stone Cottage, Coleman's Hatch, Sussex, Pound reading aloud to Yeats and penning his letters to save Yeats's eyesight, Yeats composing aloud and reading his new poems to Pound, Pound teaching Yeats to fence. From this domestic intimacy in its early stages emerged the idea for a dinner honoring Wilfrid Blunt.

"Sitting on the same hearth rug"

A cold night in Indiana propelled Pound to Yeats. In February 1908, the 22-year-old Pound, then teaching romance languages at Wabash College in Crawfordville, found a burlesque showgirl out wandering the streets during a blizzard in search of a bed and allowed her to sleep in his room ("safe as in her mother's arms," Pound wrote).[23] Landladies will talk . . . dismissed from his job, Pound set out almost immediately for London, hoping soon to "sit at Yeats's feet, and learn what he knew."[24] Slowly but systematically, new friend by new friend, Pound moved closer to Yeats, one of "the real people in London." As he wrote his mother in August 1909, "I don't know that my doings are much more than meeting people."[25] Through visiting Elkin Mathews's bookshop in late summer 1908 he had met Mathews, who introduced him to the minor poet James Griffyth Fairfax, who introduced him to the salonnière Eva Fowler, at whose tea he met Olivia Shakespear, Yeats's close friend and first lover.

After Pound's first tea at Mrs. Shakespear's, he wrote Mary Moore, his friend back in New Jersey, that he had been "sitting on the same hearth rug" where Yeats sat: Shakespear's rug connected Pound's bottom with the bottom of Yeats, the man he had gone to London to meet.[26] Shakespear's daughter Dorothy viewed Pound as a miniature Yeats: in February 1909 Pound was reading Yeats's poetry aloud "in a voice like Yeats's own," an unusual feat considering that Pound had not yet met Yeats. His accent, oddly, sounded "half American, half Irish." Dorothy's girlish diary (she was 22) recorded her infatuation with the new man in her family's house:

"Ezra."

Listen to it—Ezra! Ezra!—And a third time—Ezra! He has a wonderful, beautiful face, a high forehead, prominent over the eyes; a long, delicate nose, with little, red, nostrils; a strange mouth, never still, & quite elusive; a square chin . . .[27]

. . . And so on. "I do not think he knows he is beautiful." Allowing the daughter of the house to fall in love with him was part of the route to Yeats. The Shakespears promised an introduction, and Pound sent his father regular bulletins on the long-deferred meeting: "Yeats is coming over from Ireland soon," he wrote in March; and then, "Yeats . . . couldn't or didn't get here"; and finally, at the end of April, "Yeats has at last arrived and I had about five hours of him yesterday." The fateful day was 29 April 1909.[28] Soon Pound was "taking charge" at Yeats's Monday evenings at Woburn Buildings, pouring the wine while he "laid down the law about poetry." By the autumn of 1913 they had progressed to the intimate status of housemates in Sussex, sharing meals, books, and first drafts of their poems.

In the absence of established institutional structures for learning how to be a poet, Pound had created his own informal ones. Through conversations, teas, visits to bookshops, "Mondays," "Sundays," and dinners, Pound was forming the network of literary acquaintances he might have found in the "school of the arts" he had written about. The locus of culture, he assumed, was the poet himself, in his person; and proximity to Yeats would be his route to becoming a poet. The language of body parts—"sit at Yeats's feet," "sitting on the same hearth rug"—suggests that intimacy and proximity make up an important part of the plan, that the transmission of culture takes place through the body. Pound's famous description (in Canto LXXXIII) of Yeats in the process of poetic composition takes on significance in this context:

> so that I recalled the noise in the chimney
> as it were the wind in the chimney
> but was in reality Uncle William
> downstairs composing
> that had made a great Peeeeacock
> in the proide ov his oiye
> had made a great peeeeeeecock in the . . .
> made a great peacock
> in the proide ov his oyyee

> proide ov his oy-ee
> as indeed he had, and perdurable
>
> a great peacock aere perennius[29]

. . . . . .

The repetition of Yeats's line (with small differences) indicates the intimacy in which the two poets lived at "Stone Cottage in Sussex by the waste moor": they are so close that Pound can hear Yeats's voice even when he is "downstairs" and Pound is not in the room with him. Pound hears the poem as it comes from Yeats's breath, as if it were direct from his imagination. Poetic culture is transmitted through the air, up the chimney.

"The grandest of old men, the last of the great Victorians"

It was partly a matter of timing. Blunt's name had come up in Yeats's reading only two weeks before the letter to Gregory suggesting the dinner. On 9 November, Yeats wrote Lady Gregory urging her to get Katharine Tynan's memoir *Twenty-Five Years: Reminiscences* from the library. This was the volume that irritated Yeats because Tynan, his old friend, had used long portions of his letters to her without his permission; it was "careless & sometimes stupid," he wrote Lady Gregory, but "contains a great deal that moves me." He took particular care to mention Blunt's presence in Tynan's book: "there is something about almost everybody I knew in those days & about Blunt & some other people that you know."[30] Tynan describes "a week-end at Crabbet Park with the Blunts" in 1889, where she noticed

Byron relics everywhere, pictures, portraits, a cast of his hand, delicately feminine. Crabbet in that July was in strange contrast to Galway Jail, where Mr Blunt had, not long before, spent three months in Vindication of the rights of free speech.[31]

But it was Lady Anne who made the bigger impression on Tynan: "I admired Mr Blunt immensely, but I was in love with Lady Anne. She looked so good, so much of the open air, so wholesome, so simple."

Through an accident of timing another event may have reinforced the idea of giving honor to Blunt.[32] In the same week as the letter proposing the dinner for Blunt was written, Yeats was preparing for a meeting of the Royal Society of Literature at which its Edmond de Polignac Prize, selected by the Academic Committee, was given to the Irish writer James Stephens (28 November 1913). From Coleman's Hatch, Pound wrote Dorothy Shakespear that Yeats talked of the Academic Committee's "passion for the absolutely harmless" (30 November 1913). At that time Stephens was famous for publishing fairytales like *The Crock of Gold* (1912). He had not yet, of course, written *Insurrection*, his sympathetic account of the 1916 Rising in Dublin, which would not have endeared him to the Royal Society. Perhaps an even more important qualification for the prize, given Yeats's power on the Academic Committee, was Stephens's defense and praise of Yeats, who had been attacked in *The New Age* in 1912. With the phrase "the absolutely harmless" Yeats may also have been remembering the visit to Hardy with Henry Newbolt. Whatever the reason, Dorothy Shakespear, who attended the ceremony, found this honor to the harmless "entertaining beyond description" and described the Society's dusty Victorian literary formality in a letter to Pound.[33]

To organize a literary event around Wilfrid Blunt was to make a different kind of statement altogether. Blunt was not "harmless": he was openly, outspokenly, and provocatively anti-imperialist. His support of the Egyptian nationalist leader Urabi and his imprisonment in Ireland during the Land War would have sufficed to make him anathema to the Royal Society, and letters from Blunt attacking imperialist policies could be found regularly in *The Times* and elsewhere. He was the same age as Hardy, and he had written a lot of pastoral verse in praise of West Sussex, but he would never even be on the short-list for the Royal Society's gold medal. In 1911 Yeats had tried to muster the votes to get Blunt elected to the Academic Committee, enlisting the help of Sturge Moore. Moore supported Blunt because "he is a horse dealer, a calling which should foster insight," but he was not elected.[34]

To imagine, plan, construct, and then publicize a dinner honoring Blunt was a major intervention in the literary world. The poets gathered to honor him would share in his notoriety. The dinner would constitute a deliberate de-centering of cultural power, a challenge to the Royal Society. It implied that a cultural opposition might be formed and flaunt its formation. The praise of Blunt and the aggressive publicizing of that gesture would make the dinner provocative. The idea for the dinner also derived from a less disruptive and flamboyant impulse, the wish to dine with another poet. That wish—for an encounter, proximity, maybe friendship—was Pound's. In December 1912 he had written of Blunt as one of the men who

contribute liberally to the "charm" or the "atmosphere" of London: Wilfred [*sic*] Scawen Blunt, the grandest of old men, the last of the great Victorians; great by reason of his double sonnet, beginning—

> He who has once been happy is for aye
> Out of destruction's reach . . .[35]

Pound's interest in meeting Blunt derived from the same impulse as his longing to meet Yeats, in part the American need to seek European cultural celebrities, in part the need to affiliate with a poet and define his work in relation to a living literary tradition: "Swinburne my only miss," as Pound wrote in Canto LXXXII.

In spite of Pound's expressed admiration for Blunt's double sonnet "To Esther," it was probably more of a general homage than a desire to learn poetic style that drew Pound to Blunt. To the unillusioned reader, Blunt's poems manifest all the defects of style Pound's Imagist "tenets" were designed to prevent: "Direct treatment of the 'thing' whether subjective or objective," "Go in fear of abstractions," "Don't chop your stuff into separate *iambs*."[36] Even the poem by Blunt that Pound explicitly singled out for admiration in *Poetry* in January 1913, sonnet 51 in the sequence *Esther, A Young Man's Tragedy*, might not qualify by Imagist standards, with its archaisms, non-colloquial syntax, and imprecise images:

> When cities deck their streets for barren wars
> Which have laid waste their youth, and when I keep
> Calmly the count of my own life and see
> On what poor stuff my manhood's dreams were fed
> Till I too learned what dole of vanity
> Will serve a human soul for daily bread,
> Then I remember that I once was young
> And lived with Esther the world's gods among.[37]

Blunt was a literary conservative, and it is unlikely that his conventional poetry alone would have caught Pound's attention or inspired his admiration. But Blunt had glamor and notoriety, and by modeling himself on Byron had fashioned himself into a poet who appeared to be a conduit for a "live tradition," the kind of poet that an Anglophile American would want to visit.

A major source of Blunt's glamor was his association with Byron, an association constructed by Blunt himself, guided by assumptions not unlike those that guided Pound. In the absence of any institutions to connect aspiring poets with established ones, Blunt, too, had assumed that the locus of poetic culture was in the poet's person, and he forged material connections between himself and the great romantic poet who had died sixteen years before he was born. Blunt claimed that his father had been at Harrow with Byron, and by accident and by design he found himself often in places where Byron had been: the villa at Albaro where Blunt's family stayed in 1852 was "only a stone's throw from Byron's Casa Saluzzo." As a young diplomat in Athens in 1859, he felt he must be seeing Albanian "pallikars, among whose names Byron had counted those of his brethren in arms;" and he met George Finlay, a historian "who had often conversed with Byron." Although he couldn't breathe the same air as Byron and gather a "live tradition" from it, and although he couldn't get an "unconquered flame" directly from Byron's eyes, he could come pretty close:

He sat at the feet of George Finlay the historian of Greece, and once Byron's guest on Cephalonia. In the great heat of summer he would sail in a caïque to Sounion, lie in cool caves by day and by moonlight skim past the isles of Greece. He was soon writing a lyric highly imitative of Byron . . .[38]

And even closer: in 1869 he married Lady Anne Isabella King-Noel, Byron's granddaughter. Lady Anne was the only one of Byron's grandchildren to have grandchildren herself, so Blunt's DNA and Byron's are joined forever in a single line of descent. Marriage to Lady Anne functioned for Blunt as living with Yeats did for Pound: it gave a younger poet intimate access to an older one whom he aspired to emulate. Soon Blunt was acting with Byronic personal authority. In 1871 Blunt and Lady Anne visited Count Arthur de Gobineau at his chateau in Normandy. Gobineau was a "poet, novelist, philosopher, orientalist," diplomat, and Byronist, modeling his poetry on Byron's as he modeled his fiction on Scott's. Lady Anne gave

Gobineau "a handsome copy" of Byron's poems, and Blunt signed it himself: "Genealogy / Lord Byron / Lady Lovelace / Lady Anne Blunt / Presented to Count de Gobineau / August 21th. 1871." The inscription, placing Blunt and Gobineau in a genealogical sequence, flatteringly attempts to connect Blunt's host directly to Byron through the persons of his guests.[39]

In spite of these many points of contact with his great predecessor, Blunt was a kind of Byron *manqué*: poetry was not the central passion of his life, as it had been for Byron. His list of lovers is much shorter (closer to 50 than to 500) and more limited in many respects (only women, and primarily titled ones from among the same circles). He sired only two illegitimate children, not three, and he did not drink. Nor did he die, as Byron did, "in action" for a romantic nationalist cause at age 36: he died at home in bed, aged 82. But the potent mixture of sex, politics, aristocracy, and poetry that Blunt embodied was one Byron had concocted and Pound admired. Like Byron, Blunt led an exciting, visible, exotic life, traveling extensively by camel with Lady Anne in Arabia, Persia, and Egypt, accompanied by an entourage of native guides and roughing it considerably. Visitors to Newbuildings were frequently treated to the sight of Blunt in his Arab robes, and after 1882 he spent many winters at his (and Lady Anne's) estate Sheykh Obeyd near Heliopolis outside Cairo. Even when he was too old for dramatic political activities, such as giving banned speeches and getting arrested, he continued to annoy the government with letters to the paper.

To some extent Blunt had even copied from Byron the idea of constructing himself as a celebrity. Byron was a celebrity *avant la lettre*, exploiting his social status as a peer, his good looks, personal charm, the high-volume sales of his poetry, and his tabloid life, obliquely referred to in his poems.[40] Byron encouraged and developed the notion that his poetic self was coextensive with his person. He dieted to slim down his chubby body, kept his hair in its famous curl, and dressed with great care, displaying himself at various times as a Turkish boy with "a diamond crescent glittering in his brocade turban," in women's clothes (in Greece), and—as he was famously painted—in Albanian dress. The plumed Homeric helmet he designed and commissioned for the armed struggle he anticipated in Greece bore the family motto, "Crede Biron."[41]

So successful was Byron in creating public interest in his person that the young American George Ticknor included Byron on his list of literary celebrities to meet during his grand tour in 1815. (Ticknor also met Wordsworth, Sir Walter Scott, Southey, and Goethe.) In 1823 Lady Marguerite Blessington traveled to Genoa with her entourage for the sole purpose of meeting Byron: "I never felt before the same impatient longing to see anyone known to me only by his works. I hope he may not be fat . . . for a *fat poet* is an anomaly in my opinion."[42] As in the case of the peacock dinner, the impulse to see the great man was followed by the impulse to publish an account of it, and Lady Blessington's *Conversations with Lord Byron* confirms that Byron was not fat, though his appearance was disappointing. Byron seemed to have looked more like Thomas Gray's bard with his "haggard eyes" and "hoary hair" than the curled darling of London salons: he was so thin that his clothes "hung strangely on him," and his curls were grey and needed trimming. Blunt's appearance in 1914 did not disappoint.

"Too many women—it lowers the tone"

"Ezra Pound has a project which he wants me to ask you about," Yeats wrote Lady Gregory on 24 November 1913.

> He and some of the younger writers would like to get up a dinner in honour of Wilfrid Blunt. Of course I approve of the scheme.
>
> He wants to know if you think Blunt would come and if he would care about it.
>
> It would be entirely a men's dinner and so would escape the usual air of Hampstead and of literary men's wives.
>
> We went over a possible list of people last night and I think he would have no difficulty in getting a very good gathering.
>
> He proposes to hold the dinner at "Dieudonné" just before I start for America.
>
> Yours
>
> WB Yeats[43]

The Shakespears, Olivia and Dorothy, had provided Pound's access to Yeats, and Lady Gregory, Blunt's intimate friend and former lover, would provide access to Blunt. The path is embodied in the small complexities of the letter: the first-person is Yeats's; the handwriting is Pound's; the signature is Yeats's; the addressee is Lady Gregory; and the ultimate goal is Blunt (Figures 4 and 5).

The route required Lady Gregory, but this was to be "entirely a men's dinner." At the dinner for Hardy the gender discrimination had happened unplanned (unplanned by Newbolt and Yeats, at any rate), as Hardy "invited" his wife "to leave us" several times, and finally (in Newbolt's excellent prose) she "gathered up her cats and her train with perfect simplicity and left the room." The artistic circles Pound and Yeats moved in included many women: H.D. for instance, Harriet Monroe, the salonnières Olivia Shakespear and Eva Fowler; not to mention Yeats's many close women friends— Katharine Tynan, Lady Gregory, and Florence Farr, among others. The modernist writers had subtler styles of exclusion than Hardy.

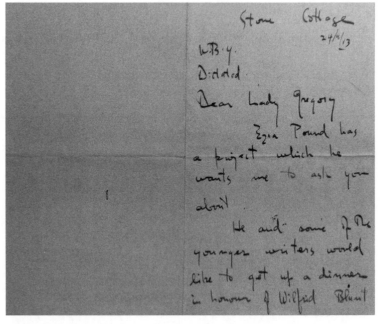

Figure 4. The first mention of the dinner in a letter from Yeats (in Pound's handwriting but signed by Yeats) to Lady Gregory, 24 November 1913. Reproduced by permission of the Henry W. and Albert A. Berg Collection, New York Public Library, Astor, Lenox, and Tilden Foundations.

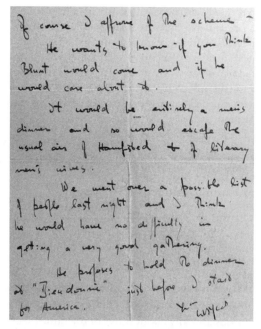

Figure 5. The second page of the letter from Yeats to Lady Gregory, 24 November 1913. Reproduced by permission of the Henry W. and Albert A. Berg Collection, New York Public Library, Astor, Lenox, and Tilden Foundations.

Writing to Pound in September 1917, T. S. Eliot complained about the essays by Dora Marsden that opened each issue of *The Egoist*, and then referred to a recent gathering:

Thursday—I thought too many women—it lowers the tone: not up to the Café Magry; perhaps there should be a special evening for males only, as well as this.[44]

The preference for a "men's dinner," then, was not unique to Pound; the word "Hampstead" may provide a clue.

Pound was possibly thinking of the literary gatherings held at the Hampstead house of the editor Ernest Rhys and his wife Grace. In his memoir, Rhys tells what has become a famous story about the time Pound ate the floral decoration at the Rhyses' supper party:

During the supper, Willie Yeats, always a good monologue, held forth at length on this new art of bringing music and poetry together, and possibly

Ezra Pound, who could also be vocal on occasion, may have felt he was not getting a fair share of the festivity. So, in order to pass the time perhaps, and seeing the supper table dressed with red tulips in glasses, he presently took one of the flowers and proceeded to munch it up. As Yeats, absorbed in his monologue, did not observe this strange behavior, and the rest of us were too well-bred to take any notice, Ezra, having found the tulip to his taste, did likewise with a second flower. Now, memory I admit is an artist, but not always to be trusted, and may have deceived me into recalling that by the end of supper all the tulips had been consumed.[45]

Arundel del Re remembered the episode slightly differently: the flowers were roses, not tulips; and at the time, Pound and Mrs. Rhys "were hotly discussing the merits of Ancient-Irish and Anglo-Saxon epic poems."

By the time we reached dessert, most of the roses had lost their petals and Mrs. Rhys, with a charming smile and a wicked twinkle in her bright blue eyes, turned to him and said, "Would you like another rose, Mr. Pound?"[46]

It seems unlikely that this generous offer would be the reason Pound would want women excluded from the dinner for Blunt; and Pound had written enthusiastically about Rhys in the same piece in *Poetry* in which he had called Blunt "the grandest of old men." But possibly the atmosphere *chez* Rhys was too genteel for him. As one of the founders of the Rhymers, Ernest Rhys might have been considered *passé* by Pound, old-fashioned, not modern; and in his memoir Rhys writes that he invited Rhymers to the gatherings and "usually some woman writers to join the company."[47]

Another possibility among Hampstead literary men's wives was Constance Masefield. Invited to the dinner but not present for it, John Masefield had lived with his family at 12 Well Walk, Hampstead, since 1912; Sturge Moore lived at 40 Well Walk. When it emerged that Masefield would not be able to attend, Lady Gregory remarked he was "under the thumb of a wife who will not let him go anywhere."[48] There is no evidence of such a ban, and in fact the Masefields together visited Blunt in April, and Blunt wrote, "I like them extremely."[49] But not everyone liked her extremely. Mrs. Masefield visited George and W. B. Yeats in Oxford in 1920, and George wrote to Ottoline Morrell, "Mrs. Masefield has just departed & left us such bad headaches!"[50] Yeats wrote to John Quinn that Masefield's daughter Judith was "not allowed to know us because we might talk astrology, or magic, or say something unclassifiably wicked. She was sent out when we were expected to tea . . ."⁵¹

The exile of Judith Masefield was (it seems) not attributable to her father. But of course those encounters had not yet occurred in 1914, at the time of the Blunt dinner. Whoever was the wife or wives Pound had in mind, to his way of thinking—as to Hardy's at the cat dinner, and Eliot's at the "Thursday" occasion at Café Magry—the presence of a woman seemed to diminish or threaten the professionalism of the event.

The Guest List

In his own account of the dinner, published in *Poetry* magazine, Pound lists the poets who might have attended "a large dinner of honor" had Blunt been amenable to such an event, a dinner with "all the reputable poets of England save those who hold official positions"—an allusion to Robert Bridges, the new Poet Laureate, who had refused the invitation. The "unavoidable omissions" were

Mr. D. H. Lawrence, who is in Italy; Mr. Padraic Colum, now in Ireland; Mr. James Joyce, in Austria, and Mr. Rupert Brooke, somewhere in the South Pacific.

"Still," wrote Pound, "it was a fairly complete sort of tribute, representing no one clique or style but a genuine admiration for the power behind all expression, for the spirit behind writing."⁵² What a wonderful photograph the large group with all the "omissions" would have made, and what a complex literary hierarchy the relative positions of all these writers would have revealed; a hierarchy completed also by the two other omissions, John Masefield and Frederic Manning, poets who at the last minute were unable to attend.

A dinner for Blunt with Yeats, Pound, Lawrence, Joyce, and Brooke would now be better remembered than the dinner with Yeats, Pound, Sturge Moore, Plarr, Aldington, and Flint. The latter poets lived in London and so were readily available, but they were a mixed bag, not all the best-known poets of the day, not members of a single poetic school, not all admirers of Blunt or his poetry, and never to meet again as a group. Each one had his eccentricities and his *Times* obituary; each one brought a different kind of interest to the peacock dinner. Their poetries were as radically different from one another's as their hair styles, and only two of the poets, Yeats and Pound, acknowledged Blunt as a precursor.

The disparities in social position and income were marked. Four of the poets had ties to old wealth, but different kinds of ties. The only survivor of three siblings, Blunt owned 4,000 acres of land in West Sussex and had the use of his wife Lady Anne's considerable wealth.[53] Yeats at this time earned money from his literary work and in 1909 had been awarded a Civil List pension, a permanent source of income from the British government. He also enjoyed Lady Gregory's pecuniary support as well as the comforts of her big house every summer. Pound received a regular allowance from his father and occasional professional support of various kinds from his future mother-in-law, Olivia Shakespear, and her wealthy friends; in 1912 he earned money from academic talks on the troubadours given in the elegant London house of Lord and Lady Glenconner.[54] Thomas Sturge Moore, a poet and engraver, received a legacy from "two wealthy maternal uncles" and, as his philosopher brother G. E. Moore wrote, this gave all the brothers and sisters "sufficient private means to enable us to live in moderate comfort, without needing to earn anything."[55] In 1919 Sturge Moore, too, was awarded a Civil List pension. It was he who made the beautiful cover illustration for Yeats's 1928 volume *The Tower*.

The three other poets did not have the benefit of old money; they had actual jobs, but not poetry-writing jobs. Aldington had had to leave University College London when his father met with financial difficulties, and since then had earned a living in journalism. At the time of the peacock dinner, Aldington was assistant editor of the *New Freewoman*, which had just become the better-known *The Egoist*.[56] The two men at the margins of the photograph—the two of whom biographies have never been written—earned their livings in non-literary jobs. (Their obligations at work determined the day of the dinner: "Plarr and Flint could only come on a Sunday," Pound wrote Lady Gregory.)[57] Victor Plarr, son of an English mother and Alsatian father, was the librarian of the Royal College of Surgeons.[58] Frank Flint had worked since childhood. Born into a large, impoverished family in Islington, Flint as a small boy had worked as a "barber's lather-boy."[59] At the age of 13, Flint left school to take on full-time work. In 1904 he began work in the Civil Service as a typist; at the time of the peacock dinner he was working for the Post Office. He continued work in the Civil Service for the rest of his life, ultimately becoming Chief of the Overseas Section, Statistics Division, in the Ministry of Labour.[60] And yet of the peacock poets listed in the 1911 "England Census," only Flint listed his occupation as poet. Under the heading "occupation," he wrote "SHORTHAND WRITER AND TYPIST POET AND MAN OF LETTERS."[61] His list of occupations sends the message, *I may be earning a living as a civil servant, but I'm a POET AND MAN OF LETTERS.*[62]

The Laureate Says No

Yeats had written Lady Gregory that he and Pound would "have no difficulty in getting a very good gathering," but the constitution of the party shifted until the last minute. Although the final four—the Imagists Richard Aldington and Frank Flint, the former Rhymer Victor Plarr, and Thomas Sturge Moore— would not now be considered major literary figures, they were close friends of the two organizers. The Australian poet Frederic Manning contributed a poem to the marble box and had been expected to attend, but at the last moment did not turn up. His biographer speculates that asthma may have been the cause, "but on this occasion the moral indignation of Arthur Galton at the idea of paying homage to a radical, womanizing, pro-Irish, anti-Britisher may have barred the path."[63] Galton, a Church of England clergyman who was Manning's tutor and good friend, was pleased to let people know that the Duke of Fife was his second cousin, and the Earl of Northumberland a "connection," so if his opinion about the dinner was solicited, it certainly would have been a definite negative. But no record of the "regret" remains; Pound wrote his mother only "Manning had to go back to lincolnshire [*sic*]."[64]

One little fuss around the invitation showed that the dinner had already begun to provoke. On 7 December 1913 Robert Bridges, who had just become Poet Laureate in July of that year, responded to Yeats's invitation with a firm "no." "As for your main matter," he wrote,

I really can have nothing to do with Restaurant dinners. You can't imagine how I dislike them & all their adjuncts. I admire Wilfrid Blunt's work, but he has unfortunately a very political or impolitical side, & I do not know enough about that to feel quite comfortable about what one might let oneself in for if one was to magnify him ostensibly. So pray excuse me.[65]

Yeats and Bridges had a stable though not intimate friendship, and the letter is diplomatically organized: the comments on Blunt are placed between cheerful and friendly remarks that emphasize the continuity of their acquaintance. In the final paragraph, Bridges invites Yeats to visit him in Oxford in the spring. But the "no" is rich with significance: Bridges's shudder is almost audible. The idea of a dinner at Dieudonné, as the occasion still was in early December, a dinner in the heart of Bohemia, and for Blunt, inspired such a strong repulsion that Bridges capitalized the R.

If the implicit purpose of the dinner was a de-centering of poetry, a gesture intended to make the case for a radical, avant-garde literary culture, then the letter from Bridges signified a very palpable hit. As Poet Laureate, Bridges was the lyric voice of the nation and the monarchy. He was situated at the center; he *was* the center of the geopolitical map of poetry. Although he tended to avoid involvement in international politics (and to avoid London when possible), Bridges engaged in patriotic cultural reforms of a preservationist nature. Only a year earlier he had founded the Society for Pure English to ensure "that our language in its future development should be controlled by the forces . . . which have formed it in the past; that it should keep its English character," and he was one of a committee advising the BBC on pronunciation in 1926. His wife, Monica Bridges, was a handwriting evangelist, an earnest advocate of italic script. Blunt and Pound both had legible and quite pleasing handwriting, but Bridges would not have known that.[66]

Blunt's "impolitical side" would never have been to Bridges's taste. And of course the dinner did "magnify him ostensibly": the feature about it on page five of *The Times*, two days after the event, surprised even Blunt himself. Bridges's letter of refusal, a cultural off-shoot of the dinner, resonated in conversations and correspondence. It echoed as far away as New York: there was a "cult" of Blunt "beginning among the young poets," Lady Gregory wrote the American arts patron John Quinn, because they "uphold him as 'an expert in life' and think the Laureate colourless."[67] In a letter to Gregory, Yeats alluded to the "eclipse" Bridges "suffered . . . when he refused to honour Blunt," an eclipse, it seems, in Pound's estimation.

Bridges was a great one for opening lines: "Whither, O splendid ship, thy white sails crowding"; "Awake, my heart, to be loved, awake, awake!"; "Thou didst delight my eyes"; "Beautiful must be the mountains whence ye come"; "I have loved flowers that fade," and so on. Void of irony and edge, his upbeat, beauty-loving, idealistic poems remain upbeat and beauty-loving through the final lines. In 1915, fulfilling his role as Laureate, Bridges edited an anthology called *The Spirit of Man*, intended to keep up the spirits of British subjects and their allies during the war. It was dedicated "by gracious permission to His Majesty the King." Bridges would not have fitted in at the peacock dinner, but his utter unsuitability might have enriched literary history with anecdotes.

2

Lady Gregory's Ideas

I told him how Yeats had once been tempted to go to a reception at some London house by the rumour that a roast peacock was always a feature of the supper; and in his disappointment at not finding this . . .

Lady Gregory, *Seventy Years*

In the fifty-five days between the first mention of the dinner in the letter to Lady Gregory and its occurrence, its ceremonial aspects and not its intimacies loomed large, as it evolved into an event of some significance. The rituals for the cat dinner had been decided hastily, on the spot, by Newbolt and Yeats, whose decisions came into slight conflict with Hardy's own privately determined ritual. The most important feature was the transfer of the gold medal from Yeats's pocket to Hardy's hand, and that act required little planning. The dinner was a secondary consideration, a necessity because of the timing of the transfer; Mr. and Mrs. Hardy had not, it seems, given any thought to creating a guest list. As the Blunt dinner's ritual elements—the venue, the menu, the box, the poems, the photographer—were discussed, debated, and determined, the occasion began to take on an air of glamour. It became more widely known, more of an intervention, its cultural capital growing greater with each decision.

Lady Gregory's response to Yeats's and Pound's letter introduced a paradigm shift. The original phrasing of the idea had been vague—"get up a dinner in honour of Blunt"—but the last sentence had clarified what was meant: Pound "proposes," said Yeats, to hold the dinner at the Soho restaurant Dieudonné. Soho had become the center of London's exotic, naughty, foreign pleasures, especially nocturnal ones such as nightclubs, theaters, and restaurants. As Judith Walkowitz has written, its "cosmopolitan reputation dated from the second half of the nineteenth century, when it became a multiethnic, polyglot settlement of European diasporas."

> Soho was not so much a cultural melting pot as a space of intimate and sometimes tumultuous interaction between men and women of many walks of life: rich and poor, unschooled émigrés and Bloomsbury literati, moral purity campaigners and libertarian anarchists, undercover police and dance hostesses . . .[1]

Pound was inviting Blunt into Pound's own bohemian, avant-garde space. At the time Pound frequented it, Dieudonné's, on Ryder Street, was an elegant restaurant and hotel. Its decor and cuisine were in high bohemian style: white pillars, white walls, and (in the words of a diner from 1899) "delicately-painted panels, with gentlemen and ladies in powder and silk and brocade limned upon them."[2] White shades and pink ones covered small electric lights; silver vases full of flowers stood on all the tables. In the 1880s, when Dieudonné's had been a boarding house, Mme. Dieudonné invited the famous artists and musicians who were her guests to sign the wall of her "little parlour" or paint on it: Tchaikovsky, Rubinstein, Rodin, Saint-Saens, Massenet, and the Prince of Wales had all left their mark. By the time Pound was eating there, the celebrity signatures were gone, but the "foreign" artistic atmosphere, "an impression of Italy and Paris," as Arthur Symons put it, remained. Pound evidently liked introducing other writers to his haunts. As Robert Frost described his brief friendship with Pound in 1912: "what Pound did was show me bohemia . . . He'd take me to restaurants and things." The Frost-Pound friendship did not catch fire, possibly because Pound (according to Frost) "showed me jujitsu in a restaurant. He grabbed my wrist, tipped over backwards and threw me over his head."[3]

For Pound, a poets' dinner was not simply a meal enjoyed by a group of poets; it was a gesture, usually a somewhat belligerent one, directed at the rest of the literary world. At Dieudonné's on 15 July 1914 Pound and company celebrated the launch of *BLAST,* the Vorticist magazine "blasting" some (Galsworthy, Dean Inge, Elgar) and blessing others (Joyce, James Barrie, and, curiously, Henry Newbolt). Amy Lowell, visiting from America and invited to the dinner, was surprised to discover that Imagism had been "replaced" by Vorticism. She decided to give a counter-dinner two days later, also at Dieudonné's, on behalf of *Des Imagistes*, the recently published anthology of Imagist poetry.[4] After Pound insulted her at her own dinner, Lowell decided to give yet another dinner ("in her hotel suite" on 30 July, and without Pound) to introduce plans for yet another Imagist anthology. In the view of the American *literati*—Pound, then Amy Lowell—dinners functioned as a move in a larger offensive, one designed to dominate the poetry scene. As Peter Brooker notes, "Promoting Imagism appeared to entail literally taking over the territory occupied by its rival."[5]

Pound's idea was a modernist version of the "restaurant dinner," a familiar phenomenon that a Max Beerbohm character invokes with disdain: "He wanted me to be guest of honour at some festal junket in town. Such are the signs that England has heard of one's existence. I salaam'd him off, but he was not an easy goer."[6] Dinners of this sort were aspects of the new professionalism, the gathering of experts to praise one of their own. As Brooker has shown, the sites of London modernists' meetings—tea-rooms, cafés, restaurants—had semiotic significance. Inviting Blunt to Dieudonné was an honor; it was one of the most expensive Soho restaurants: "the Baedeker considered this a restaurant of the highest class," writes Brooker; "evening dress was usual and dinner cost between 7/10 and 10/-."[7]

Blunt was never to form part of a battle of dinners. As he came to see the dinner, it emerged from Lady Gregory's visit to Newbuildings Place after Christmas and was her way of cheering him up. To both of them it was (not surprisingly) a Blunt-centered dinner, entirely separate from the agonistic discourses of London-based literary movements. Blunt was dying for company: on 13 November he had written Gregory, with a hint of self-pity, "How are you & is there any chance of your being in London this winter? I am beginning again to lead my winter life of dormouse [*sic*]. It is all that is left me at my age." (Dormice, at least the British variety, have long periods of celibate hibernation.) Since 1906, Lady Anne had been living at Sheykh Obeyd, in part because Blunt had invited his cousin's niece Dorothy Carleton to live with him at Newbuildings in a romantic relationship. Blunt had "adopted" Dorothy as his "niece" and was not altogether living like a "dormouse," but when Dorothy went to visit her non-adoptive family in London, Blunt was lonely. He wrote again on 13 December, "At this time of year I lead the life of a tortoise . . ."[8] (Tortoises are reclusive.) In close and regular contact with Blunt, Gregory was able to write immediately to Yeats in response to the suggestion of the dinner, revising it with a light but sure touch:

I am sure the invitation would please him very much. I don't think he would go to London though, I think he has sworn against it—still he likes an invitation of the sort, and from the Younger Generation—If he can't come up, it might be possible to suggest some little presentation instead of the dinner—their own books perhaps in a little case—something with a line of inscription—which they could take to Newbuildings & see him & his surroundings.[9]

Gregory knew that those "surroundings" would be impressive and that Blunt was proud of them. She happily took on the role of conduit: "I am willing to invite him," she wrote, and two days later she was writing Blunt to schedule her own visit to Newbuildings.

The style of visit Gregory suggested was more old-fashioned than Pound's avant-garde Soho get-together. Instead of Pound hosting Blunt on Pound's own bohemian territory, Blunt would host Pound and the other poets in his manor house in West Sussex. The paradigm shifted from dinner in the exotic, foreign *quartier* of the metropolis to dinner in an upper-class English manor house. At this point, then, once Gregory wrote her response on 28 November, the dinner became something of a cultural hybrid, drawing on both modernist and Victorian practices. Two upper-class Victorians, Lady Gregory and Blunt, were now involved in the planning. Making herself the messenger, Lady Gregory became part of the cultural flow initiated by Pound and Yeats. Lady Gregory did not, however, mention the proposed dinner in her letter to Blunt. That she saved for her visit to Newbuildings just after Christmas, when she could deliver the invitation face to face, the idea for the dinner appearing to issue from herself directly and personally. Lady Gregory functioned as intermediary, but the verbal delivery of the invitation to Blunt gave him the impression, one he retained, that she was its source. "I feel that I owe this most agreeable little fete to you," he wrote her the day after the dinner.[10] In a sense he was right; the event began to come into being when Blunt gave his acceptance to Lady Gregory.

As Blunt assimilated the idea, Lady Gregory's contribution was the dominant one. He wrote in his diary that she had arrived bringing

> . . . an invitation to me with which she had been charged by a group of young poets that I would accept a complimentary dinner to be given me by them. I am of course much flattered by this and still more surprised, for I have been quite unaware of having any following among the young in poetry and I wd gladly accept it if it could be given me here, but I cannot go to London for any possible consideration. Lady Gregory thinks I might invite them here. She also has agreed to help Dorothy in her literary executorship of my will and is anxious that I should forestall it in some Degree by publishing now a complete Edition of my verse.[11]

As Blunt experiences her visit, Lady Gregory brings the excitement of the cosmopolitan literary world to quiet West Sussex; she is in touch with "young poets" and the poetry market. Her authority also extends to social skills: she "thinks I might ask them to lunch with me instead." Like Yeats, Blunt defers to her superior understanding of how to arrange these things.

That the project was to be "entirely a men's dinner," as the Yeats–Pound letter announced, never seems to have bothered her. Understanding her importance in linking the eminent young poets with the eminent older poet, Gregory made herself indispensable. To Pound and Yeats she had already suggested a visit to Newbuildings Place; to Blunt she now also suggested a dinner at Newbuildings Place. She who was not to dine on the peacock was nonetheless calling the shots. Blunt hoped Lady Gregory would be a guest; "I hope you are to be of the poets' party," he wrote her.[12] She responded that she was "very sad at missing the occasion" but offered as excuse "home calls" and her brother-in-law's death. No doubt she remembered and respected the wording of the letter.[13]

As the necessary link between the chief poet of the day, W. B. Yeats, and the wealthy, upper-class celebrity eccentric Wilfrid Blunt, Lady Gregory actively maintained her position in this loop. When Yeats forgets to mail the invitation to Blunt (or so Pound reports), leaving it in London when he is at Stone Cottage, Pound writes Gregory asking her to write Blunt about the date.[14] Then at Gregory's request Blunt sends a telegram to Pound confirming the date, writing her again to say that although he has not "received the formal invitation," nevertheless preparations are under way: "I have had the peacock slain in preparation, as peacocks require a deal of hanging."[15] Lady Gregory makes it all work.

The Peacock: "L'Art et L'Argent"

The peacock, another nineteenth-century element in the dinner for Blunt, emerged collectively from the minds of the older people involved in the planning. On 25 November, the day after the letter about the dinner was composed, Yeats again wrote Lady Gregory—this time in his own handwriting—and sent her a copy of his new poem "The Peacock," the one that Pound heard him composing through the chimney. Scholars have attempted (hitherto inaccurately) to designate an inspiration for this poem. Humphrey Carpenter, Pound's biographer, writes that "on their return to Stone Cottage" from the dinner for Blunt, Yeats wrote "The Peacock," but that's impossible: the letter in the Berg Collection makes clear that when Yeats sent Gregory the poem the dinner hadn't happened yet, and anyway on 25 November there was no peacock on the menu.[16] It was Lady Gregory who later suggested this most important ceremonial detail. Nor was it, as Hugh Kenner has suggested, about the "great peacock" that James McNeill Whistler planned but never painted for the Boston Public Library.[17] It was, however, inspired by Whistler.

"What's riches to him / That has made a great peacock / In the pride of his eye?" The relation of "riches" to "peacock," and the haughty, defiant, theatrically anti-materialist pose of these opening lines, associate them with the story of the Peacock Room, which Yeats would have read about in Elizabeth and Joseph Pennell's book *The Life of James McNeill Whistler*, newly reissued in 1908. In 1876, the wealthy London ship-owner Frederick Leyland, who owned Whistler's *La princesse du pays de la porcelaine*, commissioned Whistler to make small revisions in the decoration of the dining room in his London house to better display the painting. Whistler's changes ended up costing Leyland more than he had expected to pay. When (in 1877) Leyland paid in pounds and not guineas, as artists were supposed to be paid, the insulted artist further revised his wall design and kept on painting. Whistler painted "a pair of peacocks aggressively confronting each other," and "scattered at the feet of one" of the birds were the coins "that Leyland refused to pay."[18] This additional

Figure 6. James McNeill Whistler, from *Harmony in Blue and Gold: The Peacock Room*, south wall mural. Reproduced by permission of the Freer Gallery of Art, Smithsonian Institution, Washington, D.C.: Gift of Charles Lang Freer, F1904.61.

picture he called *L'Art et L'Argent* (Figure 6). The dominant bird (on the right) wears a ruffled collar like the kind Leyland always wore; the more submissive peacock has a white feather like Whistler's lock of white hair.[19]

Thus the new picture on the dining room wall actually commemorated the fight between the rich man and the artist, and the rich man let it stay. "His ghost will be gay / Adding feather to feather / For the pride of his eye," wrote Yeats, and that was exactly what Whistler had done: underpaid, as he thought himself, he had kept on making beautiful peacocks on Leyland's dining room walls. Moreover, the room's wainscot was "embellished with a gold eye-feather motif" and its solid blue wall with a "gold breast-feather design." Quite literally, Whistler was "adding feather to feather / For the pride of his eye": these were the decorations that Leyland had never commissioned but was charged for. The magnificent Peacock Room was a work of high aestheticism: Whistler's choice of the peacock as motif has been imputed to the influential remark of Ruskin in *Stones of Venice* ("Remember that the most beautiful things in the world are the most useless; peacocks and lilies for instance").

In addition, as Linda Merrill has shown, it has visual sources in a Satsuma faience vase, nineteenth-century Japanese lacquer ware, and a Japanese woodcut.[20]

Reading Yeats's new poem the day after she read his suggestion of a dinner for Blunt, Lady Gregory possibly connected the two letters written to her on successive days and made a subliminal association. In her autobiography she gives a different reason, but the association is still between Yeats and peacocks. She is pleased to take credit for the chief element of the menu, the one by which she matched the supply of one of her two important men with the demand of the other. Blunt, she says, "had at that time a large flock of peafowl, so large that some were killed and eaten from time to time." And, she writes,

> . . . in suggesting that one would be an appropriate dish at his lunch I had told him how Yeats had once been tempted to go to a reception at some London house by the rumour that a roast peacock was always a feature of the supper; and in his disappointment at not finding this . . .[21]

Blunt's letter of 7 January confirms that the choice of *entrée* was discussed during Gregory's visit after Christmas, because he appears to be referring to an earlier exchange: "[T]here shall certainly be a peacock for luncheon. The idea is just to my fancy and one quite easy to realize at Newbuildings." Blunt's word "fancy" suggests the tradition of the nineteenth century's aestheticized peacock.

Pound's letter to his mother emphasized the way the meal fit the Olde Englishe decor of the house, especially appealing to Anglophile Americans: "We were fed upon roast peacock in feathers which went very well with the iron-studded barricades on the stairway and other medieval relics and Burne-Jones tapestry."[22] From Ruskin to Whistler to Yeats to Gregory to Blunt to Pound's gullet and all the other poets' gullets, from icon to *entreé*, the peacock moved from the nineteenth century into the twentieth. Blunt's 12-year-old granddaughter Lady Anne Lytton, a wise child, was able to inform Patricia Hutchins much later that (contrary to the poets' assumption) the bird was *not* served "in full plumage." "Regarding the roasted peacock— The one appearing in full plumage was in fact the skin of the whole bird arranged over a dummy to look realistic—the roasted bird followed on a separate dish."[23] In becoming an English country house dinner, the Soho restaurant dinner originally intended to fête "the grandest of old men, the last of the great Victorians" and co-opt him

Figure 7. The Blunt Coffer by Henri Gaudier-Brzeska (side view). Private collection.

Figure 8. The Blunt Coffer by Henri Gaudier-Brzeska (top view). Private collection.

into modernism had instead been taken over by a late Victorian symbol that would be forever attached to the occasion.

A Box of Pentelican and Siennese Marble

The idea of a container of poems was also Lady Gregory's contribution, but this conventional form of tribute became more exotic and "modern" as Pound took it over. Some "little presentation," she had written, "their own books perhaps in a little case—something with a line of inscription—which they could take to Newbuildings & see him & his surroundings." The combination of container and text was a customary form of gift: only a week before the peacock dinner, the "past and present members" of the South Notts Hunt presented the Earl of Harrington, on his 70th birthday, with "an illuminated address enclosed in a gold casket."[24] In honor of Hardy's 80th birthday (but in October 1919), each of forty-three poets wrote out fair copies of "some verses of his own, and the manuscripts, bound together in a beautiful volume, were presented to Mr. Hardy . . ."[25] (Yeats and Newbolt were among the forty-three; no cat dinners this time.)

Pound took this idea and ran with it: he commissioned a marble box from the 20-year-old French sculptor Henri Gaudier-Brzeska, a recent "discovery" of Pound's whose work had been exhibited in the summer of 1913 at the Allied Artists' Salon at the Albert Hall. The marble box was no "little case": it was 4½ × 10¼ × 4⅞ inches, the bottom made of Pentelican marble and the lid of "grey, pink-veined Siennnese marble." Gaudier did this "rush job" in "two weeks in January"; Pound paid him £6.[26] Variously called a casket, a reliquary, a trough, a marble pen-box, and a sarcophagus, this was the container in which the poetic "culture" of the young poets was transmitted to Newbuildings (Figures 7 and 8). The transfer of the gift from the visiting poets' possession to Blunt's would mark their provisional affiliation with the older poet. To Blunt's eye shockingly "Futurist," its contents incomprehensibly modern, the Gaudier-Brzeska marble box brought the fresh air of 1914 into the "sixteenth century defensible grange."[27] As T. S. Eliot wrote of the smoking and dancing "Cousin Nancy" indulged in, ". . . her aunts were not quite sure how they felt about it, / But they knew that it was modern."

It wasn't just the artistic style that was shocking; the overt sexuality made a strong and naughty statement. As the art historian David Getsy has noted, Gaudier shaped the nude female body carved on one side of the box in such a way as to emphasize its sexuality. By making the body appear "to be simultaneously reclining and fully frontal," Gaudier created "unfettered visual accessibility."

Gaudier reiterated this display of the female body through the regularized shapes of the secondary sex characteristics. Despite the approximated and deliberately crude handling of the figure, he made sure to signify its sex clearly through the addition of perfectly circular breasts. Rather than just leaving the pelvis blank, Gaudier furthermore chose to call attention to the pubis by inscribing a "V" shape that matches the breasts in its frontality and geometric regularity.[28]

The box is additionally sexual in another way: "the compression of the female figure to the rectangular format raises the implication that such a figure or form is also somehow contained within the casket itself," so that " 'the opening of the box" is made analogous to the sexual act.[29] The suggestion is that the young male poets are giving the old male poet—well known for his interest in the female form—a miniature naked woman. The word "box" in its vulgar sense emphasizes this joke.

Although we do not know precisely what Pound said to Gaudier when he commissioned the box, Gaudier seems to have picked up on the possible implications of "entirely a men's dinner" and happily exploited them. The "ribald allusion" of the box—the *Blunt coffer*, Getsy calls it—"was consistent with the still-youthful Gaudier's infamous irreverence, puckish behaviour, and predilection for sexual humor." The coffer was not the polite, functional "little case" that Lady Gregory had suggested, the respectful gift "which they could take to Newbuildings." It implicated its owner, or any male who handled it, in sexual activity, because the decoration "established a direct association between the physical object and the image of the naked female." Moreover, if the sexual was "a sign of the modern," then the box constituted a rejection of the "presumed prudery characteristic of Gaudier's and Pound's Victorian forebears."[30]

The association of female genitalia with a "box" exists not only in slang but in myth: as Getsy points out, the conjunction of "boxes and female nudes had been used for decades as the iconographic attributes of Pandora," and in her book on Gaudier, Evelyn Silber suggests the influence of Harry Bates's statue *Pandora*.[31] The shape of the female figure on top of the box in that sculpture resembles Gaudier's woman strikingly in her position (head on the left, legs on the right), a head in profile, chin resting on her neck, and long arms stretched along her legs.

The gendered guest list made a certain point, as would, later, several of the poems enclosed in the box and the poem Blunt read aloud to his guests, but the coffer, writes Getsy, was " 'the object that made the sexual the most visible." The two central emblems of the dinner, separately and almost innocently suggested by Lady Gregory as appropriate and decorous—the peacock with its emphasis on the display of male courting behavior and the "little case," the nude female in her box—embodied a message about the sexual implications of the dinner and anticipated the sexual and professional rivalry of its three celebrity poets.

"Ferocious Youth"

Another minor conflict over details indicated conceptual differences among the planners themselves. In a final pre-prandial letter, Yeats tells Lady Gregory about a disagreement over the presence of a photographer:

My dear Lady Gregory: I can do nothing about the press. Pound says "tell Lady Gregory we hate the newspaper press as Blunt hates the British Empire"[.] I spoke of a "photographer"[.] he made contemptuous allusions to Ducal shooting parties, which are photographed for the American press. I had to tell him Blunt did not make the suggestion or Blunt might have suffered the same eclipse Bridges did when he refused to honour Blunt. The others probably think as Pound does Sturge Moore is sure to. I preserved our dignity by saying we had mechanically suggested what is usual in case of plays. Ferocious Youth does however agree to my sending a report to "*The Times*" as this leaves "a record for posterity"[.] I was so sick and sleapy on Friday night that I hardly know what you said. Did you say I was to write to Miss Lawrence to get a photographer if we cannot? If she does he will not be appreciated, but I have no doubt he will be endured but I think he should not send it anything to the press. It is really more valuable to Blunt

for these young men to be at ease, & feel they have done a spontaneous fine
thing, than for him to have the compliment made more generally known
at the moment. It will get known very quickly. I think any writers of the
press might make them feel it was done with that object. Pound suggests
our bringing Nagochi the Japanese poet, as "he will make it known among
men of letters in Japan." "It concerns the world of letters" he says "& nobody
else." I hesitate about the Japanese, as I am afraid he may not know Blunt's
work & I cannot find out until Saturday till when he dines with me. He is
quite a distinguished man & Prof of English in some Japanese University.
I am afraid if full up with people, who might show ignorance & so spoil the
compliment . . .

Yours WB Yeats[32]

The famous photograph of the seven poets—famous at least among
the *literati*—was unlikely to have attracted the same audience as
pictures of "Ducal shooting parties." Probably the phrase "photographed for the American press" expressed the true source of
Pound's contempt, the vulgarity of Americans gawking at titled
people hunting or engaging in other kinds of aristocratic activities.
Pound did not want such low, uneducated people to have visual
access to his dinner for Wilfrid Scawen Blunt. If "we"—Pound and
Yeats presumably—"hate the newspaper press as Blunt hates the
British Empire," then literature is linked with anti-imperialism in
its passion, purity, and superiority to a more "popular" force. As
articulated by Pound, quoted by Yeats, belletristic values form the
sacred term to the profane "newspaper press." The profane is vulgar,
tabloid, ignorant, and American. The press feeds the low American
hunger for pictures of British aristocrats, exotic and marvelous in
their hunting gear. Imagine if photos of Blunt, Yeats, et al., the
lofty world of poetry, provided such a low form of entertainment!
The distance in value between the "world of letters" and the tabloid world can be measured in the strong feeling of that repeated
word "hate." To Yeats, Pound (twenty years younger) is "Ferocious
Youth."

Yeats's letter is a valuable one because in its fragmentary quotations
from Pound we can see how his mind works when he is talking off
the record, not issuing manifestos or framing utterances for posterity. The tone is recognizably Pound's "altaforte," but the apparent
spontaneity allows us to see how he imagined a "world of letters"
and conceived his role in it. The other term in Pound's contrast, the

realm to which the dinner should be accessible, is "the world of letters." Pound's comments on Yone Noguchi explain what he means
and illuminate the phrase. Born in 1875 in Tsushima, Noguchi had
traveled to California before arriving in London in 1902. Like Pound,
he wanted to be a poet (in English) and had made his way to the literary center of the English-speaking world. He had been Professor of
English Literature at Keio University since 1905, but Robert Bridges,
that other non-guest, had invited him to lecture at Oxford in 1913, so
he was available to dine, if asked.[33] Pound's remark "he will make it
known among men of letters in Japan" reveals how Pound's conceptual "world of letters" functions person by person. It is not an institution, nor does it have any corporate form: it exists, it comes into
being, because poets and "men of letters" talk to one another. It is
transnational: "men of letters in Japan" are simply the Japanese equivalent of Yeats and Pound, equally superior to the "newspaper press."
(Noguchi had actually worked for a Japanese-American newspaper
in California, but Pound was probably not aware of his complete
résumé.) The peacock dinner would be a small gathering of members
of that "world" to honor one of its own.

   In his published account of the dinner, Pound listed the writers
who would have come to the dinner, had they been in England at
the time: Lawrence, Joyce, Padraic Colum, Rupert Brooke.[34] By
implication Pound sketches those "men of letters" who constitute
his ideal "world of letters." Just as the phrase "he will make it known
among men of letters in Japan" implied a series of conversations, each
conveying news of the dinner for Blunt, so the list of contemporary
writers and their whereabouts suggests a "conversational commu-
nity." Pound actually knows where all these writers are; he's in touch
with them, keeping tabs on them, maintaining a flow of friendship
through correspondence, if not through conversation.

   Yeats's attitude was more forthright and practical: with Lady
Gregory in the wings, he approached the peacock dinner more prag-
matically. "I preserved our dignity by saying we had mechanically
suggested what is usual in case of plays." As founders and directors
of the Abbey Theatre, Gregory and Yeats were master publicists,
expert in "theatre business, management of men," especially management of hostile audiences, refractory players, touchy patrons,
and unpredictable reviewers. To them the "world of letters" had no
boundaries or levels: it was coextensive with the non-literary world,

articulated through social, political, and economic systems. Both "worlds" existed in the same plane: the Abbey directors regularly walked through the city to the offices of the *Dublin Evening Mail* or the *Freeman's Journal* to drop off a press release or advertising, and letters from them appeared frequently in *The Irish Times*. They were running a commercial enterprise and dependent on the press, however irritated they got at reviews or editorials.

In November and December 1913 and early January 1914, while all the details of the peacock dinner were being worked out, the dependence of the fluctuating fortunes of the Abbey on the press dominated every other concern; the dinner's value came to be seen as a usefully distracting media event. Because of the outcry in Liverpool over a traveling production of Synge's *Playboy of the Western World*, performances had to be stopped, "and," wrote Gregory to Yeats, "I mind more the bad press (evidently Irish) it will be quoted for ever." A few sentences later she wrote, "Go to the dinner to Wilfrid Blunt, I am sure the invitation wd. please him very much," and then closed, "Wilson very rightly cross at players chattering to interviewers—I think we must make some rules against it."[35] Living in a continual struggle to create good press and thereby raise the value of the theater and all attendant artistic projects, Gregory soon saw the dinner for Blunt as potentially useful. She began spinning it even before it happened. To John Quinn she wrote on 1 January 1914, "I spent my Sunday in the country with Wilfrid Blunt. He has given up politics and is writing fine poetry again." It was in this letter that Gregory referred to the "cult" of Blunt among the younger generation. Writing to Quinn, a rich, well-connected lawyer in New York, was another way of sending out press releases. Quinn was a former lover of Lady Gregory's; they had had an affair at Quinn's apartment in New York two years earlier (December 1911–January 1912), when the Abbey was on tour there. No doubt Lady Gregory (who was never to know that both men had saved in their files the poems and letters she sent them) also felt a private *frisson* at connecting her two lovers in this letter.

Gregory and Yeats were involved in two other public relations battles that would have kept them thinking about the worldliness of the "world of letters." In the January issue of the *English Review*, George Moore had published the section of his autobiography *Hail and Farewell* titled "Yeats, Lady Gregory, and Synge," a chapter unflattering to all its subjects, especially Lady Gregory. In January, while

the peacock dinner was being planned and then eaten, Moore had
been in correspondence with Gregory about her threatened lawsuit
over his representation of her as a Protestant proselytizer. As Lady
Gregory wrote Moore's editor Sydney Pawling on 5 January 1914,
the false description of her would "damage her position" as director
of the Abbey Theatre because she would appear as an "enemy of the
Catholic faith," the faith of most of the players.[36] In a postscript to his
letter of 7 January, Blunt wrote her, "I have just read George Moore's
article about you. It is an outrage and stupid too, a thing of the gut-
ter—."[37] Yeats had just written the lines that became the closing poem
of *Responsibilities*, in which he says that his "priceless things" have
become "but a post the passing dogs defile," Moore being one of
those urinating dogs. In a letter to Gregory written after the dinner, Yeats said of Moore, "People have constantly spoken to me of
the article with indignation."[38] All the more reason, then, to have a
record of the Blunt testimonial in *The Times*; not just "for posterity,"
as Pound said, but very much for the present moment.

Yet another Abbey Theatre conflict, transpiring simultaneously
with the George Moore libel and the planning for the Blunt dinner, threatened to divide Lady Gregory and Yeats. The previous
winter, the Abbey Theatre players had been on tour in Chicago,
New York, Boston, and London, accompanied by Lady Gregory.
Several benefit matinée performances had been given to raise money
for the art gallery Hugh Lane, Lady Gregory's nephew, wanted to
have erected in Dublin. He was willing to donate his entire collection of Post-Impressionist paintings if an appropriate building
could be built. At the time of the benefit performances, the Dublin
Corporation was promising to pay for a permanent building if funds
could be raised privately to buy a site. However, in September 1913
the Corporation voted not to fund the building, and Lady Gregory
and Yeats were left with a fund (they called it the Guarantee Fund)
that no longer had a purpose. In November the Abbey players began
demanding the money for themselves, because they had given their
labor free as a contribution to the fund. At first Gregory and Yeats
thought the funds should be put aside in a special trust account for
the site, to be purchased some day in the future, but as the players got
angrier and threatened to sue Lady Gregory, Yeats and the players
put the issue before the Solicitor-General to get his opinion. In the
event, on 31 January, Jonathan Pim handed down the opinion that

the money should go to the players, as it did.[39] From November 1913
through January 1914, Gregory and Yeats were exchanging several
letters a week on the subject.

These episodes—the traveling *Playboy* production, the Moore
libel, the Guarantee Fund dispute, and the dinner for Blunt—over-
lapped with one another in chronology, and viewed together, they
show the diasporic spread of the Gregory-Yeats culture business, with
publication in London potentially ruining a theater in Dublin, money
collected in Chicago and New York in a legal dispute in Dublin, and
a dinner in Sussex that might be written up in *The* (London) *Times*.
While Pound was talking loftily about "the world of letters," Yeats
and Gregory were coping with labor disputes, lawyers, money, and
the press.

With all his practicality, his vigorous engagement in battles on so
many fronts, his very worldly sense of his "trade," Yeats had good
sense about what was appropriate for a poets' dinner. He did not
want a reporter present or a photograph sent to the press and in the
end agreed only to a local photographer hired by Blunt's nurse Miss
Lawrence. Living with the ferocious young Pound, Yeats respected
the passion of his desire to meet Blunt. As one who was to be a guest
at the dinner himself, Yeats was thinking of it as a social occasion,
the beginning of a new conversation, not a publicity gimmick: "It is
really more valuable to Blunt for these young men to be at ease, &
feel they have done a spontaneous fine thing, than for him to have
the compliment made more generally known at the moment." For
that same reason, his consciousness of the reality of the occasion, the
poets sitting together around the table, Yeats was reluctant to invite
someone like Noguchi, who might never have heard of Blunt and
therefore "might show ignorance and so spoil the compliment." In
deference to Lady Gregory's pragmatism, however, or perhaps letting
his own resurface, Yeats adds that the dinner "will get known very
quickly" even without the press in attendance.

Nor was Pound entirely idealistic. In the event, Pound, having
seen the photograph, requested extra copies—four extra copies—
to send to America, where people are so vulgar they like pictures.
Pound looks good in the picture, and he is in the lofty company of the
greatest living poet (so Pound thought Yeats) and the most notorious
anti-imperialist, along with four lesser figures on the sides who con-
veniently frame the greater three. When Pound said of Noguchi, "he

will make it known among men of letters in Japan," he had imagined the imminent dinner as part of a conversation among poets, an episode that would be heard round the world; his own record of it would be published in *Poetry*, so the dinner would be made known among men and women of letters in America, and he saw to it that the account was published in four other places. In fact another American account, published in the *Boston Evening Transcript*, has recently come to light.[40] The "world of letters" was after all a notional professional organization, as worldly as any guild or association; poets were as worldly as lawyers, physicians, or clergy. It was Yeats who talked of ' "sending a report to *The Times*"; Yeats who said he had suggested "what is usual in case of plays"; and Yeats who confidently wrote Lady Gregory, "It will get known very quickly." Yeats knew the peacock dinner would be spectacle. In their distinct ways, both men knew that it would not be a private dinner. It would be eaten for an audience. It was a ritual staged by professional poets to provoke and edify other poets and all members of the "world of letters." It was already visible. In a profession as crowded, as flourishing, and as unstructured as literature, an event like this one in January 1914 would be news.

3

Victorian Adultery

. . . there are several women who amuse me, I don't care which of them it is, but I must have someone. There is Lady Gregory, Mrs Batten, Mrs Thurlow, Mrs Singleton . . .

Wilfrid Blunt, as quoted by Lady Anne Blunt

The peacock dinner was "entirely a men's dinner," but it required Lady Gregory to make it happen. She was the link, the linchpin, the conduit, the node in the network. It was her friendships with men that drew the poets together.

It wasn't simply that Lady Gregory and Sir William Gregory had met Wilfrid and Lady Anne Blunt at a few London dinner parties or corresponded about Irish politics, as Yeats may have assumed. The connection was deeper, more significant, and completely unknown to anyone but the parties themselves: Lady Gregory and Wilfrid Blunt had had an affair thirty years previously. The intimacy with Blunt changed Lady Gregory forever, in ways she could not of course have known at the time. Their romance, her only adultery, was for her a passionate awakening to sexuality, to love, and to authorship, all inextricably mixed. It enlarged her sympathy for sexual transgressions and activated her literary gifts; it made her the kind of person who would be attracted to and attractive to a high-power literary man like Yeats, who (like Blunt) was open to poetic collaboration with women. The intensity of the intimacy between Gregory and Blunt and its erotic and literary dynamics formed the necessary pre-condition of the peacock dinner.

Yeats knew about the intimacy but not its secret origin. He seems never to have suspected Lady Gregory of an affair with Blunt, or one with John Quinn, or of any sexual adventures whatsoever. For him she was, as he wrote in 1909, "mother, friend, sister and brother," "more than kin," but never a romantic figure.[1] Lady Gregory introduced Blunt and Yeats in 1898, and it was she who arranged and mediated all their meetings. It was she, therefore, who had to be consulted about Blunt's likely response to a testimonial dinner. Yeats gave the plan his blessing ("of course I approve the scheme") but deferred to Lady Gregory's familiarity with Blunt's habits and tastes.

To study the intimacy between Lady Gregory and Wilfrid Blunt is to understand the depth, intensity, and significance of the heterosexual attachment that made possible the peacock dinner's celebration of masculinity and homosocial friendship. The attachment continued even when they were no longer sexual partners, making her the natural person to deliver the invitation, and making his acceptance natural. The peacock dinner emerged from Gregory and Blunt's continuing friendship, and its narrative trajectory begins at the start of their affair, in July 1882.

"The fellow knows he has a handsome head . . ."

Because Wilfrid Scawen Blunt was an exceedingly good-looking and wealthy man with a powerful personality, his personal charisma turned him into a celebrity, the kind of man young women would become infatuated with and young men would want to meet. Blunt's distinct blend of anti-imperialist politics, sexuality, and "poetry," mixed with the exoticism of his Arab robes, Arab horses, and Arabian travels, created an irresistible form of transgressive masculinity. Mary Colum thought he was one of the three "handsomest and most romantic-looking men" she had ever seen (the others were W. B. Yeats and Roger Casement); Margot Asquith thought him "one of the four most beautiful men she had ever seen"; Lady Emily Lytton called him "strikingly handsome," even at age 53.[2] Men, also, were charmed by his looks. Sir William Gregory, according to his wife, had been struck "in the bull-ring at Madrid" by the "extraordinary good looks" of the young matador and was surprised to learn that he was "an attaché from the English Legation, Wilfrid Blunt."[3] Lord Houghton, commenting in 1882 on Blunt's dramatic anti-imperialist politics, said, "The fellow knows he has a handsome head and he wants it to be seen on Temple Bar."[4] To some his good looks were overpowering: "Wilfrid Blunt was a magnificent figure," wrote Edward Marsh in his memoirs, "especially in the Arab dress which he wore whenever he could—to me too alarming for easy intercourse" (Figure 9).[5]

According to Elizabeth Longford, Blunt had at least thirty-eight *recorded* lovers.[6] Even before Lady Gregory, Blunt had

seduced one married lady many years younger than her husband, fallen passionately in love with another, lived with a third in South America, helped to ruin the marriage of a fourth in Sussex, and been himself drawn from the arms of a little madrilène by the famous Anglo-Irish courtesan, Catherine Walters, known as 'Skittles.'[7]

In the romance novel *Belgrave Square*, a character refers to one of these events: "Look at Doll Zouche and that miserable business with

Figure 9. Wilfrid Blunt on Pharaoh, painted by Lady Anne Blunt. Private collection.

Wilfred [sic] Scawen Blunt. Amusing in its fashion, but all quite unnecessary."[8] (She was the wife in the marriage ruined in Sussex.) The term "cad" has been used of Blunt, as has the phrase "insatiable womaniser," but both categories gloss over a set of sexual practices that are more culturally complex.[9] Blunt's grandson writes more tolerantly, "Perhaps the sins of sex are among the least of the deadly ones," adding an interesting notion: "Perhaps there are differing grades of adultery . . ."[10] To some extent Blunt's grandfather-in-law Lord Byron functioned as a model: the poetry, the anti-imperialism, the dashing and visible political engagements, the series of sexual partners, and the self-conscious construction of himself as "a lover" are all Byronic, but Blunt was never self-destructive, violent, or "mad" like Byron. Blunt was desperately eager for children and would never have smashed furniture, fired pistols in the room below that of his pregnant wife, as Byron did, or attempted to rape her.[11] Blunt did not fall in love with his sister, though three of his most important loves were cousins.[12] Mark Girouard characterizes Blunt's style as "modern courtly love." Some poets, he writes, "exalted love without sex as the purest form of it; but more often the ultimate aim was a consummated love with a mistress who was not necessarily, or even usually, a wife."[13]

Like the lovers Girouard discusses, Blunt's affairs were conducted in a "style of high literary romance."

He believed (or persuaded himself that he believed) in what he called the "passion of the soul," in which a spiritual relationship was what really mattered, but a physical one was a necessary part of it. Sexual intrigue was only worthwhile to him if conducted with high drama, and on an elevated literary and artistic plane.[14]

Certainly Blunt's courtship of Lady Emily Lytton fit this pattern. She was the 18-year-old daughter of his best friend, Lord Robert Bulwer-Lytton, former Viceroy of India and Ambassador to France, who died in 1891. Less than a year later, Blunt began a romance of a sort with her. The dalliance included, among other features, an acrostic on her name:

> Enshrined within my heart of hearts she lies,
> Mysterious, secret, by the world unguessed.
> Ideal love is sealed in her blue eyes,
> Love without words, the sweetest, holiest, best.

So far, pure and elevated. But then comes a *volta* after which the love
is less pure:

> Yes. She is thus. But there comes a day
> Looked for yet feared, when Love shall rend the veil.
> Young summer calls us to the woods away.
> There will I venture my soul's passionate tale,
> There kneeling crave a first ungrudging kiss.
> O Sun, shine bright today on hill or dale.
> Nurse, O soft wind, tonight my happiness.[15]

The day "Looked for yet feared" never came with Lady Emily, but
the four years of flirtatious letters, furtive kisses, hand-holding under
the table, and small gifts, not to mention numerous poems, show how
the apparatus of courtship was a great part of the pleasure for Blunt.

The achieved consummation also merited romantic language. In
his private diaries Blunt wrote hyperbolically about his night with the
hitherto virginal Margot Tennant (later to become Mrs., then Lady
Asquith), who (according to Blunt's account) had been the aggressor
in their one-night stand:

Of all the nights of my life I remember not one more perfect, soul and body.
Not that Margot is a *great* beauty, but she has a sweet little body, and I found
her a virgin still . . . Of her soul who can tell except that it is unique in all
the world. People may say what they will, but a night like this is the purest &
most exquisite delight our lives can give. To be ashamed of it is to be unwor-
thy of all that is noblest & best & tenderest in our possibilities of feeling. . . .
What a treasure to have won from Time![16]

Here Blunt sounds Paterian, as in some of the phrases from the famous
coda to *The Renaissance*: "While all melts under our feet, we may well
grasp at any exquisite passion, or any contribution to knowledge that
seems by a lifted horizon to set the spirit free for a moment . . ." or
"Great passions may give us this quickened sense of life, ecstasy and
sorrow of love," or even "For art comes to you proposing frankly to
give nothing but the highest quality to your moments as they pass,
and simply for those moments' sake."[17] What art can offer to Pater,
sexual love—especially, most significantly, a single night of sexual
love, unassociated with any long-term romantic commitment—can
offer to Blunt, "the purest & most exquisite delight." This is needless
to say a secular view, the "treasure to have won from Time" briefly
offsetting our mortality. As if it were rhetorically inevitable, Blunt

mentions Margot's "soul" after mentioning her "sweet little body," but all he has to say is that it is "unique."

Blunt spoke somewhat less aesthetically of his sexual rivals, whom he tended to disparage. Lady Mary Elcho, married to Lord Elcho, bore a child by Blunt but also had an "accepted" lover, the conservative politician Arthur Balfour: Blunt, believing they had never consummated their love, remarked of Balfour, "he must be something more or less than a man."[18] H. H. Asquith (another prime minister and rival), was, wrote Blunt, "a good creature but distinctly bourgeois."[19] And again of Asquith, Blunt wrote: "Truly he is a dull fellow though he tries his best to be amiable and sprightly."[20] And Edwin Lutyens, who married Lady Emily Lytton in 1897, was "a rather inferior little young man."[21] Blunt claimed that Sir William Gregory's temporary failure to support the Egyptian nationalist cause was due to concern to protect his reputation "as a clubman and diner-out."[22] And of Yeats (whom Blunt may have suspected of being Lady Gregory's lover, though he was not), Blunt noted in his diary, "Though doubtless a man of genius, he has a strong touch in him of the charlatan."[23]

Romance and sexuality were inseparable from the category of the literary not only for Blunt but for some of his women also. They did not copy his style, but their romantic entanglements with Blunt inspired them to write. Locked up in trunks in stately houses or in manuscripts in the British Library or in safe deposit boxes in London, there may possibly be unpublished manuscripts by titled Victorian women who were among Blunt's many lovers. The tradition, if it can be called that, is a hidden one. But Lady Anne Blunt, Lady Gregory, and Lady Emily Lytton (as the married Lady Emily Lutyens) all wrote about Blunt, though they did not publish everything they wrote about him. Blunt caused existential crises in their lives, crises directly occasioned by his sexual involvement with them. In order to make sense of the intense but impermanent experience of being loved by Wilfrid Blunt, the women had recourse to the most private of literary genres—poems (unpublished), diaries, and letters.

At the end of their one-year love affair, in August 1883, the morning after their last night together, Lady Gregory put into Blunt's hands a twelve-sonnet sequence, its tones remorseful, heart-broken, abject, ashamed, and, just briefly, realistic: "I staked my all upon a losing game / Knowing thy nature and the ways of men."[24] It was also a "losing game" for Lady Anne, more "losing" because she was the neglected wife: "I don't agree to the position of Lady G. having all the rose leaves while the thorns are kept for me," she wrote in her journal in December 1884. Her husband had "said something about my 'disliking' Lady Gregory. I don't dislike her, I *did* like her."[25]

Lady Anne was already an author, having written (in collaboration with her husband) *Bedouin Tribes of the Euphrates* and *A Pilgrimage to Nejd* (Figure 10). She had also translated "The Celebrated Romance of the Stealing of the Mare" from the Arabic for Blunt to put into English verse. But Blunt's affair with Lady

Figure 10. Lady Anne Blunt in Dublin, 1888. Reproduced by permission of the British Library Board.

Gregory inspired Lady Anne to write something more personal. At almost the same time as Lady Gregory was giving Blunt the sonnets, on 10 August 1883, Lady Anne was writing the pages of traumatized self-expression—"two pages of lined foolscap"—that she, too, put in his hands three days later.[26] The affair with Lady Gregory gave Lady Anne "the shock of discovering that I have spent many years under a false impression . . . I accept harsh truth, preferring it to a false dream."[27] Lady Anne's statement uses a series of metaphors to explain her feelings. An earthquake has destroyed her house, "of which nothing remains but a heap of ruins. Ivy may grow up and hide the ruins but they will never be a house again." She is like "some traveler deceived by a mirage floating over & hiding a desolate waste . . ." She had a dream

of two ships together steaming round the world—their courses parallel together weathering waves and fierce storms until, as I thought, they reached a great calm sea. Then a sudden fog shut out the other ship from mine. All night long my ship signalled. No answer came. Nothing was there but a sunken rock & my ship struck it & went down & with it perished all my treasure.

All was lost "but my compass & a scroll of Arabic. I sit alone now in an open boat & must learn to row against the waves . . . I strain my eyes for a sight of land."[28] There is no record of what, if anything, Blunt wrote his wife in response to her eloquent missive. Lady Anne was always to row alone; in 1906 she began living separately from her husband, and in 1915 she left England and moved permanently to Sheykh Obeyd, where she died in 1917.[29]

In August 1893, almost ten years to the month after inspiring these outpourings, Blunt was occasioning another crisis: he was attempting to seduce Lady Emily Lytton. Although Blunt toyed with Lady Emily and she was infatuated with him, the romance was never consummated, and he, at least, appeared not to take it seriously. At the time of the Lyttons' summer visit to the Blunts at Crabbet in 1893, the dalliance was at its most intense (Figure 11). During an early morning stroll à deux in the woods behind his house, Blunt asked Lady Emily about the novel that she and his daughter Judith were writing. As she describes the encounter,

I told him I had as yet no plot, and that he was to be the villain. He asked if I came into it and whether I married. I said I had not yet decided that. He then took my hand and said, "Won't you let the villain love you, the villain

Figure 11. Lady Emily Lytton in Blunt's coat (1892).

does love you and will you love the villain?" I told him I would see as the plot worked out. We talked on in this way, he holding my hand and kissing it, and telling me that he loved me . . .[30]

The novel was never completed, but much later Lady Emily did indeed write a book in which Blunt was the villain. In 1953 she published *A Blessed Girl: Memoirs of a Victorian Girlhood Chronicled in an Exchange of Letters 1887–1896*. Unbeknownst to Blunt, she had been sending a play-by-play account of his attempts to seduce her in letters to the Reverend Whitwell Elwin of Booton Rectory, Norwich, "His Rev" to Lady Emily, her mother Lady Lytton, and her sister Lady Betty. His Rev, she writes, "was my sole confidant," and his letters to her "saved me from what might have been disaster." Like a character in a morality play, the young Lady Emily is pulled in two directions, toward the handsome, seductive Blunt (thirty-five years her senior), who kisses her, holds her hand under the table, gives her a ring and tells her she is his "Mahomedan wife," and toward "His Rev," who warns her that "His whole design towards you is that of a demon."[31] Blunt, wrote Reverend Elwin, "continues bent upon effecting your ruin, and . . . the whole of his pretended affection has no other object but to accomplish it."[32]

Lady Emily's "ruin" was not accomplished; it was as a 79-year-old grandmother, the widow of the famous architect Sir Edwin Lutyens, that she published her memoir.[33] Blunt is its villain but also its muse: what drives the narrative, what gives the book its drama and suspense, is the tale of this "corridor-creeper," as he was once called, and his designs on Lady Emily's innocence.[34] Once he tried to open her (locked) bedroom door; Judith Blunt (wrote Lady Emily), hearing the story, immediately "took me off to see a priest," but what His Rev said is not known, because Lady Emily visited him in person to talk over this episode.[35] His Rev is also an ambiguous figure, with an almost voyeuristic interest in the unfolding story. The Reverend Elwin had many "blessed girls" who made him their confidant; Lady Emily may not have been the only one whose hand he held on her visits to Norwich, while his wife watched, sitting "as far away as possible . . ."[36] But from Blunt's attentions and the consequent correspondence with her moral guide, Lady Emily got a book so well written, so witty and charming, such a period piece, that it sold 10,000 copies; more copies indeed than any of Blunt's books sold.[37]

Wilfrid Blunt and Augusta Gregory

For Wilfrid Blunt, the romance with Lady Gregory in the year between "that summer day" in 1882 (her phrase in Sonnet I) and August 1883 was another fling. As he reportedly said to his wife the following year, "I have now got to the age when I like to be amused without giving myself much trouble and there are several women who amuse me, I don't care which of them it is, but I must have someone. There is Lady Gregory, Mrs Batten, Mrs Thurlow, Mrs Singleton, etc., I don't mind which of them."[38] In his diary he referred to it in more idealistic terms as "the passionate element in our intercourse" while they worked together on Egyptian politics.[39] But for Lady Gregory it was important and life-changing, a "love which now is all my life," as she called it in Sonnet III.[40] What her Blunt-related writings show is the way she transformed her sexual passion into her literary career. The "passionate element" in their "intercourse" released the writer in her. Her first publication, a feature on the Egyptian nationalist Colonel

Ahmed Urabi, was occasioned by Blunt, written with his supervision (as well as her husband's), and printed in *The Times* in 1882.[41] A torrent of poems (some of them published under Blunt's name) followed in the wake of their romance. A short story under her own name followed later; and for many years Blunt remained a hidden presence in many of Lady Gregory's canonical Irish works. As Blunt wrote in his diaries when she delivered the invitation for the poets' dinner in his honor, neither her late husband Sir William "nor anyone cd. have guessed then the important part she was to play in the world. Her connection with me was her first emancipation . . . she has been the real inspirer of the Irish literary movement . . ."[42] Blunt also thought that Lady Gregory was the "real inspirer" of the peacock dinner; in letters written after the event, he was constantly thanking her for all she had done.[43]

Men were school, university, and professional training to Lady Gregory, the gateways to the cultural world in which she became one of the most important figures of her generation. Unlike Pound, she had not got a university degree; unlike Yeats, she had not grown up in an artistic family or even gone to school; unlike Blunt, she had not been employed in a diplomatic mission; and unlike Byron, she had not entered Parliament. She grew up in an Anglo-Irish family in County Galway, one of thirteen children, the "plainest" of its five daughters. The men were interested in horses, the women in religion. Educated at home by unmemorable governesses, she was not given access to metropolitan culture. Her mother "did not consider book learning as of any great benefit to girls . . . Religion and courtesy, and holding themselves straight, these were to her mind the three things needful."[44]

Through marriage in 1880 to her 64-year-old Galway neighbor Sir William Gregory, owner of the large estate Coole Park and a house in London, an MP, former colonial governor of Ceylon, member of the Athenaeum, a popular "diner-out" and "club man," 28-year-old Isabella Augusta Persse was introduced to the drawing-rooms and dinner parties of the most powerful families in London, the political and intellectual leaders who constituted the caste of "public moralists," as Stefan Collini calls them (Figure 12). She met Browning, Tennyson, Gladstone, Oscar Wilde, all the most famous and infamous Victorians. With Sir William she traveled in Europe, India, and the Middle East, visiting museums, dining with ambassadors, partying

Figure 12. Lady Gregory in her youth; drawing by Lisa Stillman. Reproduced by permission of Colin P. Smythe.

with royalty. In May 1881 she gave birth to their only child, William Robert. The Irish winter was bad for Sir William's health, and he decided that they would spend the winter in Egypt: it was a warmer, cheaper, and more stimulating place to be. Lady Gregory was not happy to be leaving her new baby, but she had to acquiesce; Robert was left with her sister Adelaide Lane in Cornwall.[45] However, there were compensations: as she put it in her autobiography, during their stay in Cairo in 1881–2, Sir William and Lady Gregory "tumbled into a revolution."[46]

Sir William and Lady Gregory met the Blunts at the house of Sir Gerald FitzGerald, the Director General of Public Accounts in Egypt. Like the Gregorys, the Blunts had no official diplomatic position; they were living in Egypt because, in the words of David Cannadine, Blunt was "attracted to distant lands by a combination of romance, chivalry, and alienation that was almost knight-errantly in its self-indulgent and quest-like intensity."[47] More immediately, they had been diverted from another trip to Nejd (modern Saudi Arabia) by the interesting political situation in Egypt.[48] Lady Gregory's diary entry for 2 December 1881 reads, "Lunched with the Fitzgeralds, Mr & Lady Anne Blunt."[49] By 2 February Lady Gregory's diary entries about Blunt sound warmer and more flirtatious: "Wilfrid sat looking unutterably dejected & I gave him the Arabian Nights & some bonbons to console him."

Lady Gregory's erotic interest in Blunt developed around her political interest in the Egyptian nationalist army colonel Ahmed Urabi (Figure 13). Although the Turkish Khedive still maintained nominal control of Egypt, his policies had left the country bankrupt, and to generate cash he had sold shares in the Suez Canal to British and French interests. As European economic control of Egypt became stronger, alliances among Egyptian, Turkish, British, and French powers were continually shifting. During this time of political instability, Urabi, a native Egyptian, emerged as the leader of a popular nationalist movement and in 1882 was made Minister of War. Sir William had met Urabi and was sympathetic to his political goals, a restored legislative assembly and reform of the army, where the careers open to native Egyptians had recently been limited by the Dual Control, France and England, which managed Egypt's finances. Sir William and Lady Gregory discussed Urabi on many occasions and heard varying opinions of him: he was the subject of conversation when they "dined with Sir E. Malet," British Consul-General in Cairo, and when they went "with Lord Houghton and Mrs. Fitzgerald" to lunch with the Blunts in their tent at Heliopolis.[50] Dining at the Van der Nests, they "heard the account of Arabi's reception at the Feast of the Sacred Carpet in the morning."[51] When Lord Cawdor, the Duliers, and the Goldsmids came to tea, stories were told of Urabi, as they were again when Zohrab Bey came to dine.[52]

Lady Gregory visited Urabi's family on two occasions; on the first of these Lady Anne Blunt served as interpreter and explained

احمد ابى العرابى

Ahmad Arabi the Egyptian

for Lady Gregory October 1883

Figure 13. Ahmed Urabi; signed photograph formerly in Lady Gregory's possession. Reproduced by permission of Colin P. Smythe.

what Urabi's wife and mother were saying.[53] She was just as interested as her husband in all things Arab and spoke Arabic more fluently than he. (This was perhaps the period when, in the words of her journal, she "*did* like" Lady G.) In the spring of 1882, both families, the Gregorys and the Blunts, returned to London. In June, a riot in Alexandria was blamed on Urabi (who had not been present and had no role in it). In July the British, purportedly protecting their interests in the Suez Canal, attacked and defeated Urabi and the army forces loyal to him in a series of battles that lasted until

September. Urabi surrendered and was imprisoned by the British. It was in large part due to Blunt's maneuvers in London that Urabi was not executed: Blunt wrote letters to *The Times*, called on journalists and politicians, organized a legal defense fund, and contributed £300 to it himself. Blunt engaged Mark Napier and A. M. Broadley to defend Urabi, who was banished to Ceylon; he returned to Egypt in 1901.[54]

During the summer and autumn of 1882, when Urabi was a prisoner of British forces in Egypt and his fate uncertain, Sir William's opinion changed several times; "Not, however, his wife," wrote Blunt, whose "woman's constancy" kept her sympathetic with Egypt and Urabi.[55] Her continuing support for Urabi and the Egyptian nationalist cause was inextricable from her attraction to Blunt. As he recorded, her loyalty

naturally drew us more closely than ever together, and at the climax of the tragedy by a spontaneous impulse we found comfort in each other's arms. It was a consummation neither of us, I think, foresaw, and was a quite new experience in her quiet life. It harmonized not ill with mine in its new phase of political idealism and did not in any way disturb or displace it. On the contrary to both of us the passionate element in our intercourse at this time proved a source of inspiration and strength.[56]

It was during this affair, at the height of it, that Lady Gregory composed the essay that became her first publication.

"Arabi and His Household"

The publication of "Arabi and His Household" in *The Times* (23 October 1882) marks Lady Gregory's first professional literary effort. The piece is a sly mixture of deference to men and assertion of womanly authority. To explain why a woman rather than a man should write on Urabi's behalf, she quotes an unnamed Englishman who has expressed his support of the cause privately but cannot say it in public: "A lady may say what she likes, but a man is called unpatriotic who ventures to say a word that is good of the man England is determined to crush . . ." Thus Lady Gregory may speak, because "I, like Master Shadow, present no mark to the enemy." Having established her insignificance as well as her Englishness with the allusion to *Henry IV, Part 2*, Lady Gregory presents Urabi as a simple, truthful man, said by English officials to have "the gentleness of the fellah" (peasant). He is Anglicized by association with the nineteenth century's favorite Shakespearean hero: "Report me and my cause aright to the unsatisfied," Lady Gregory says she has written on a photograph of Urabi, quoting Hamlet's dying words to suggest Urabi's idealism.[57]

"Arabi and His Household" is framed by the two visits Gregory made to Urabi's house. Seen in the light of her later work, this essay anticipates Lady Gregory's visits to cottages in the west of Ireland to collect folklore: a powerful woman visits a vulnerable family in their dwelling. She serves as the mediator between the little family and the great outside world; she "reports" them "aright." The little girls and Urabi's old mother, as well as his wife, treat her as an honored guest; the son Hassan, "a bright-eyed little imp of four years," is present also. The family is "simple, honest, hospitable," and they are religious Muslims: "God will preserve me!" Urabi has said earlier. The article's final line belongs to the wife: "Why should the Christian Powers want to harm my husband?" She, too, presents "no mark to the enemy" and pleads for him while he is in prison and cannot speak for himself.

To some extent Urabi stands in for Blunt, the man at the center of Lady Gregory's thoughts. She cannot write about him directly, of course, but she can focus on the male figure of Urabi, who occupied Blunt's thoughts day and night as he worked to save him from execution: to write about Urabi was to keep her attention on Blunt.[58] To help Blunt in his endeavors, to make Urabi an attractive figure to the English, Lady Gregory had to de-exoticize him, not only presenting him as another Hamlet but constructing him as a Liberal Victorian *pater familias*, with devoted wife, mother, and children, not a rebellious soldier but as unthreatening (to upper-class English males, that is) as an English family man. Lady Gregory publishes her recollections "hoping to interest Englishmen in this family." Urabi is present only in the middle of the piece, speaking in language that no right-thinking Englishman could disagree with: "They must know some day that it is the good of the people that we seek." He then kisses a photograph of the young Robert Gregory that Lady Gregory has shown him and hopes that Robert "would some day come to Egypt to be the friend of his children." In this remark Urabi, as quoted by Lady Gregory in her earliest recorded anti-imperialist writing, articulates the trope of "the undivided friends," as E. M. Forster does at the end of *Passage to India*: " 'Why can't we be friends now?' " But the world isn't ready for that: the earth, the rocks, the buildings "said in their hundred voices 'No, not yet,' and the sky said, 'No, not there'."

Wisely, Lady Gregory does not tell all she knows, that (as she mentions in her autobiography) this is Urabi's third wife, nor, in her emphasis on the simplicity of the rooms, does she mention a photograph of Urabi framed in diamonds.

In its authorship and its content, the article emphasizes its reliance on women's voices, but its field of production was entirely masculine. A husband, a male lover, male editors, and politicians, and readers determined the article's path from manuscript to publication. In late July Lady Gregory wrote to Blunt, "I am writing from memory an account of Arabi and his household and will publish it someday" and asked him, "Do you think any of the magazines would take it?"[59] Blunt wrote back two days later saying the account was "excellent" and suggesting the *Contemporary Review* and *Fortnightly*.[60] Initially Sir William authorized publication of his wife's article, which had already been vetted by Blunt. "Rather to my surprise," Gregory wrote Blunt on 29 August, "Sir Wm. said he saw no objection to my publishing my article in my own name if one of the magazines will take it. I shall be glad to say a word for Egypt and Arabi when there are so few to do so. If it is refused you must keep it for your full history of the revolution which must be written someday when all is over." Blunt submitted Lady Gregory's essay to John Morley of the *Fortnightly*, prefixing "a few opening sentences" of his own "as the beginning seems hardly to explain itself."[61] The piece was about to be published when British forces invaded Tel El Kebir and accepted Urabi's surrender on 14 September. Writing to Blunt from Vienna, where the Gregorys were touring, Lady Gregory announced, "I am very sorry but Sir Wm. now says he does not wish my article to appear as he thinks it too late to do any good."[62] When Blunt agreed that at this juncture, with Urabi a British prisoner, there was no point in publishing the essay, Lady Gregory was palpably relieved: "I am very glad to get your telegram and to know that you approve of my paper being suppressed. It could not do any good now and Sir Wm. was quite decided about it. I felt like a coward withdrawing it just after the defeat."[63]

By the middle of October, however, the possibility of Urabi's getting a fair trial seemed unlikely, and the Queen's counsel hired (and partially funded) by Blunt to represent him risked arriving too late to help. Sir William, genuinely sympathetic to Urabi and wishing the colonial authorities to be fair to him, changed his mind. Believing in his wife's "power of writing well and piquantly," he encouraged her to publish the article so the British public would understand the true nature of Urabi's position. As cautious in her old age as her husband was in his, Lady Gregory omits all this complicated triangulation from her autobiography, where she casually says, "I don't remember if it was at Hayward's suggestion that I wrote an account of Arabi and His Household."[64] Submission and publication, as she reconstructs the situation, came about as an easy, natural function of social life. Hayward suggests and Chenery accepts; Lady Gregory is one of the guys: "I took it to friendly Chenery," she writes with deceptive ease, "and on the 23rd it was printed in *The Times*." Abraham Hayward was a distinguished barrister and journalist, and Thomas Chennery was editor of *The Times*. The network of "public moralists" works for Lady Gregory, and she becomes one of them. In the paper, Chenery introduced the article with respectful neutrality: "We have been favoured by Lady Gregory with the following interesting account of Arabi Pasha and his family." As Lady Gregory tells the story in her autobiography, the success of her publication is determined by the response of its male readers:

It really was a success. Sir William was pleased when he went to the Athenaeum because so many of his friends, Dicey and Chenery among them, paid him compliments about it; and especially because when someone had said it was so good that people would think it was written by him, W. E. Forster had growled, '"I know you didn't write it because I know you couldn't." And Hayward came on Sunday saying he had dined at Downing Street the night before to meet the Granvilles, and they were all talking about it, and Gladstone had said it was "very touching."[65]

Lady Gregory's wifely pride in Sir William's husbandly pride ("Sir William was pleased") does not prevent her from including Forster's compliment that she writes better than her husband does. But the highest compliment of all is that at the prime minister's dinner party, "they were all talking about it." Lady Gregory's first publication became table talk at the premier table in London. Presenting no mark to the enemy, writing obliquely about Blunt but beholden to Sir William for license to publish, surrounded by men and pleasing them, Lady Gregory created a public voice for herself and entered the world of professional authorship.

4

A Woman's Sonnets

I wish I could remember that first day,
First hour, first moment of your meeting me,
If bright or dim the season, it might be
Summer or Winter for aught I can say . . .
    Christina Rossetti, Sonnet I of *Monna Innominata*

Ah! could I bear those happy hours to miss
When love began, unthought of and unspoke
That summer day when by a sudden kiss
We knew each other's secret and awoke?
    Lady Gregory, Sonnet I, *A Woman's Sonnets*

The middle and late nineteenth century saw a resurgence of the "amatory sonnet" sequence: Elizabeth Barrett Browning's *Sonnets from the Portuguese* (1850), George Meredith's *Modern Love* (1862), Wilfrid Scawen Blunt's *Songs and Sonnets by Proteus* (1875), Dante Gabriel Rossetti's *The House of Life* (1881), and Christina Rossetti's *Monna Innominata* (1881) are the best known. So when, at the end of their affair, the morning after their last night together, Lady Gregory gave a twelve-sonnet sequence to Blunt—put them directly in his hand, he writes—she was following a poetic fashion of the time. Victorian women, especially, were writing love sonnets, and the form, "generally assumed [to be] . . . a vehicle for truthful revelations," offered the perfect space for a literary woman to process a love she sought to understand.[1] Barrett Browning's and Meredith's sequences were assumed, like Shakespeare's, to construct "a psychological interiority."[2] Certainly Blunt's reference to the sonnets suggests their "authenticity":

She wrote them for me as a farewell to our passion and put them in my hand the morning that we parted after a last night spent together in the room over the bow-window at Crabbet . . . they tell all our love's history that needs the telling.[3]

In 1892, with Lady Gregory's permission, Blunt published the sonnets (significantly revised by himself) under his own name, with the title *A Woman's Sonnets*, an ambiguous phrase that is simultaneously true and false. They *were* "a woman's sonnets," but not *A Woman's Sonnets* by W. S. Blunt. Only in 1972, when Blunt's private papers at the Fitzwilliam were opened, was Lady Gregory's authorship revealed: the "twelve originals . . . were written out by Augusta Gregory herself though in a disguised handwriting."[4]

Because the last night that Lady Gregory and Blunt spent together was 7 August, the sonnets were probably written in July 1883. They are Lady Gregory's second Blunt-related literary work, and in some respects they mark an advance from "Arabi and His Household." For one, they require more skill. A sonnet is a *tour de force*, and to write twelve connected ones is ambitious. To deliver them to a published poet, the author of the *Sonnets of Proteus*, is to make some claim to literary authority. The abjectness of the sonnets' tone is balanced by the achievement of their existence; at the same time as Lady Gregory was expressing regret at the end of their affair, she was presenting herself to Blunt as a fellow poet. The moment Lady Gregory put the sonnets in Blunt's hand, she shifted the ground of their relationship; the literary conversations that had begun over "Arabi and His Household" were implicitly offered as a way to define their intimacy in the future. Theirs was no longer an intimacy between lovers but between writers.

In addition, the genesis of the sequence shows more authorial autonomy. The composition of "Arabi and His Household" was overseen by men with varying political and social interests, and Lady Gregory struggled to please all of them. Its final form had to be approved by Chenery at *The Times*, and the prime minister's good words were the final seal of approval. The sonnet sequence was written in solitude and attempted something verbally more complex than she had written before. Because Lady Gregory had no thought of publication for the sonnets, she had no one to please but herself. When, in 1891, Blunt asked her permission to publish them under his own name, she wrote diffidently, "I see no reason why those twelve sonnets should not be published if you think them worth it—merely calling them 'Sonnets written by a Woman'.⁵ The route to publication was still patriarchal, but publication was incidental, because Lady Gregory did not want to expose her own adultery: the sonnets were her own in conception and execution.

Blunt wrote that the sonnets "tell all our love's history that needs the telling," but that is not altogether accurate: the poems attempt to make sense of the mixed feelings of one person only in the relationship. Blunt confided to his diaries later that the affair was "a quite new experience in her quiet life" and "harmonized not ill with mine in its new phase of political idealism and did not in any way disturb or displace it."⁶ Lady Gregory's feelings were not so calm; in the very first sonnet she writes about "the pain / Debate and anguish," and (in the fifth) the "hard conflict" that "rends her soul."⁷ To a large extent, she uses the sonnet sequence, a private space provided by a literary form associated with interiority and the process of thinking about love, to figure out what she thinks about the choices she has made. Apparently Lady Gregory didn't tell anyone at all about the affair, and the sonnets offered her only opportunity to mull over a romance that was sexually exciting but morally traumatic; so traumatic that, as she says in one of them, if her secret were ever to become known, she could not "live the scandal down" but "must die."

The idea that she had committed adultery shocked Lady Gregory, and she asks repeatedly, in the poems, if she would make the same decision again:

> If the past year were offered me again,
> And choice of good and ill before me set,
> Would I accept the pleasure with the pain
> Or dare to choose that we had never met? (I)

She cannot get used to her changed self: "Where is the pride for which I once was blamed? / The pride which made me hold my head so high?" (III). She asks herself "What have I lost?" and answers, in so many words, that she has lost her moral grounding:

> What have I lost? The faith I had that right
> Must surely prove itself than ill more strong.
> For all my prayers and efforts had no might
> To save me, when the trial came, from wrong. (VI)

She also asks "What have I gained?" and the answer is put judgmentally: she has learned "charity," not to be critical of others' faults. Even the pleasure she has had—"one moment's glimpse of Paradise" is judged: she knows "the flavor of forbidden food" (VII). In reasoning that makes self-interest sound like self-abnegation, she says she would still "undo" all the past, if it were not for the fact "That I once made some happiness for you." But her moral universe has changed: she leads a "double life" and tosses and turns in bed (VI).

Two other voices besides the ethical super-ego speak in the poem. A worldly-wise voice seems to understand that Blunt's attitude to their affair is quite different from her own. "And time and fate bring near our parting hour," she writes in the second sonnet, "Which well I know thy love will not outlast." And in the eighth sonnet she acknowledges, "I staked my all upon a losing game / Knowing thy nature and the ways of men." But a pathetic, dependent, abject voice, the kind that makes a modern reader cringe (or want to give Lady Gregory a good shake), dominates. She is distraught at the idea of parting from Blunt, and the sonnets offer a vicarious way of holding on to Blunt physically, or at least, so she would like to think, prolonging their proximity. They are a "long goodbye," written with the knowledge that when he read them, their love affair would be over. For Lady Gregory the sonnets lengthen the goodbye: as she says in the second one, "Ah, my own dear one, do not leave me yet! / Let me a little longer hold thy hand." In the penultimate sonnet, she writes, "Wild words I write, wild words of love and pain / To lay within thy hand before we part." She also writes several times about their physical closeness in bed. In the third sonnet, she is "Petitioning a touch to smooth my sleep." In Sonnet VI, similarly, she says, "No longer will the loved and lost I mourn / Come in my sleep to breathe a blessed word" and "In thy dear presence only have I rest." All the sonnets are full of the language of corporeal positioning, speaking metaphorically of their bodies as if they were close together: "As at thy feet I subject, pleading lie," and "bowing my head to kiss the very ground / On which the feet of him I love have trod." I'm afraid she's not being metaphoric there.

When Blunt published the sonnets under his own name, the changes he made in them were not improvements. His revisions turn

the speaker's pained reflections into platitudes and weaken the intensity of her emotions. Her clear-eyed vision of his philandering is trans-
muted to a vague acknowledgment of the male sex generally: "which
well I know thy love will not outlast" becomes "Though well I know
Love cannot Time outlast" (II), and "Knowing thy nature and the
ways of men" becomes "Knowing the nature and the needs of men,"
generic men, that is (VIII). Her precise, vivid memory of the beginning of their romance ("That summer day when by a sudden kiss /
We knew each other's secret") is made vague ("That first strange
day . . .") (I). Her memory of the consequent "pain, / Debate and
anguish" is revised to the excessively poetic "that fell agony" (I). Her
direct "I lead a double life—myself despise" is weakened to "Behold
me here to-day / Leading a double life, at shifts with lies" (VI). And
one of her best lines—"Wild words I write, wild words of love and
pain"—is ruined with awkward, hyper-poetic diction ("Wild words
I write, and lettered in deep pain"), thereby losing the emotion and
alliteration of the repetition (XI).

The final sonnet as written by Lady Gregory imagines the great
future ahead of Blunt as he leaves Lady Gregory: "Go forth dear!
Thou hast much to do on earth; / In life's campaign there waits thee
a great part"—lines which Blunt left intact, no doubt agreeing with
them. But it was Lady Gregory for whom a "great part" waited, as
Blunt acknowledged in the diary entry he wrote when she came to
deliver the peacock dinner invitation: neither Sir William nor anyone
else, he wrote, "cd. have guessed then the important part she was
to play in the world." He added that she was "an admirable writer"
and "something of a poet"—that "something" no doubt being the
sonnets she handed to Blunt, poems he considered good enough to
publish as his own.[8]

The Galway Gaol Poems, 1888

One "great part" that "life's campaign" held in store for Wilfrid Blunt
was his arrest at Woodford, County Galway, 23 October 1887. Like
his support for Urabi, Blunt's support for evicted Irish tenants constituted a direct, practical, and unambiguous anti-imperialist statement.
In order to protest Chief Secretary for Ireland Arthur Balfour's July
1887 Crimes (Ireland) Act, which had outlawed the Land League,

Figure 14. The arrest of Blunt in Galway, pictured on the front page of the *Illustrated London News*, 5 November 1887.

Blunt went on Sunday 23 October to speak at a banned anti-eviction meeting on the notorious Lord Clanricarde's estate. Twice he began his speech—"Men of Galway!"—and twice the police pulled him down from the platform. Finally he called out, "Are you all such damned cowards that not one of you dares arrest me?" After that apparently spontaneous line, a wonderfully theatrical challenge, the police had no choice but to arrest Blunt. At his January trial he was sentenced to two months in jail.[9] Balfour was not only the "official" though possibly not adulterous lover of Mary Elcho, but also a member of the cluster of friends, lovers, and family who visited Blunt's cousins Percy and Madeline Wyndham's house Clouds. In October, before Blunt had been sentenced to prison, Balfour wrote to Mary, "We are trying to get your cousin in gaol. I have not heard whether we have succeeded—I hope so for I am sure Blunt would be horribly disappointed at any other consummation—."[10]

Blunt's women friends were excited and enthusiastic about his political activism; all of them wrote him. "You are so brave and good," wrote Skittles, the courtesan who was the "Esther" of his Proteus sonnet sequence. "What a splendid commotion you have made!" wrote Janey Morris, another former (and future) lover; and Lady Gregory, in similar language, wrote him from Venice, where she and Sir William were wintering: "How bad of you to get into such a commotion! The first accounts in the papers were horrible . . . I was more anxious and upset than you deserve your friends should be—" and, knowing her man, she continued, "I suspect you are rather enjoying the trial now, & taking up so much of the papers—so I won't waste my sympathy any more—."[11] He took up even more of the papers: the following week the *London Illustrated News* sported a dashing full-page drawing of Blunt on its front page (5 November 1887) (Figure 14).

The drama of Blunt's Irish activities seemed to call for a literature to celebrate or at least to record it, and Lady Gregory was alert to that possibility. He was, after all, staging his protests in her home county, in a place that was not only where she lived, but where her cousin Henry Persse was a visiting magistrate.[12] Blunt's proximity was exciting, even if, because she was in Italy, he was not in close proximity to her at the moment. "You will have to write a poem about yourself in prison," she encouraged him, and in fact Blunt did just that. Incarcerated in Galway Gaol, he wrote the sixteen-sonnet sequence *In Vinculis: Sonnets written in an Irish Prison, 1888.* He was quite proud of being the first Englishman to have "taken the Celtic Irish side in any conflict, or suffered even the shortest imprisonment for Ireland's sake."[13] Blunt sent Lady Gregory the proof sheets because, as he wrote her, "I trust your judgment more than I do anyone else's."[14]

Lady Gregory fetishized the material traces of Blunt's time in Galway Gaol. After Blunt was released, and the Gregorys

WILLIAM LAWRENCE.   DUBLIN.

Figure 15. Wilfrid Scawen Blunt in prison garb, 1888. Reproduced by permission of the Syndics of the Fitzwilliam Museum, Cambridge.

were back home at Coole, she had herself (with some difficulty
persuading the officials) admitted to the cell he had occupied,
sketched it, and sent the sketches to Blunt, who wrote her (with
a subtext to add to the *frisson* she probably felt already just by seeing his handwriting on the envelope), "I am having them framed
to remind me of you & of other things and shall hang them in
my bedroom."[15] ("Other things" indeed!) The sketches were only
one item in a continuing exchange: at Lady Gregory's suggestion Blunt had had a photograph taken of himself in prison garb,
and she wrote requesting a copy: "Please send me your prison
photograph. I wd send to Dublin for it but that having one from
you with your name on it wd give me more pleasure than the
enclosing it in an envelope can give you trouble."[16] In his will
Blunt left Lady Gregory his prison diary, and she put in it a piece
of oakum that he had picked and given to her. Gregory noted in
her diary that he was "looking none the worse for his imprisonment."[17] Blunt had made the same observation himself: "As to my
women friends, my prison adventures, I soon found, had done
me no real discredit with them . . . [T]he episode was a title to
romantic interest . . . Their kindness did me full amends and for
the next few years strewed my path with flowers . . ."[18] Possibly
Janey Morris was one of those women whose "kindness" Blunt
was thinking of. Like Lady Gregory, she was excited by his time
in prison, and designed a cover for *In Vinculis* "with shamrock
leaves."[19] They renewed their affair when he visited Kelmscott
Manor in 1889. His handsome prison photo appears to have been
widely distributed among women (Figure 15). Katharine Tynan
writes, "Mr Blunt was arrested and sentenced to three months
in prison in Galway Gaol. I have a picture of him in his prison
garb."[20]

Blunt's time in Galway Gaol rekindled Lady Gregory's romantic
excitement; her insistence on being admitted to his cell was only
one sign ("I had great difficulty . . . there are very strict anti-visitor
rules enforced now—but I was determined to see your place of
abode—").[21] Two of the four poems she wrote for him show that
his imprisonment had a major, indeed lasting effect on her writing: Blunt Gaelicized Lady Gregory's literary imagination. Irish
locations and poetic tropes entered her literary repertoire through

Blunt and thereafter retained a mild but persistent erotic excitement. Lady Gregory's sonnets had drawn on the traditions of the
English, Victorian "amatory sonnet" sequence, but with the poems
celebrating Blunt as an Irish hero, she writes herself into an Irish literary tradition. Their foundational role in her literary career could
not have been known while she was alive, because the only texts of
these poems were filed with Blunt's papers in the Fitzwilliam; they
were not published until 1994. Her poetic influence shifted from
Barrett Browning to *The Spirit of the Nation*. In the second stanza
of "A Triumph" it's possible to hear a weak echo of Young Ireland
motifs:

> Let sons of Erin cry your fame
> And call for blessings on your days
> And in their cities set your name
> And sing your memory in their lays.[22]

As Lady Gregory says in her autobiography, as a child she would
spend the sixpences earned reciting Bible verses on "the paper
covered collections of national ballads, *The Harp of Tara, The Irish
Song Book,* and the like." She was obviously proud of what "the old
bookseller" at Loughrea said: "I look to Miss Augusta to buy all
my Fenian books." For her birthday, an older sister gave her *The
Spirit of the Nation*.[23] So in writing about Blunt, she may have been
remembering songs like "The Forlorn Hope: A Song of the Irish
Brigade" ("The green flag on the air / Sons of Erin and despair") or
"Awake and Lie Dreaming No More" ("Not the want of green fields
nor of countless resources / The sons of Sweet Erin have cause to
deplore").[24] Lines like these had lain in her memory for years; it was
Blunt's imprisonment in Galway that made them echo in her own
writing.

The poem "Without and Within" is the best of the lot; its "refer-
ences to the salmon fishermen, 'Gaelic jests,' 'hast'ning nuns',"
and the bridge over the River Corrib situate it explicitly outside the gate
of Galway Gaol.[25] This poem makes literal the speaker's position in all
the poems: Lady Gregory ardently waiting at the jail gate, longing for
the moment of Blunt's release, but in the meantime using the opportunity of his imprisonment to write about their relative locations, he
"within," she "without." The trope even appears in a letter she wrote

him at the time: "Oh! I shall be so glad when you are on the right side of the walls again!"[26]

1

Without the gate, without the gate
The patient fishers antedate
The dawn and watch with eager eyes
The flashing sudden salmon rise
Without the gate, without the gate.

2

Within the gate, within the gate
A prisoner wakes to poor estate
The barren light of morning falls
Upon the narrow whitened walls
Within the gate, within the gate.

. . . . . .

6

Within the gate, within the gate
What dreams the captive's sleep await!
A couch of honor is his bed
A glory rests about his head
Within the gate, within the gate.

7

Without the gate, without the gate
I early come, I linger late,
I wait the blessed hour when he
Shall come and cross the bridge with me
Without the gate, without the gate.[27]

Of course, if any woman were going to "cross the bridge" with Blunt when he emerged from jail, it would have been his wife Lady Anne; but in fact he was transferred to Kilmainham Gaol in Dublin on 8 February and released from there on 6 March, and Lady Gregory was not present on that occasion.

As in "Arabi and His Household," Lady Gregory positions herself between a nationalist prisoner, a "rebel," and the world from which he is cut off, the world to which she proclaimed his "couch of honor" and the "glory" about his head. In the essay she had defined her position as "merely" female ("a lady may say what she wants"), enabled to write "freely" because she had no political power. In all the Galway poems, but most explicitly in "Within and Without," Gregory speaks from a free space outside the jail, because the man is locked up and cannot speak for himself. Of course, Blunt was in there writing the poems she had urged him to write, but her lyric does not mention the fact that they are *both* poets: she speaks for him. He is the muse, and she is the poet.

The Irish felon becomes thereafter the primary muse of Lady Gregory's literary career. He is the inspiration behind her essay "The Felons of Our Land" (1900), in which she speaks "without the gate" on behalf of all the felons in Irish tradition. Blunt lurks here too, his secret presence hiding the original reason for Gregory's excitement at the thought of felons. He is hidden in a quotation: asserting that the ballads "written by the felons themselves . . . stand outside criticism," she writes

As some old lines say:

> *And he was also in the war,*
> *He who this rhyme did write;*
> *Till evening fought he with the sword,*
> *And sang the song at night.*[28]

Figure 16. Painting of Galway Gaol by Lady Gregory. Reproduced by permission of Geoffrey O'Byrne White.

But the lines were not old at all, or anonymous; they had recently been inscribed by Blunt in Lady Gregory's copy of his poem about Egypt and Urabi, *The Wind and the Whirlwind*.[29]

The felon "within" and the women "without" inspire the structure of Lady Gregory's 1906 play *Gaol Gate*, which is in fact a dramatizing of the secret poem. In the play, two illiterate country women wait "outside the gate of Galway Gaol," says the stage direction, for news of their son and husband, who has been arrested for "moonlighting," some kind of agrarian violence that is never specified. The two women are both named Mary, and thus they are reminiscent of the Irish tradition of the "three Marys" who keened Christ, himself considered a "felon." As in the low-angled perspective on the jail in her painting, here also much drama focuses on the gate (Figure 16). The mother says, "I'm in dread of it being opened," and when it is, they hear "the rattling of keys."

After learning that Denis Cahel, the prisoner, is dead, and believing that he died after informing on his friends, the mother and wife mourn him in shame. However, when they learn from the gatekeeper that he never informed and was hanged as a felon, there is great joy. As a felon, he immediately inspires poetry, and the mother utters a paean of praise for him: "I will go through Gort and Kilbecanty and Druimdarod and Daroda; I will call to the people and the singers at the fairs to make a great praise for Denis." Denis's political death is his mother's artistic opportunity. The mother takes the place of the (absent) adulterous lover Lady Gregory, who had urged "sons of Erin" to sing praise of Wilfrid Blunt. *Gaol Gate* is a de-eroticized version of the poems, because it is the mother, not the widow, who gets the long final speech.[30]

Gregory's Pearl for Blunt's Oyster

One other Galway poem by Lady Gregory is more hidden even than these, because there is no manuscript of it. If it were not for a letter of 27 August 1888 from Blunt to Lady Gregory, no one would know she wrote it, because it was published by Blunt under his own name. "I think I never wrote to you abt your lines 'The Eviction'," he wrote her, which is really an extraordinarily good thing. I am putting my poems together with a view of publishing them this autumn . . . and it wd. be nice if I might put your "Eviction" in with them. Of course if you are ever likely to publish a volume of your own I wd. not do it, and I have altered a few lines & added a couple of verses. But it wd. be pleasant to me to have this little pearl in my oyster.[31]

The image of the last sentence suggests an unattractive possessiveness, the desire of a dominant person to appropriate something beautiful belonging to a weaker one. Blunt's oyster did get that pearl, but because there is no manuscript, we can never be sure what the unaltered poem looked like. As published in Blunt's *Poetical Works*, it has six stanzas:

The Eviction

Unruly tenant of my heart,
    Full fain would I be quit of thee.
I've played too long a losing part.
    Thou bringest me neither gold nor fee.

'Tis time thou shouldst thy holding yield,
    Thy will and mine no longer meet.
With cockle hast thou sowed my field,
    With squanderings all the public street.

Thy presence doth disturb my pride.
    Let me be owner of my own.
I fling thee with thy goods outside
    And bar re-entry with a stone.

Begone and hide thee from my face.
I will not see thee chiding there.
Away, to live in my disgrace!
Away, to die in thy despair!

O impotence of human wit!
    The law is mine, the fault in thee,
And yet in vain I serve the writ,
    In vain I scourge thee with decree.

For lo, in stillness of the night,
    O'erturning stone and guard and door,
Thou art come with thy lost tenant-right
    And hast possession as before.[32]

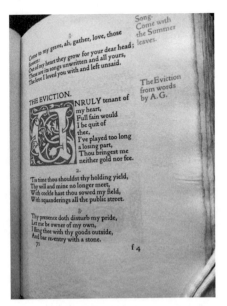

Figure 17. The Kelmscott edition of *The Love-Lyrics & Songs of Proteus* by W. S. Blunt, with Lady Gregory's initials in the margin.

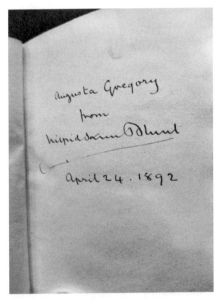

Figure 18. Blunt's signature in the copy of the Kelmscott edition of *The Love-Lyrics & Songs of Proteus* given to Lady Gregory. Figures 17 and 18 reproduced by permission of the Henry W. and Albert A. Berg Collection, New York Public Library, Astor, Lenox, and Tilden Foundations.

If in adding "a couple of verses" Blunt was true to his usual over-blown poetic diction, it seems possible that he added stanza four, which seems like padding in terms of the poem's narrative, and either two or five, which do not advance the argument. ("O impotence of human wit!" does not sound like a line Lady Gregory could ever have written.) It may also be possible to hear Blunt's rhetoric in words like "squanderings," "begone," "chiding," and "scourge." But without a manuscript, there is no way of knowing. In the Kelmscott edition of *The Love-Lyrics & Songs of Proteus* (1892) Blunt coyly acknowledged Lady Gregory's authorship by adding her initials in a marginal note (Figures 17 and 18). There was no such note, however, beside the series *A Woman's Sonnets*, which was also printed in that edition.[33]

At any rate, the central metaphor must be Lady Gregory's, and it is a brilliant Irish metaphysical conceit, linking the interior, erotic realm and the exterior, political one. The erotic is the primary narrative of the poem, and the political the metaphor. In the erotic realm, the poem expresses Gregory's feelings about Blunt: she can't get him out of her "heart." But without the word "heart" in the first line, the poem would be entirely political. After that first line the poem never returns explicitly to the erotic, and so her mixed feelings are articulated entirely through the little drama of the political realm. The metaphor, then, attributes agency to the "unruly tenant" (Blunt) rather than to her uncontrollable feelings about him and thereby makes the spatial dynamic of the metaphor implicitly sexual. The heart becomes both a house and (in the sexual analogy) a body, i.e., a space to which she cannot "bar re-entry" by a male tenant who breaks down barriers. The nocturnal—"in stillness of the night"—links these realms, because it is the time of released desires, both sexual and political, adulterous longings and "moonlighting."

In spring 1888, when Lady Gregory wrote the poem, her feelings about this double transgression were ambivalent and unstable in both realms: she was still attracted to Blunt but feeling she shouldn't be, and sympathetic to the tenants but not yet ready to overturn the whole system of landlordism. As her letters make clear, she still identified with the landlords, but Blunt's imprisonment tilted her politics to moderate support of the Land League's aims. When two of the Coole tenants were arrested and accused of moonlighting, one of them "at the door of Galway Gaol . . . called out to his mother in the crowd 'Go to Lady Gregory to help me' but I had already done what I could—for I think he is innocent—and every day I hope to hear of his release!"[34]

The interesting question is how the two narratives of the poem function together. Because Blunt had been in jail for protesting evictions, he features as transgressive—and *aggressive*—in two realms, the erotic and the political. She resists him in both, but his aggression is stronger than her resistance, and he has "possession as before." The eviction metaphor adds aggressive maleness and externalizes the agency in the erotic realm; the tenant's forced re-entry, "o'erturning stone and guard and door," makes clear the speaker's sexual attraction to him. But the emotional "heart" adds a sympathy for the individual "unruly tenant" in the political realm, because he is also her lover. In this respect, the politics of "The Eviction" resembles the politics of "Arabi and His Household": Lady Gregory shows her sympathy to nationalism not in relation to a large system of oppression but in relation to a single figure in his domestic site.

Considered as part of the trajectory in Lady Gregory's Blunt-inspired writings, "The Eviction" shows an advance in its speaker's autonomy and assertiveness. She's not asking him to go away or to come back to her. It is an attempt to understand an interior dynamic, her inability to overcome her infatuation. It may seem as if she is again the romantically powerless speaker of the sonnets, but the ability to analyze the emotional dynamic indicates an advance in understanding.

"Dies Irae," 1896

In March, 1896, Lady Gregory published in the relatively new London-based magazine *The Sketch* a story that appears to be her last explicitly Blunt-related piece of writing.[35] No doubt she would not have published a piece with such daring content—adultery—while Sir William was still alive, but he had died in 1892. The plot shows how far her moral thinking had advanced in the thirteen years since her sonnet sequence. The cruel husband in the story, an appropriately named "Dr. Iron," has, years earlier, required his wife to sign a confession admitting that she ran off with another man for one week. Dr Iron "consented" to her return on the condition that she remain in the house only for ten years, until the children were grown up. As the story begins, he hands her tickets for an exile on the continent: "I thought you would perhaps like to give a trial to Brussels. It is cheerful, not expensive, and you will find quite an English colony." She begs to be allowed to stay, flinging herself at his feet and clasping his knees, but he rings for the servant in order to end their conversation.

The wife is full of misery and guilt, until she learns at the last moment that he has showed the children ("Alice," eighteen, and "Hubert," seventeen) her signed confession. Hearing that news changes her tone to outrage:

"You treacherous man!" she cried passionately. "You had not the right to speak to them without my knowledge and without giving me the chance of escape I have asked for. If I had thought you were so cruel and so cowardly as this, I would have killed you. It would have been better for me to have had a second stain on my soul than to leave my darlings in your hands . . . I never made an excuse for myself before. I despise the plea of madness. I was not mad; I think now I was wise. I think now it was what was good in me that shrank from all that was bad in you and made me throw myself on another. I would to God I had stayed with him! I would I had taken my children with me, and gone out in the wide world with him and them. I am glad I gave myself to him; it is the week of my married life that redeems the rest. You need despise me no longer. Take back your contempt! I despise you!"

As she leaves the room, the children have just come into the house, "the cold, dark fog entering with them." The daughter shrinks back and will not embrace her, but the son sobs and begs to go with her. However, the mother "pushed him gently from her, and in a moment had gone out, alone and silently, into the darkness."

In the years since the end of her affair with Blunt, Lady Gregory must have been thinking "What if . . . ?"[36] There is no evidence that Sir William knew about the affair, and his biographer points out that "Surviving letters to Augusta for this period are affectionate in tone and he continued to employ tender diminutives when he addressed her."[37] One detail is slightly suggestive of Lady Gregory's life: she had met Blunt in December 1881; in the fictional wife's signed confession, the date her affair began was 16 January 1881. The story's significance lies in the wife's dramatic defiance of her husband and passionate assertion that her one week of adultery "redeems the rest" of her married life. Adultery was no longer, as it had been in Lady Gregory's sonnet sequence, such a shame that a woman would have to "die" if the scandal became known; on the contrary, it could be claimed as valuable, significant, even "redemptive." The wife's secular, anti-patriarchal outburst was something new for Lady Gregory to put in print; but then, she was a widow, and independent. She had already met Yeats in 1894, and soon after "Dies Irae" was published came the famous and more consequential meeting with Yeats in August 1896, when the idea for the Irish Literary Theatre was born.[38]

Mazzini

In his presentation poem at the peacock dinner, Ezra Pound praised Blunt because he had "Upheld Mazzini and detested institutions." But Blunt had never "upheld Mazzini" or ever engaged in Italian politics; the name was a mistake for "Urabi." Most likely Lady Gregory, over the fire at Coole, had told Yeats about Urabi and Blunt's Egyptian involvements before introducing the two poets on 1 April 1898.[39] (She had not told Yeats about "the passionate element" in their "intercourse.") And most likely Yeats, talking to Pound over the fire in Stone Cottage about Blunt, had misremembered the name he heard from Lady Gregory. At any rate he had not corrected the error in the poem, which Pound had showed him before the dinner. "Urabi," then, was intended, even though the name wasn't mentioned, and in that intended reference Lady Gregory was present, however obliquely and invisibly, at the peacock dinner. Through a chain of conversations, partly misremembered, her passionate memories of Blunt had made their way into the poem Pound read aloud.

Lady Gregory and Ezra Pound are strange cultural bedfellows, but Blunt was a muse for both of them; they wrote poems to and about him over a period of years. A totally transgressive figure, Blunt implicitly gave both Gregory and Pound license to be transgressive also. His influence, or rather his inspiration, was textual and extra-textual; for better or worse, he inspired their politics and sexual behavior as well as their poetry. Gregory and Pound were also drawn to Yeats, and both spent time under the same roof with him, at Coole Park and at Stone Cottage, working closely together at their writing. Lady Gregory because she was a woman, and Pound because he was an American, found much that they needed professionally and personally in these tall, good-looking, pleasingly masculine celebrity poets. It is no surprise that Lady Gregory took Pound's idea of a dinner for Blunt and ran with it.

5

Alliances and Rivalries

*I propose the health of Mr. Yeats especially, as I have said the most disagree-
able things to him.*

Wilfrid Blunt at the peacock dinner

Wilfrid Blunt and W. B. Yeats had met one another face to
face many times before the day of the peacock dinner, and
each time Blunt wrote something sniping in his diaries. Their first
encounter had not been promising. On 1 April 1898—5.00 p.m. to be
exact—they were introduced by Lady Gregory. Blunt called him "an
Irish mystic of an interesting type. He is tall, lean, dark, good looking . . ." In his diaries Blunt described the event in detail:

Yeats experimented magically on me. He first took out a notebook and
made what he called a pyramid in it which was a square of figures, then he
bade me think of and see a square of yellow as it might be a door, and walk
through it and tell him what I saw beyond.

So 1890s! There were three such options, but Blunt "failed to see"
what Yeats's magic was offering: "The performance was very imper-
fect, not to say null."[1]

A later encounter evoked a more explicitly negative critique. "We
had an afternoon of poetry," Blunt wrote in 1902, "but all agreed that
Yeats's theories of recitation were wrong, useful only for concealing
indifferent verse. When he recites it is impossible to follow the meaning."[2] The following year, Blunt reacted strongly to a production of
Yeats's play *The Hour-Glass*: "What Yeats can mean by putting such thin
stuff on the stage I can't imagine." But Lady Gregory's play *Twenty-Five*,

which Blunt stayed to watch, was "quite the most perfect work of art and the most touching play I have ever seen acted."[3] And the year after that, 1904, Blunt's diaries recorded yet another snipe at Yeats. After dining with Lady Gregory, her son Robert, Yeats, and the translator Gilbert Murray, Blunt wrote of Yeats, ". . . Gilbert Murray is worth ten of him as poet . . ."[4] Murray was not even known as a poet; he was a classicist and translator. His rhyming translation of *Hippolytus* was about to be performed in London: "Hail to thee, Maiden blest, / Proudest and holiest: / God's Daughter, great in bliss, / Leto-born Artemis!"[5] Not bad, but "worth ten" of Yeats? (Blunt, connected to almost every titled family in England, had flirted in his youth, around 1860, with Rosalind Stanley, who would later become the mother of Gilbert Murray's future wife, Lady Mary Murray.)[6]

By 1910, when Yeats's poetic success had to be acknowledged, Blunt, after dining with Lady Gregory and Yeats, conceded this much praise to Yeats in his diaries: "He is an extremely pleasant fellow, and has a more prosperous look, and is fatter and rosier than formerly. Lady Gregory has been the making of him."[7] The week before the peacock dinner, Blunt was evidently gearing up for an encounter with Yeats and other modern poets. At that point Blunt believed that Masefield would be among the guests. His companion Dorothy Carleton read him Masefield's "Everlasting Mercy," "which is a very powerful poem, worth all that Yeats and the rest of them have written twenty times over . . . I unhesitatingly put him first among our living poets."[8]

What was it about Yeats that inspired such antagonism in Blunt? Possibly it was his good looks, which Blunt always commented on also: his first impression that Yeats was "tall, lean, dark, good-looking" was followed by the observations that he was "beginning to get fat and sleek; he has cut his hair and his cheeks have a pink colour, and he is well dressed." And no doubt Blunt felt rivalrous because of Lady Gregory's intimate (though non-sexual) friendship with Yeats; Blunt may have assumed it was sexual. Murray, ten times better than Yeats, Lady Gregory, the better playwright, and Masefield, twenty times better, are all stand-ins for Blunt himself, writers victorious over Yeats in the literary contest. And if "Lady Gregory has been the making of him," then maybe Blunt himself deserves a little credit for Yeats's success, because Blunt, in a sense, was the (literary) making of Lady Gregory.

Figure 19. Period photograph of Newbuildings Place.

Blunt's uneasiness about Yeats (and Yeats's about Pound, and Pound's about Yeats) found its way into the testimonial meal they ate together. The peacock dinner was a ritual of affiliation organized around ceremonial exchanges. Pound especially, with the other poets accompanying him, came to Newbuildings Place to construct, in person, a poetic genealogy, to find an ancestor for the kind of poet he wanted to become (Figure 19). In gratitude for the poetry that Blunt had given to the world, the poets brought a marble box of their own poems. In response to the invitation to dinner in London, Blunt invited them to his house in West Sussex. After dinner, Pound read a poem in Blunt's honor; Blunt gave a speech thanking Pound; and Yeats gave a speech thanking Blunt. "In return for their verses," Blunt wrote in his diary, "I could think of nothing else to read them out than Gobineau's 'Leporello' in my new translation." But these rituals constituted more than assertions of affiliation in a spirit of "artistic freemasonry," as Roy Foster calls it.[9] They also offered opportunity for conflict and competition. The gendered nature of the gathering elicited an aggressive masculinity: throughout the afternoon, affiliations gave way to rivalries and rivalries to new affiliations. As the seven poets encountered one another in formal rituals and informal conversation, they were implicitly calibrating their own and one another's celebrity. What more they said, what jokes they cracked, how they sat at the table, or how they communicated paralinguistically we can never know; but the jostling for status, the oblique antagonisms, and the hierarchical alignments are visible in the photograph and audible in the speeches.

The "most famous literary photograph"

The poets had arrived promptly at 12:30, all together in a car rented for £5 from Harrods. Blunt's neighbor Lord Osborne Beauclerk (an explorer and "adventurer" in Canada and Alaska, and later Duke of St Albans) joined the poets for lunch, and his account of the occasion in a letter to Sydney Cockerell is the only one by a guest who was not himself one of the poets. "It took some time to break the ice," he wrote, "(as you know W.B. is very shy) . . . it was all quite interesting, though Yeats would interview W.B. for the benefit of the company."[10] After lunch, "The sun came out and we were photographed in the open air in a group," Blunt wrote to Lady Gregory.[11]

The simultaneous rivalry and affiliation is nowhere more obvious than in the photograph taken of the whole group, taken in spite of Pound's concern about the tabloid vulgarity of "Ducal shooting parties." Rejecting the invitation to the dinner, Frederic Manning missed (says one of his biographers) "the most famous literary photograph of the Edwardian [sic] era."[12] The photo has a curious "composed" quality: each man occupies his own space; they are not touching or interacting or even seemingly aware of one another's proximity. They are arranged yet separate, in a symmetry that is complex and highly significant (Figure 20).

The photograph represents the group constructed by the dinner. The arrangement makes visible the poets' differing degrees of status and the structure of their professional network, namely, a hierarchy of homosocial friendships created by heterosexual intimacies. In the design formed by the men, the photo shows the routes by which "culture" has been transmitted: it reveals both the complex interconnections among the central three poets and the significant, almost visible distinction between the inner three and the outer four.

Figure 20. After the peacock dinner. Reproduced by permission of the Syndics of the Fitzwilliam Museum, Cambridge.

Yeats and the poets of his generation stand on the viewer's left, and Pound and the younger poets on the right. Victor Plarr, on the far left, was a former Rhymer, but in 1914 he was closer to Pound than to Yeats, entertaining Pound with stories of the late alcoholic Rhymer Ernest Dowson. Thomas Sturge Moore was at the time designing a bookplate for Yeats.[13] The younger generation, to the right of the photo, on Pound's left, were the Imagists Richard Aldington and (on the end) Frank Flint.

But to read the photo as right versus left is to get only a small part of its meaning. Interpreted as center and periphery, the arrangement of the poets tells much more. The three important poets are in the center, and the less important on the edges; the arrangement is a horizontal dominance hierarchy. The difference in status and celebrity is striking. To some extent the disparity was an accident: had Robert Bridges been one of the guests—never very likely, but he had been invited—his celebrity as Poet Laureate would have eclipsed Pound's, and possibly he would have been standing next to Blunt.

And had Masefield dined on the peacock, the dynamics would also have been quite different. He would have offset the great power center Yeats/Blunt/Pound for a number of reasons; he, too, might have stood on Blunt's left instead of Ezra Pound. *The Everlasting Mercy* had come out in 1911 and *Salt-Water Ballads* just recently, in 1913: Masefield was, as J. C. Squire wrote in *The New Statesman* in 1913, "undoubtedly the poet of the hour."[14] At the death of Alfred Austin (in June 1913), his name was mentioned as a candidate for Poet Laureate, though in the end Robert Bridges got that honor. (Masefield was named Poet Laureate in 1930 after Bridges's death.) Moreover, Masefield admired Yeats and considered him his mentor: on 5 November 1900, a date with memories Masefield "cherished," Masefield dined with Yeats for the first time and thereafter became a regular at his "Monday evenings."[15] With his gruff sailor's vernacular, Masefield was neither a Rhymer nor an Imagist; Aldington had even written a parody of Masefield.[16] What the undercurrents would have been had Masefield been present can only be imagined.

Absent Bridges and Masefield, the arrangement of men embodied a distinct pattern. For the three central men, the ones with the most cultural capital, marriage and adultery constituted professional networking. Their erotic histories show how heterosexual intimacy functioned as a means of transmission of culture and led to homosocial friendships with other poets. Blunt (to begin with the senior member of this "family") had in 1869 married Lady Anne, attracted not only to her but also to her grandfather, Lord Byron. Even before he met Lady Anne, he had courted Alice Noel, another (though collateral) Byron kin.[17] Once Blunt was married into the family, he took a great interest in family papers, stories, relics, and everything else connected with the Romantic poet. In love with a cousin, as he occasionally was, Blunt thought of Byron's feelings for his half-sister Augusta; and as he fought British imperial tyranny in Egypt, he thought of Byron in Greece.[18] The exchange of bodily fluids with Lady Anne constituted a symbolic cultural exchange with the great poet, a transmission for which the woman was the conduit.

Blunt and Yeats might never have met, or certainly not so often as they did, without Lady Gregory: she formed the link between them. Blunt's diaries make clear that every time he saw Yeats, it was Lady Gregory who organized the gathering. Her intimate friendship with Blunt authorized her to extend to him Pound and Yeats's invitation to dinner. Like Lady Anne, though in a more active and deliberate way, she functioned as the conduit between male poets.

The Shakespear family also proved important in this way. Yeats's first lover was Olivia Shakespear, the cousin of the Rhymer poet Lionel Johnson: Yeats met her at a party for the 1890s quarterly *The Yellow Book* in 1894. It was after a tea at Mrs. Shakespear's, in 1909, that Pound had written Mary Moore that he had been "sitting on the same hearth rug" where Yeats sat. Pound married Shakespear's only daughter Dorothy in April 1914, two months after the dinner for Blunt; and Yeats, through his renewed friendship with Olivia Shakespear, strengthened by his friendship with Pound, met Dorothy's step-cousin Georgie Hyde Lees, whom he married in October 1917. Pound was best man at the wedding.

In 1918, four years after the peacock dinner, Pound "seduced," or "relieved of her virginity," or was the first lover of (depending on how one reads the sexual politics involved) Iseult Gonne, daughter of Maud.[19] Thus Pound slept with *the daughters* of two of Yeats's most important lovers; and the first congress between Pound and Miss Gonne most likely occurred in Yeats's rooms at Woburn Buildings.[20] Whether it was inspired by competition or emulation or both, this pattern shows the combination of affiliation and rivalry that characterized Pound's attitude to Yeats. Blunt's private sniping at Yeats may also have had its origin in sexual jealousy; and in the cases of both Pound and Blunt, it was probably not only Yeats's good looks that inspired this attitude, but also his superiority as a poet.

The Pound–Yeats competition over the Shakespear women seems to have made a final appearance in November 1937, when Yeats wrote Edith Shackleton Heald about a dream:

I had a delightful dream three nights ago in which I had simultaneous affairs with an unknown eastern lady & the wife of Ezra Pound & then the Sultan, who was interested in both ladies, found out & when I woke up I was envoled [*sic*] in explanations.[21]

In this "delightful" dream, Dorothy Shakespear Pound may have stood in for her mother, Yeats's first lover, or may simply have indicated Yeats's rivalry with Pound. The Sultan adds the note of male rivalry, and in a particularly powerful way, because he's a *Sultan*; and the two women may have been the dreaming mind's way of alluding to any of the lesbian women in whom Yeats was then interested. And might the Sultan have stood in for Blunt, who often dressed in Arab robes?

At any rate, the three men in the center were linked in networks that were at the same time erotic and professional. Standing one man over from the center on the right side of the picture, between the center and the periphery, is Richard Aldington, who was linked to Pound in a similar, though less complex, network. Aldington and Pound met in 1911 at the salon of Brigit Patmore, who was later to become Aldington's lover.[22] In 1912, Pound introduced Aldington to his own former fiancée, the American poet Hilda Doolittle, who had recently arrived in London to visit Pound. In October 1913, H.D. had just married Aldington.

Like all the other women who functioned as routes between the male poets, H.D. (as is well known) was no mere conduit: she was a serious poet and later a novelist and memoirist. Lady Anne Blunt was a violinist, a linguist (fluent in French, German, Italian, and Arabic), an excellent water-colorist, an expert in the knowledge and breeding of Arab horses, and the author of several books.[23] Lady Anne's obituary (the "correspondent" who supplied it may have been her daughter or grandson) also praises her "perfect horsemanship."[24] Almost seventy years after her death, her eloquent *Journals and Correspondence, 1878–1917* were published. Lady Gregory was of course a folklorist, playwright, and a major cultural figure in the Irish Revival. Olivia Shakespear was a novelist, her daughter Dorothy a painter, Georgie Hyde Lees a cultured, unconventional, witty woman with a dry sense of humor, and Iseult Gonne, as Yeats famously put it, "knew all Dante once." The celebrated poets chose for their lovers aristocratic or haute-bourgeoise women, sophisticated and artistic. Lady Anne, Dorothy Shakespear, and George Yeats also had incomes that at various times supported their husbands. That Pound did not want women present at the dinner for Blunt did not mean he was ignorant of their professional value to himself and other male poets. *Au contraire*; they might have taken up too much oxygen and distracted attention from the men.

That the arrangement of the poets in the photograph is a dominance hierarchy becomes clearest when one concentrates on the men at the ends. Sturge Moore was slightly alienated from what seemed to be the dominant view expressed by the dinner. He did not feel that the presentation poem Pound read spoke for him in its "we." As Yeats (no doubt amused by the objection) wrote Lady Gregory, "Sturge Moore is a little unhappy about Ezra's verse verses [*sic*] as he says he respects a lot of things & Ezra has made him say he does not." Nor had Sturge Moore married to advance his artistic and poetic career, though some rivalry may have been involved: he was happily married to his first cousin, who had previously been engaged to his brother.[25] And—to add to the complex ties of likes and dislikes connecting the men at the dinner—Sturge Moore was on record as disliking Hilaire Belloc, who arrived for tea that afternoon. In 1911, Yeats had sought Sturge Moore's support for nominating Belloc to the Academic Committee of the Royal Society of Literature, and Moore had, in response, urged the nomination of E. M. Forster: "Why go for people hopelessly prostituted in politics and journalism when one could have a man like that? It is insane! Belloc? No! a thousand times no! It is disgusting. You read *A Room with a View* and see what you think."[26]

The men on the far edges were the lowest in status: for one thing, they were the only two who had regular, non-literary jobs. On 8 January 1914 Aldington wrote to Flint, "Dear Flint, That Blunt affair is to come off on Sunday, 18th. We are all to go down to Blunt's place for lunch. I am instructed to see that you turn up." Pound had also written Flint about the logistics, but the fact that Aldington was delegated to organize Flint shows him to be closer to the center of power. Of course Flint was less significant: in 1909 he had married his landlady's daughter.[27] His "error" in this choice of bride formed the subject of a letter H.D. wrote to Pound's mother in 1912. Ezra had introduced her to

celebrities and lesser oddities—he always has some underdog on hand. On Thursday it was a derelict poet named Flint who made the fatal mistake of marrying his landlady's daughter, a hapless little Cockney.[28]

H.D.'s comments on Flint and his wife make it clear why Flint is at the edge rather than the center: he is poor and he married a working-class woman. An "underdog," he is clearly, from H.D.'s point of view, marked for life. Although H.D. was soon to change her mind, "writing affectionately to Flint from Paris," at first meeting she felt sure of Flint's utter lack of cultural capital or any other kind of capital.[29]

By a curious symmetry, Victor Plarr (at the far left of the photograph, balancing Flint exactly in the horizontal line-up of poets) was said to have committed the identical error. Yeats told the story in his post-prandial letter to Lady Gregory:

All the poets behaved modestly & said what they should except for Plarr, a survived Rhymer, who has deteri[or]ated through marriage with his cook & has the most mechanical & foolish small talk. As we came away Blunt asked all there to invite themselves down from a Saturday to Monday any time they chose. As we got into the motor I thought 'all will be too modest to accept but Plarr & he will go[.]' [A]t that moment Plarr said 'I will accept that invitation.' On the way home the poets kept Plarr out of all the conversation—they would not give him the clue to anything—he had become an ordinary person, an enemy, & next day or the day after Ezra said 'Plarr has made his last public appearance.' He was silent & modest in the days of the Rhymers, but having a story to tell & the cook have undone him.[30]

Like Flint, Plarr did not have the wit to marry up, to marry into aristocratic or at least *haut bourgeois* literary circles, allying himself with a wife whose money and connections would help his career. Nothing about him lent importance to the world of letters. Even his body language in the photo is too eager.

The Daughters

And yet there is no evidence that Plarr's marriage had ruined his power of repartee, because he had been married to the same woman, Helen Marion (Shaw) Plarr, since 1892; their daughter Marion was born in 1893. If his "small talk" had deteriorated, marriage could not be the reason. Perhaps Pound had by now heard all Plarr's stories about Ernest Dowson and had found more important people to spend time with. Certainly Mrs. Plarr's background was not the kind from which Pound, Yeats, or Blunt would ever have selected a wife. Mrs. Plarr's father, Albert Shaw, was a railroad stationmaster and then a construction worker, and her mother ran The Bugle Inn on the Isle of Wight.[31] But Mrs. Plarr's provenance was more colorful than Pound allowed, because at age 24, in 1891, she had been working as a domestic servant in the Bloomsbury house of the Rev. Stewart Headlam, the famous Christian Socialist, Fabian, friend of Annie Besant and Arthur Symons, admired by Shaw, and present in a cameo in Yeats's *Trembling of the Veil*, rescuing Wilde after the first trial.[32]

Headlam's somewhat remote association with the peacock dinner offers yet another instance of the dinner's relation to the poets of the Nineties. At the time the future Mrs. Plarr was working for him, Headlam was known for founding the Church and Stage Guild, intended to legitimize the social and professional position of actors and dancers. (One of the boarders in his house is listed in the 1891 census as an "artist dancer.") Through his interest in the arts, Headlam became friendly with all the Rhymers, especially Selwyn Image, Dowson, Symons, and Plarr. In his *Reminiscences* of Dowson, Plarr mentions Headlam's

Church and Stage parties, which took place always in January, and were a brilliant and picturesque episode in the crowded artistic life of the early nineties. They should be put on record. The customary scene in his beautiful drawing-rooms will remain impressed on the minds of his many grateful guests.[33]

This, then, was the atmosphere—radical, socialist, artistic, bohemian—in which Plarr met his wife.[34] The 1891 Census shows him living with his parents in Tonbridge, Kent, and he appears to include himself among the "grateful guests."[35] That Helen Shaw was (in the words of the Census) "House & Parlour Maid Domestic Servant" and yet was courted by a guest may indicate the liberal ways of the household or the open-mindedness of Plarr (a graduate of Worcester College Oxford). Nothing in their daughter Marion Plarr Barwell's charming memoir of her childhood (the first section of *India Without Sentiment*) gives any indication that her mother was uneducated; on the contrary, she mentions that her mother taught her Blake's "Songs of Innocence."[36] In her novel *Cynara* she calls her mother "English as a primrose."[37] The photograph of the dinner, at any rate, shows maximum distance between the honored host, whose wife died a baroness, and the guest whose wife began her adult life as a domestic servant.

The elitist eugenic implications of Yeats's and Pound's remarks about Plarr and of H.D.'s initial response to Flint are consistent with the affiliational purpose and the genetic subtext of the dinner. The aim for Pound, at least, was to create a literary genealogy, to ally himself with a poetic "father" and follow in his cultural path. In that sense, the photograph shows a father and brothers. The two "runts" are the little brothers who didn't understand "breeding," in the active sense of the verb. It is no accident that the dinner celebrated a man who exemplified successful breeding: he had married the wealthy granddaughter of a great romantic poet who was also a titled aristocrat, and along with his wife he had established the Crabbet Stud and become expert in breeding Arab horses.[38]

Such were the implicit purpose and values of the dinner. A look at some of the offspring of these men, however, indicates that they were all, all seven, successful in "breeding," and that they passed on artistic skills and various competencies to their daughters.[39] In fact it could be said that several of the daughters channeled their fathers, keeping their reputations alive professionally, in that sense acting as conduits like the women who linked the poets in the first place. Catherine Aldington Guillaume, who grew up mostly in France, translated her father's poetry into French and managed the permissions for her father's poetry. Ianthe Flint Price also managed her father's permissions. Mary de Rachewiltz, Pound's daughter, edited his letters to his parents and translated the *Cantos* into Italian; she is also a poet and author of the memoir *Ezra Pound, Father and Teacher: Discretions*.

In this context Marion Plarr is no different from the others: she inherited her father's talents (her mother's genetic legacy, whatever it may have been, notwithstanding) and produced two books that in different ways gave a nod to his life and interests. She was closely associated with male poets from her birth, the subject of Ernest Dowson's poem "On the Birth of a Friend's Child; for Victor and Nellie Plarr." Years later she returned the compliment by writing about him: her novel *Cynara* (1933) told the story of Dowson's love life. Dowson was, of course, Victor Plarr's close friend, a man Marion remembered meeting, and the man Pound liked to hear stories about ("he was silent and modest in the days of the Rhymers . . ."). Marion Plarr turned those very stories into fiction. Dowson's infatuation with the 11-year-old waitress was an "inappropriate" romance that Marion Plarr told sympathetically; Adelaide Foltinowicz was the "Cynara" of Dowson's famous poem. Marion Plarr's memoir *India Without Sentiment* (published in 1960 under her married name Marion Barwell) begins with affectionate reminiscences of her parents, her father especially, but then goes on to chart her own distinct intellectual and spiritual development; she channels her father only so far. However, before she describes her own choice of Hinduism, she cites many examples of her father's anti-imperialism and his multicultural sympathies *avant la lettre*.[40]

The other poets' daughters also inherited family talents and interests but did not serve as keepers of their fathers' flames: Blunt's daughter Judith Blunt Lytton managed the Crabbet Stud and published many books, among them a volume of sonnets (1913), *Thoroughbred Racing Stock and its Ancestors: The Authentic Origin of Pure Blood* (1938), and other books on horse-breeding. Yeats's daughter Anne was a distinguished painter and stage set-designer. Sturge Moore's daughter Riette (Henriette Hélène Rebecca Sturge Moore) was also a set-designer as well as an interior decorator and design teacher. To some extent the daughters appear to have perpetuated the photograph's hierarchy into the next generation, with the most celebrated professionally those whose fathers were in the center. Marion Barwell authored two books, the second published under her married name; but under either name she is as an author almost invisible, whereas Mary de Rachewiltz is well known as Pound's daughter, organizes conferences to perpetuate his literary legacy, and makes herself accessible to those studying his poetry. Anne Yeats's paintings hang in the National Gallery of Ireland, in the Yeats Collection, and she donated the Yeats Archive to the National Gallery.

The Speeches

Although Lord Osborne wrote that Yeats "would interview W. B. for the benefit of the company," Blunt never mentions feeling "interviewed" by Yeats.[41] The account in his private diaries makes the dinner sound like a successful combination of the formal and the informal. "I had arranged to give them luncheon," he wrote, "and there was a Peacock served up in full plumage on the table for them and they eat [*sic*] with excellent appetites and we had good conversation and I think they all enjoyed themselves after which the address was intoned by Pound and I responded in a brief speech and Yeats made another . . ."[42]

Like the photograph, the speeches embodied masculine competition, in this instance not explicitly over women but over poetry. In a ritual of turn-taking, the three poets in the center of the photograph spoke to one another: Pound read his presentation poem to Blunt, Blunt responded to Pound and toasted Yeats, and then Yeats responded to Blunt. They spoke in three different discourses expressing three entirely different visions of the profession of poetry. In these exchanges, they engaged with one another's personalities in a manner that was superficially friendly but expressed an undercurrent of aggression. Flint took detailed notes on the formal speeches, so all that was said was recorded.

Pound's presentation poem—quoted in full in *The Times*'s account published two days later—offered a rationale for affiliation that attributed to Blunt the kind of masculinity Pound himself wanted in a poetic ancestor:

> Because you have gone your individual gait,
> Written fine verses, made mock of the world,
> Swung the grand style, not made a trade of art,
> Upheld Mazzini and detested institutions;
> We, who are little given to respect,
> Respect you, and having no better way to show it,
> Bring you this stone to be some record of it.[43]

Working on the poem three days earlier, Pound had told Yeats that "poems of salutation are obsolete."[44] With its awkward, accidental final rhyme ("show it," "of it"), uneuphonious repetition ("little given to respect, / Respect you"), and ugly, desperate directness ("having no better way to show it, / Bring you this stone to be some record of it"), the poem does not rank as one of Pound's best. The phrase "having no better way" sounds almost self-referential, as if Pound himself had given up on writing a better poem. In addition, Pound had gotten the patriarch's biography wrong, as Blunt realized when he read the poem later in solitude. It was of course the Egyptian Urabi, not the Italian Mazzini, whom Blunt had "[u]pheld."

But here, in a mediocre, inaccurate poem, Pound had constructed a precursor: this was the man who "hates the British Empire." The chief quality that Pound admired in Blunt, according to the poem, was his iconoclasm, which was enhanced by his poetry writing and the bravado of his personal style (in Canto LXXXII, Blunt's youthful triumph in the bullring is mentioned). The poem turns the act of writing poetry and Blunt's anti-imperialist politics into physical motion, a way of walking and moving through the world: "gone your individual gait," "swung the grand style," "upheld Mazzini." Everything Blunt did is perceived as an action, done with a swaggering masculinity. Pound says little about Blunt's poetry except "swung the grand style, not made a trade of art." The operative word is "swung," which implies a kind of swagger as well as the physical effort of writing "grand" poetry; the weaker verb "write" is not used. The pattern of stresses in the short, brisk, parallel verbal phrases—gone, written, made mock, swung, not made, upheld—sounds defiant, as if each action is a moral triumph on Blunt's part. Blunt as constructed by Pound is a source of value in a politically corrupt world.

The wording of this praise is interesting for a number of reasons. It's curious that Pound of all people would consider not making "a trade of art" worthy of praise: who more conscious of money, marketing, publicity, the fluctuation of reputation, than the young Ezra Pound? To praise someone for not making "a trade of art" sounds odd from a poet who—in publishing anthologies, seeking out the friendship of major poets, befriending bookstore owners, organizing poets' dinners, soliciting poems and reviews for anthologies, and bringing the methods of public relations to bear on the field of poetry—was doing more to professionalize poetry than any other poet alive. Pound allowed his first book, *A Lume Spento*, a small print run of only 150 copies to ensure that it would soon be "a rarity": he wrote his father, ". . . when I state as I hope to before long 'First edition exhausted' I wish to give the impression of a larger circulation."[45] Or, as he put it even more directly to his father, ". . . no vulgarity of publicity need be shunned."[46] The best advertisement for the first edition of *A Draft of XVI Cantos*, Pound wrote the publisher William Bird, would be to say that "at auction recently a copy of Mr. P's 'A Lume Spento' published in 1908 at $1.00 (one dollar) was sold for $52.50."[47] Perhaps by the phrase "not made a trade of art" Pound means that the words were not written with the design of making money; and perhaps

Pound intended not to get rich but only to boom his reputation with his rare volumes and high auction prices. Blunt had "not made a trade of art" because he did not publish trade editions of his books; did not, that is, until the two-volume collected edition of 1914 that was in large part inspired by the peacock dinner. It can be argued that Pound helped make Blunt into the kind of poet who "made a trade of art."

Yeats put it another way when, in 1926, he characterized Blunt in a letter to Herbert Grierson as "mostly an infuriating amateur."[48]

Blunt's response was less to Pound's poem, to which he was listening carefully—waiting "for a rhyme that did not seem to come," as he put it—than to the whole notion of a testimonial dinner for him with the purpose of honoring his poetry. This was the longest speech of the afternoon; Flint's transcription appears to give an excellent account of Blunt's idiomatic style, which certainly—in extemporaneous prose, at least—was not "grand." It was charming, witty, and not entirely truthful, but then, the guests did not have access to Blunt's diaries. Pound read his poem aloud and presented the marble box, to which Blunt responded:

Well, I suppose I must say a few words of thanks for it. The only thing I feel about this visit—which flatters me immensely—is that I am to a certain extent an impostor. I have really never been a poet. I have been all sorts of other things. I have never been a poet. I was not brought up that way at all. I was never at a public school nor at a college. I never met a literary man who had so much as written a letter to a paper or an article for a magazine until I was twentyfive [*sic*]. I did not write any verse. I never published a single thing—prose or verse—with my name till I was past forty. I think it is very difficult to call a man a poet who has that sort of record behind him.[49]

This was a bit disingenuous. Blunt's private diaries from 1894 record his thoughts as he sat among the guests at Violet Maxse's wedding: "I counted six poets in the church, including myself, Alfred Austin, George Meredith, Alfred Lyall, Oscar Wilde, and Edwin Arnold." On 22 June in the same year Blunt lists his guests at a dinner party: "Lady Granby, Lucy Smith, d'Estournelles, Alfred Lyall, and Godfrey Webb, all of us more or less poets. After dinner we read and recited poetry . . ."[50]

The response continued:

I have written a certain amount of verse; but I have only done it when I was rather down on my luck and made mistakes either in love or politics or some branch of active life. I found that it relieved my feelings. But I never wrote any of it with the least idea of getting it published. I did not even show it to my friends. My first little anonymous work published was when I was thirtyfive [*sic*] or thirtysix [*sic*], and it was not much of a thing then. I did not publish a single verse with my name till I was, I think, about 43.

Blunt's indifference is a bit exaggerated: in 1892 he complained in his diaries, "A trouble to me is the apparent failure of 'Esther.' It is not reviewed, for which I care little, but even my friends are silent about it, and several of them disapprove."[51] And in 1908 he wrote regretfully in his diary, "Meynell thinks that I . . . shall be given a permanent place as a poet twenty years hence, but I am doubtful. Certainly I have no such place of any kind now."[52]

My life has been an active one in various connections; and people write to me sometimes: 'We have great admiration for you.' But it is never about poetry. It is the first time in my life that I have ever had any admiration for my poetry expressed to me. It is either because I have taken up the cause of the Indian or the Egyptian, or more generally because I bred horses. That is what I am generally known as—a breeder of horses. So when I received your flattering invitation, and there was nothing expressed about what kind of admiration it was, I was very much puzzled. I did not know whether it was from some of my horsey friends or political admirers. When I learned that it was for my poetry, I was all the more flattered and astonished. It was so very unusual.

This is to a great extent my fault. I think it is because in one of the very first things I wrote, I was ill-advised enough to say, 'I would not if I could be called a poet,' and that has stuck to me ever since. If anybody has thought of me as a poet, they have always had that answer: I did not think myself as a poet [*sic*]. It was quite incidental. However, I have come round from that now. Within the last year I have entirely washed my hands of politics and all forms of public life; and even withdrawn to some extent from horse-breeding; and having nothing to do I have taken up again with verse-writing, to console me for a new disappointment. I have been writing a certain amount of verse in the last year, and I am very pleased now to be considered a poet. It is quite a novelty to me. I am seventy-three years of age, and it is late to begin. That is all I can say in my excuse.

I very much appreciate the verse that you have written to me—if they are verses. I could not quite make out whether they were or not. I waited for a rhyme that did not seem to come. I am old-fashioned enough to expect rhyme in verse. I believe it is coming into fashion again. Spanish poetry runs a good deal into assonance, which I admire very much, and I have tried to write things [in] assonance. I am a great believer in assonance. I must say with all respect to Mr. Yeats that I do not like blank verse. To me it is quite a black beast—a thing I quarrel with.

Mr. Yeats is a great advocate of blank verse. I recollect one occasion he had asked me to write a play for the Abbey Theatre—or perhaps it was before the time of the Abbey Theatre. I sent him the play. He approved of it; but he said it would have been very much better if it had been in blank verse. I had put it into rhyme. He was good enough to offer to turn it into blank verse. I should have been most flattered and pleased to have had it turned into blank verse by Mr. Yeats. But as it was an Irish play, I wrote to him my objections, or views, I think, in a letter. I said: I am an Englishman; I do not pretend to have anything Celtic in my composition. I was asked to write a play about Ireland, and I wrote it in what I conceived to be something approximating to an Irish metre. And I said that it was a curious thing that Mr. Yeats—who was a representative of Ireland and of Celtic culture and literature—should have chosen such an essentially Anglo-Saxon metre as blank verse. He writes blank verse very much as Shakespeare did and people of that day; and I believe quite as well, if not better. But still it is an ~~unusual~~ English metre, and I thought it very inappropriate for the occasion.

That was my objection. Not that I did not appreciate the kind motive (laughter). I maintain that rhymed metre is better than blank verse. I think that blank verse is the essence of dulness [*sic*]. However, I will not say anything more, because I feel that I am treading on dangerous ground. I can only add that I thank you most heartily, and that I hope that you have enjoyed your lunch, and that if any of you will come down and spend a week-end with me I shall be very grateful indeed. ~~I am rather dull.~~ I lead a very solitary and dull life. I have all my life intended to end it as a hermit, and I feel that I am doing that now.

Like other poets of his time, especially male ones, Blunt attributes "Englishness" to blank verse, assuming that national culture inheres in meter.[53] Here, as in his successful effort to be the first Englishman to have "taken the Celtic Irish side in any conflict, or suffered even the shortest imprisonment for Ireland's sake," Blunt attempts to remake himself as Irish.[54]

In the context of this binary, then, to write in blank verse would be imperialist. Blunt's notion of "an Irish meter" is rhymed iambic hexameter couplets, not recognizably Irish, but not recognizably English either, as Blunt posits the nationalities of meter. Blunt may have been thinking not of verse in the Irish language but of nineteenth-century poems by Mangan and Ferguson, such as Mangan's "I saw her once, one little while, and then no more / 'Twas Eden's light on Earth a while and then no more" or Sir Samuel Ferguson's "The Hawthorn stands between the ashes tall and slim, / Like matron with her twin grand-daughters at her knee."[55] And for what it's worth, Blunt had indeed a small bit of something "Celtic" in his "composition." According to his obituary in *The Times*, his father, Francis Scawen Blunt, had been at his death "the eldest representative of the ancient Cornish family of Scawen of Molennick."[56] At the time when the Abbey received Blunt's play (7 May 1905, to be exact), Yeats had indeed complained to Blunt about the meter: his excuse was the difficulty for the actors. The alexandrines, he wrote, "will throw a great deal of work upon everybody who has to speak it for their experience in blank verse will not help them very greatly." And in a rather irritable note at the end, Yeats wrote, "I wish you had written the play in blank verse, but I imagine that you felt the necessity of breaking from the English tradition of dramatic speech." And finally, just a tad too patronizingly perhaps, "Some day I shall probably have to discuss with you the placing of some of your caesuras, but it is too soon for that."[57]

Blunt continued:

But a hermit without a hermitage is not a very delightful thing. I have to bear it as I can, and so I wish you good health, and should like to drink one toast in your honour. I propose the health of Mr. Yeats especially, as I have said the most disagreeable things to him. I thank all the members of the committee most heartily.

How much of a hermit was Blunt, indeed, considering that since 1906 he had had as his companion, domiciled with him at Newbuildings, the youthful and lovely Dorothy Carleton. She was 34 years younger than he, and "Their relations he described as 'in everything but name a marriage'."[58] Dorothy was in London visiting family at the time of the peacock dinner, but her presence at Newbuildings ensured that Blunt was by no means a "hermit." She inherited Newbuildings and left it to Lady Anne Lytton, one of Blunt's grandchildren.

Blunt's natural hospitality and tact could not quite contain his dislike of Pound's poem. His dislike of all the poems in the marble box, not just the presentation poem, was expressed more clearly in his diaries, after he read carefully the poetry he had been given: "The modern poetry represented by these young men is too entirely unlike

anything I can recognize as good verse that I feel there is something absurd in their expressing admiration for mine." The critique
of Pound's poem is slight, and Blunt puts the blame on himself for
being "old-fashioned enough to expect rhyme in verse."

Blunt lights into Yeats with more energy, expressing his characteristic antagonism to Yeats obliquely, as wit, in a funny story. The
guests, of course, were not aware of Blunt's rivalrous feelings about
Yeats, but put in the context of the diary entries, the speech has particular significance. In his diary, Blunt pitted Lady Gregory, Gilbert
Murray, and Masefield successively against Yeats, asserting in each
instance Yeats's inferiority to the other writers. Here, with Yeats in
his presence, and compelled to make a speech thanking him as well as
Pound, Blunt pitted himself against Yeats directly. His mind seemed
to have moved automatically from his dislike of Pound's poem—or
at least his preference for rhymes—to a "quarrel" with "blank verse"
and thence to an old quarrel with Yeats.

What arose spontaneously ("I recollect one occasion . . .") was
a disagreement about poetry that Blunt evidently remembered in
detail; a quarrel, a disagreement, or perhaps just a fight, this was a
conflict about poetic practice and skill. Who could write better? Or,
to catch the edge in Blunt's tone, who could write *Blunt's play* better? In 1902, Blunt began making a play out of "one of the Cuchulain
episodes for Yeats to bring out next year" at the Abbey.[59] The topic he
chose was one close to his heart, adultery. Blunt's *Fand*, a well-shaped
play, dramatizes a moment in Cuchulain's life when he must choose
among Emer (his wife), Eithne (his mistress, or rather, "beloved of
Cuchulain," as the list of *dramatis personae* more delicately puts it), and
Fand, a married fairy ("wife to Manannan," the sea king). Blunt's
diaries give no hint of the argument about meter. What they quote,
instead, is Yeats's ambiguous compliment:

Lady Gregory writes that Yeats has read my play "Fand" to his company
and that they are anxious to act it . . . Yeats, she says, has declared that if
I had begun to write plays when I was thirty, I should now have a European
reputation. (115)[60]

In the event, Blunt did not see the play produced. On 23 April 1907 he
was "astonished" to read in the paper that *Fand* had been "performed
at the Abbey Theatre at Dublin with great success." Lady Gregory
had not given him warning, but "It is only in Ireland, I suppose,"

Blunt wrote in some irritation, "that a play could be performed for the first time and the author know nothing about it."[61]

It's possible to imagine his guests' laughter at Blunt's comment about Yeats and *Fand*, "He was good enough to offer to turn it into blank verse," but it's an edgy remark. One further comment about blank verse—and there are quite a few here—is a more direct attack on Yeats's knowledge of meter: Yeats writes blank verse well, Blunt concedes, but it's an "English metre, and I thought it very inappropriate for the occasion." Curiously enough, Yeats did in fact turn "Blunt's" play into blank verse. On 16 June 1902 Yeats wrote to Lady Gregory, "Blount [*sic*] is quite bent on the Cuchullin play and proposes to take 'the only jealousy of Emer' for his subject . . ."[62] Whose was the phrase in quotation marks? Blunt's title was *Fand*. But in 1917, only a couple of weeks after his marriage—when Yeats's own life had caught up to Cuchulain's and Blunt's in that respect—Yeats began *his* play on the subject, *The Only Jealousy of Emer*. The subject resonated in Yeats's life at that point in the same way as it resonated (for many years) in Blunt's: the "theme of jealousy, wifely sacrifice, and a man torn between three women had an immediate personal relevance."[63] The struggle over Cuchulain "by his wife, Emer, his mistress, Eithne Inguba, and the supernatural Fand" reflects Yeats's own struggle among his new wife George Hyde Lees Yeats, and the two other women he had recently proposed to, Maud Gonne McBride and her daughter Iseult Gonne.

And Yeats's play was written in that "essentially Anglo-Saxon metre," blank verse. It's worth reading a few lines of both plays, Blunt's rhyming hexameters—

> *(Emer)*
> What is your Eithne to me, or all womankind,
> That she should fear to see me? Think you my peace of mind
> Is of such unstable stuff it should be over-set
> By a girl's folly, a man's fanciful regret
> For youthful joys remembered, and the sickly need
> Of a new maiden bosom for his aching head?[64]

—and Yeats's blank verse—

> *(Eithne)*
>   He loves me best,
> Being his newest love, but in the end

Will love the woman best who loved him first
And loved him through the years when love seemed lost.
(Emer)
I have that hope, the hope that some day somewhere
We'll sit together at the hearth again—[65]

—to hear the longer nineteenth-century lines of Blunt and Yeats's shorter lines, which (possibly because they are unrhymed) sound more enjambed and therefore more fluid. Apparently Blunt's speech at the peacock dinner, an insistence on his status as amateur poet that mutated into jestingly aggressive remarks about Yeats, triggered memories (in Yeats) of the play in question. Three years later, just after he had married Pound's wife's step-cousin, and before Pound took the virginity of Yeats's muse's daughter, Yeats wrote his delayed response to Blunt's sally in their continuing argument about meter. Of course Blunt's entire speech was no doubt made in a jesting tone enriched with smiles, and the poets no doubt laughed to indicate they understood the tone; the paralinguistic elements of meaning were not recorded by Flint. As Blunt did in all his diary entries about Yeats, so in his toast, having expressed his antagonism, Blunt made nice: "I propose the health of Mr. Yeats especially, as I have said the most disagreeable things to him."

Yeats did not pick up on the antagonism in the slightest. And even though Blunt's play had proved "unactable," and even though he had in fact (see the letter of 7 May 1905) complained explicitly about the unactability of the alexandrines, Yeats praised the play as well as Blunt's lyric poetry:[66]

Mr. Blunt's alexandrines formed a very effective stage metre. I have since used rhyme myself with a few extra syllables thrown-in in a play called 'The Green Helmet.' Dryden said that rhyme in drama added speed to the dialogue, and it has that curious effect. I think that Mr. Blunt's work moves some of us—myself, Ezra Pound, we represent, I should say a school, he at one end of the stocking and I at the other, a very remote antithesis.

When you published your first work, sir, it was the very height of the Victorian period. The abstract poet was in a state of glory. One no longer wrote as a human being with an address, living in a London street, having a definite income, and a definite tradition, but one wrote as an abstract personality. One was expected to be very much wiser than other people, and to represent the people of all the ages. The only objection to such a conception of the poet is that it was impossible to believe that he had existed. This abstraction was the result of the unreal culture of Victorian romance.

Now, sir, instead of abstract poetry, you wrote verses which were good poetry because they were first of all fine things to have thought and said in some real situation of life. They had behind them the drama of actual life. We are now at the end of Victorian romance—completely at an end. One may admire Tennyson, but one cannot read him. The whole movement is over, but the work that survives is this work which does not speak out of the life of an impossible abstract poet, but out of the life of a man who is simply giving the thoughts which he had in some definite situation in life, or persuades us that he had; so that behind his work we find some definite impulse of life itself.

If I take up to-day some of the things that interested me in the past, I find that I can no longer use them. They bore me. Every year some part of my poetical machinery suddenly becomes of no use. As the tide of romance recedes I am driven back simply on myself and my thoughts in actual life, and my work becomes more and more like your earlier work, which seems fascinating and wonderful to me.

A great many of us feel the same. Just as the Victorian time recedes, your work becomes younger and more fascinating to us. I say that for myself. We represent different schools and interests. To Sturge Moore, for instance, the world is impersonal. He does not dramatise himself but centaurs and great beings of that kind—he is neither the Victorian abstract poet nor the definite poet. Ezra Pound has a desire personally to insult the world. He has a volume of manuscript [*sic*] at present in which his insults to the world are so deadly that it is rather a complicated publishing problem.

Like Pound's poem, Yeats's speech constructs Blunt as a precursor, but a very different kind of precursor indeed. Each man creates the Blunt he required: Pound needed a man with a swaggering, hostile, macho style, a man of action and oppositional politics, and Yeats, as befit the poems he was writing for the volume that would be *Responsibilities* (1914), needed a poet changing his diction from that of "the unreal culture of Victorian romance" to that of "a man who is simply giving the thoughts which he had in some definite situation in life."

Whether Yeats was blithely unaware of the note of irritation in Blunt's speech, or chose to appear so, his response expressed a genuine affiliation: ". . . my work becomes more and more like your earlier work, which seems fascinating and wonderful to me." But Yeats's final words, as recorded by Flint, before the official turn-taking became general conversation, participate in a different continuing argument as they express a critique of Pound. "Yeats's impulse to insult the world was always more dignified than Pound's," writes Longenbach, "a difference in mode that despite the two poets' common arrogance created a tension in their relationship."[67]

The quarrel between Yeats and Pound over the tone of Pound's "insults" had appeared in print only weeks earlier, in the 1 January issue of *The Egoist*, where Pound dramatized it as an argument between a young man ("Porrex") and his older friend ("Ferrex"). In the first of two pieces, Porrex writes, "My gracious, superior and I need scarcely say elder friend constantly remonstrates with me for the petulance of me and my generation." The elder friend claims that the young man will never "have any effect on superior circles unless [he] lay aside all petulance." The disagreement is about the appropriate literary style for anger, and the young man asks, how can he be "expected to stretch the one word *merde* over eighteen elaborate paragraphs?"[68]

Defiantly, Porrex says at the end, "We have gone our own gait." The word "gait," in company with the word "gone," appears also in the presentation poem ("Because you have gone your individual gait, / Written fine verses, made mock of the world"), and its use in both texts, composed only days apart, links Blunt with Pound himself as a poet whose tone of righteous anger—whose "individual gait"—is justified. The phrase "individual gait" distinguishes Blunt from conventional Englishmen of his class, as well as from patriotic, imperialist poets. In the piece in *The Egoist*, the phrase "own gait" differentiates Porrex from Ferrex, that is, the angry Pound from the temperate Yeats.

In his response to Blunt's speech, then, Yeats was continuing the debate, but in a different site. The third of the three speeches at the peacock dinner cycled the belligerence that ran through all three of them back to the first speaker, at the same time as, publicly and officially, the three men were praising and toasting one another.

6

The Naked Muse

*The poem I have selected was once put, with poems by a certain group
of poets all friends, into a marble box designed by Gaudier Brzeska &
presented by those poets & myself to Wilfrid Blunt . . . We lunched with
Blunt & eat a Peacock.*

W. B. Yeats, 15 July 1933, to an American who
had asked for a poem in Yeats's handwriting

When, in 1933, Yeats sent a holograph copy of his poem
"When Helen Lived" to Chief Justice Walter B. Beals of the
Washington State Supreme Court, he was evidently reminded of
the last time he had written out a gift copy of the same poem. In the
letter, Yeats seems to be delighting in the occasion as he remembers
it, enhanced by the exoticism of "a marble box designed by Gaudier
Brzeska" and the consumption of a peacock. The few details make
a charming story; they are more interesting than the poem itself.[1]

In her response to Yeats's initial letter about a London dinner in
honor of Blunt, Lady Gregory had innocently suggested "their own
books perhaps in a little case—something with a line of inscription . . ." So she was in a sense to blame for the marble box with an
"absurd Futurist bas relief of a naked Egyptian woman" that Blunt
disliked so much he turned the side with the bas-relief to the wall.[2]
Pound had dutifully taken her advice; but the avant-garde sculptor
Henri Gaudier-Brzeska, whom Pound had commissioned to make
the container, put his own modernist spin on the traditional mode of
presentation.

Giving Blunt a box containing poems written by younger men,
Pound enacted a transmission of culture that made visible the

connection present obliquely in the photograph: a woman whose sexuality was her chief feature constituted the link among the men. Lady Gregory, the likely source of Blunt's rivalrous feelings toward Yeats, was the unmentioned source of the box. The naked woman suggested, perhaps accidentally, Blunt's adulterous activities and made proleptic allusion to the adulteries of Pound himself and of Yeats. Because the testimonial dinner implied (however inaccurately) that Blunt's poetry had inspired that of the younger poets, the gift also implied a fertile female figure pregnant with poems, a pregnancy engendered by Blunt. Although the event was designed to honor Blunt for his poetry, implicit honor was also given to Blunt's potency and an analogy made between poetic and erotic power. The muse had no clothes on. United in homosocial intimacy inside the box where their poems lay, the young men presented the old one with one more box to admire.

The Poems

When, the next day, Blunt opened the box, he appears not to have been titillated at all. He found eight poems, those by the six visiting poets as well as by two additional poets, Masefield and Frederic Manning:

> Richard Aldington, "In the Via Sestina"
> F. S. Flint, "The Swan"
> Frederic Manning, "Koré"
> John Masefield, "Truth"
> Thomas Sturge Moore, "The Dying Swan"
> Victor Plarr, "Ad Cinerarium"
> Ezra Pound, "The Return"
> W. B. Yeats, "When Helen Lived"[3]

The poems constituted one aspect, a significant one, of the cultural exchange. It is worthwhile considering all together the poems proffered that day by the various poets, not only the visitors but also Blunt, who read a poem to his guests, and Hilaire Belloc, who was invited for tea and entertained the others with a song of his own composition. Although Blunt dismissed the poems collectively as "word puzzles," they would not have puzzled anyone whose taste had been formed after 1890. Five of them—those by Yeats, Manning, Aldington, Plarr, and Pound—were classicist in different ways, taking as their subjects Helen, "Koré" (originally "Persephone"), Isis and Osiris, a "cinerarium," and the mysterious " 'Wing'd-with-Awe,' " the "Gods of the wingèd shoe." In addition, all the poems except the one by Flint focus on one of two subjects, women and poetry, the two sites most contested by the poets.

The poems by Yeats, Aldington, and Manning (as well as the translation of Gobineau that Blunt read to the poets, and Belloc's song) all focus on a single female figure and consider the mixture of high and low registers available to a man gazing at pure sexuality. Yeats's and Aldington's contributions, however accidentally, engage thematically with the same issue as the aggressively sexual figure on the box. In a sense the high formality of the box, with its elegantly carved marble in two colors, contrasted in aesthetic register with the overtly sexual breasts and private parts of the woman carved on the outside. Yeats's "When Helen Lived" considers explicitly the proper register for addressing "Beauty that we have won / From bitterest hours."

> We have cried in our despair
> That men desert,
> For some trivial affair
> Or noisy, insolent sport,
> Beauty that we have won
> From bitterest hours;
> Yet we, had we walked within
> Those topless towers
> Where Helen walked with her boy,
> Had given but as the rest
> Of the men and women of Troy,
> A word and a jest.

Helen of Troy, always a proxy for Yeats's beloved Maud Gonne, is revered by some ("Beauty that we have won / From bitterest hours") and disrespected by others (". . . men desert, / For some trivial affair"). In syntax and sound, the fourth line anticipates the way Yeats described John McBride in "Easter 1916": "noisy insolent sport" and "drunken vainglorious lout." There is a hint of male rivalry in the poem. Gonne had indeed been "deserted" by such a man. Yet however the speaker might "despair" that other men desert his beauty for "noisy, insolent sport," his own stance might also have been inadequate. Had he been "within / Those topless towers / Where Helen walked with her boy," he might also have spoken in a register inappropriate for such a beauty, uttering only a "word and a jest."

Aldington's "In the Via Sistina" also considers the mixture of poetic registers available to a man gazing at sexuality.

> O daughter of Isis,
> Thou standest beside the wet highway
> Of this decayed Rome,
> A manifest harlot.
> Straight and slim art thou
> As a marble phallus;
> Thy face is the face of Isis
> —Carven
> As she is carven in basalt.
> And my heart stops with awe
> At the presence of gods,
> For there beside thee on the stall of images
> Is the head of Osiris
> Thy lord.[4]

With its classicized female figure in modern idiom, its body "a marble phallus" and "carven," Aldington's poem appears to speak directly to Gaudier's sculpture, which of course he had not seen when he wrote the poem. Unlike Gaudier, Aldington isn't jokey. Shocking as the lower register of "harlot" and "phallus" might have seemed to some readers, Blunt for instance, the effect of the poem is to transmute the low sexual into the high mythic. The "manifest harlot," seen by the side of the highway in contemporary "decayed Rome," is elevated before she is so identified by the lofty appellation of the opening line and by the archaic "thou."

Like Yeats's and Aldington's poems, Manning's also constructs a classical sexuality. Manning's "Koré" offers a sensuous vision of a highly sexualized harvest goddess. The poem has some of the 1890s weariness and longing of Dowson's "Non Sum Qualis Eram Bonae Sub Regno Cynarae," but not its infidelity and aura of substance abuse. Pound liked this poem so much that he sent a copy to his parents; the poem, he wrote Ford Madox Hueffer, was "quite beautiful."[5] No doubt Pound requested from Manning a copy of this poem for the marble box. In the second of its three stanzas, the beauty and sensuality of the woman are reminiscent of the figure in a Pre-Raphaelite painting, but the loose gowns of Rossetti's and Burne-Jones's women (such as the ones on the tapestry in Newbuildings) do not reveal even the outlines of "small breasts":

> With slow, reluctant feet, and weary eyes,
> And eye lids heavy with the coming sleep,
> With small breasts lifted up in stress of sighs,
> She passed, as shadows pass, among the sheep;
> While the earth dreamed, and only I was ware
> Of that faint fragrance blown from her soft hair.

This fertile figure has passed "while no man wist," and the speaker writes at the end, "Only I saw the shadow on her brows, / Only I knew her for the yearly slain." He alone recognizes her meaning. Unlike the poems by Yeats and Aldington, Manning's makes no reference to different levels of diction. The sexuality of the female figure, with her "small breasts lifted up" and the "faint fragrance blown from her soft hair" is not acknowledged within the poem as sexual. These details are interpreted in idealized language as aspects of a pagan myth; she is Persephone, "the yearly slain."[6] In three stanzas the woman with breasts passes before the poet, her sexuality temptingly revealed to him, and then disappears into mythology. In the final line, the speaker says he "wept, and weep until she come again." He means, of course, that she will come in the spring, but it seems to be the possibility of sexual fulfillment that she also takes with her into the underworld.[7]

The poems by Pound, Plarr, Masefield, and Sturge Moore manifest no interest in women; not that the poets did not have that interest. Their poems are about the ways a poet can organize sound to create meaning. To some extent all poems *embody* that notion, but these poems take up the topic of sound more explicitly. All are on "high" subjects—death, a dying swan, a funeral urn, "Gods of the wingèd shoe"—but the poems' greater interest is in sound. Pound's mysterious poem "The Return" is probably the best poem in the box, and no doubt also the one most puzzling to Blunt, puzzling because, as Yeats wrote years later, Pound writes here as if he were "a brilliant improvisator translating at sight from an unknown Greek masterpiece."[8]

See, they return; ah, see the tentative
Movements, and the slow feet,
The trouble in the pace and the uncertain
Wavering!

See, they return, one by one,
With fear, as half-awakened;
As if the snow should hesitate
And murmur in the wind,
                    and half turn back;
These were the "Wing'd-with-Awe,"
                    Inviolable.

Gods of the wingèd shoe!
With them the silver hounds,
                    sniffing the trace of air!

Haie! Haie!
        These were the swift to harry;
These the keen-scented;
These were the souls of blood.

Slow on the leash,
                    pallid the leash-men!

Precisely what is "returning" in "The Return" is never made explicit, but as Christine Froula has written, the poem is about "the recurring patterns which compose its nonrepresentational harmonies."[9] The poem begins with "tentative / Movements," as the phrases "slow feet," "The trouble in the pace," "uncertain / Wavering," and "hesitate" all suggest. The cretic feet in "tentative," "wavering," and "hesitate" are imitative and embody this idea in sound. Then as "they" gradually "return," the words associated with pace speed up ("Gods of the wingèd shoe," "swift to harry") in a metaphor of hunting dogs. The men following the dogs are sluggish and can't run fast enough to keep up with the lively and eager dogs: they are "slow on the leash." The entire poem is about metric "feet," as the "wingèd shoe" suggests; that is, about the pace and "movement" of words.

Like Keats's "Ode on a Grecian Urn" or Donne's "We'll build in sonnets pretty rooms / As well a well-wrought urn becomes the finest ashes / As half-acre tombs," Plarr's "Ad Cinerarium" considers the aesthetics of an urn, in this case one with ashes in it. The urn Plarr constructs has nothing engraved on it; it is "dumbly cold," and thus it is impossible to discover whose the ashes are. Like Keats but with less genius, Plarr does the speaking for the urn, asking a series of rhetorical questions and then accepting the silence of his "cinerarium": "It scarcely matters / What is sleeping in the keeping / Of this house of human tatters."

To counteract the silence of the dumb urn, Plarr creates a rollicking, bouncy rhythm and lots of feminine rhyme, in triplets rhyming ABA, with a feminine double B-rhyme inside the second line:

> Who in this small urn reposes,
> Celt or Roman, man or woman?
> Steel of steel, or rose of roses?

He imagines the "artificer" of the urn requesting silence (a silence Plarr has filled with feminine rhymes):

> Let them score no cypress verses,
> Funeral glories, prayers, or stories,
> Mourner's tears or mourner's curses . . .

Sustaining this form for ten triplets, Plarr's poem is an athletic feat, but the pace is too excited for the grave subject. The triplet

> Sure some mourner deemed immortal
> What thou holdest and enfoldest,
> Little house without a portal!

sounds unfortunately reminiscent of the popular variation of Frank Crumit's "prune song": "Little seed inside the prune / What's in there, whatcha doin' / Is it night or is it noon / Little seed inside the prune / Whatcha doin' prune, stew-in'?" Plarr's "Ad Cinerarium" is a silly *tour de force*, the opposite of Pound's "tentative movements" and "slow feet." Just as Longfellow's *Evangeline* is really about the hexameter line, its most aggressively prominent feature, so Plarr's "Ad Cinerarium" is really about the feminine rhymes. It was, however, an appropriate poem to place in a marble "coffer."

Sturge Moore's "The Dying Swan" is about the sound that the dying swan is said to utter, according to legend, as it dies. Here, as borrowed by Yeats in "The Tower," the swan of course suggests or represents the poet. In his short lines and his repetitions especially, Sturge Moore attempts to construct a verbal equivalent of what the song of a dying swan might be like:

> O silver-throated Swan
> Struck, struck! a golden dart
> Clean through thy breast has gone
> Home to thy heart.
> Thrill, thrill, O silver throat:
> O silver trumpet, pour
> Love for defiance back
> On him who smote!
> And brim, brim o'er
> With love . . .

The short lines suggest a lack of breath, the inability to sustain a long line such as might occur in the case of a bird struck by a dart through the breast. The repetitions suggest a limited degree of representation, the simple syntax-limited discursiveness, and the fancy, almost sonnet-like rhyme scheme, an artifice making the sound more elegant. Phrases like "Struck, struck," "Thrill, thrill," and "brim, brim" imply a greater interest in sound than in complexities of meaning.

Masefield's "Truth" doesn't have the tang of "Everlasting Mercy" or the swing of the old chestnut "Sea Fever." It is a "well-wrought" poem, three stanzas with a complex rhyme scheme: ABCDBACC. Every line is trimeter except the final A and C lines, which are dimeter. The poem posits the need to "build a ship of Truth" in order to "sail on the sea of death." But it's not a very Masefieldy ship: there's no flung spray or blown spume. In fact it seems a very aesthetic kind of ship, not made of wood but "the ship my striving made":

> Stripped of all purple robes,
> Stripped of all golden lies,
> I will not be afraid.
> Truth will preserve through death:
> Perhaps the stars will rise,
> The stars like globes.
> The ship my striving made
> May see night fade.

Edward Sapir quotes this stanza to illustrate a "weak, rhyme-compelled line," the one ending in "globes."[10] The whole poem is weak, with trite phrases ("burning soul," "For death takes toll," et al.) and an embarrassingly hackneyed idea; it should have been embarrassing to Masefield, but he had to put something in the box, and this was a relatively new work. The only point of the poem appears to be what Sapir called "a rather difficult verse-pattern." What the speaker "builds" is not a ship but a complex poem that has indeed lasted over 100 years; the poem is about its own elaborate formal structure, which Masefield made with a bit too much "striving."

Flint's "The Swan" has the same subject matter as Sturge Moore's, though Flint's swan is alive and healthy; and like Aldington's poem, Flint's is Imagist.[11] It does have in common with Plarr's and Manning's poems, however, that Pound urged (or ordered) its author to copy it out for the Gaudier box. Pound wrote Flint, "Bring a hand written and signed copy of your Swan, last version, that's all you ll need to bother about, we are each to put one mss poem into the marble coffer."[12] The "last version" was the version Pound had pared Flint's original down to. As Helen Carr explains, Flint's poem, with Pound's editorial guidance, went from sixty-eight lines to ten, "reducing the poem to its most telling phrases."[13] Pound appears to have practiced on "The Swan" what he did at greater length with *The Waste Land*, pruning and cutting to release the Imagist poem within the larger, wordier original. Including his own poem, then, Pound was responsible for four of the eight poems in the box; he had told Plarr, Flint, and Manning which poems to contribute. Pound was presenting his own school of modern poetry to "one of the last of the great Victorians." Contrasted to the contributions of the day by Belloc and Blunt, the poems in the marble box were lofty and idealized.

Hilaire Belloc's Song

In 1936, The Cuala Press was publishing broadsides, and Yeats wrote Hilaire Belloc to solicit one from him:

When I met you at Wilfred [*sic*] Blunt's before the war, or during the war, you sang a delightful song about a delightful Mrs. Rees. I do not think you have ever published it.

The Cuala Press is bringing out a series of Broadsides, with songs and music. Hitherto we have only had Irish poets, but now we are having English poets as well . . .

May I have Mrs Rees and its music?[14]

There is only one record of a visit by Yeats to Newbuildings Place "before the war" at a time when Belloc was also there, and only one such during the war, so it seems likely that it was at the peacock dinner that Belloc sang the song Yeats refers to here.[15] He was a singer: writing his parents about a meeting of the Poets' Club in April 1909, Pound remarks, "Hillaire [*sic*] Belloc sang to illustrate his points."[16] As it turned out, Yeats did not like the text of the song he had heard twenty-two years earlier. Ten days later he wrote Dorothy Wellesley, who was helping him edit the Broadsides, "What did you think of the Belloc poem? It is not as good as I thought; I thought it was naiver, simpler. Shall I have it typed & sent to you? It is amusing but too deliberately so—too facetious. Perhaps on the whole I am for it; but it is your province, not mine, for you are English editor."[17] In the event the ballad was published as one of the Cuala Broadsides in 1937.[18]

Hilaire Belloc's song "Mrs Rhys" is a mocking, lightly nasty take on adultery and male rivalry. It imagines a flirtatious liaison with— so it appears—the very Mrs. Rhys possibly alluded to in Pound's original letter about the dinner, an all-male occasion in order to avoid "the usual air of Hampstead and of literary men's wives." In the song, Belloc imagines leading Mrs. Rhys on a naughty jaunt that lands both of them in debtors' prison. The thrill is imagining the irritation of her husband:

> Star of my wanderings Mrs Rhys,
> When Mr Rhys shall hear that we
> Were going on like little geese,
> It will annoy him damnably.[19]

And the arrest of his wife will disturb him as much as the infidelity: "When Mr Rhys shall hear that you / Are in the hands of the police / It will disturb him not a few." The joke, presumably, is the thrill of disturbing such an uxorious couple, tame, sweet, and well-behaved, to judge by Ernest Rhys's memoir. The song's lightly misogynistic tone, the competition for women, the jokey thrill of cuckolding Mr Rhys, or rather of *pretending to cuckold* Mr Rhys—all of these themes are consistent with the tone of the all-male occasion, at least as embodied in Blunt's own contribution. Like the poems in the box and like Blunt's translation of Gobineau, this lyric vacillates between two registers, the higher and faux-whimsical "I love to roam from mere caprice" and "Star of my wanderings," and the lower "going on like little geese," as well as the sexualizing of Mrs Rhys, the apparent ruining of her reputation and that of her husband. The juxtaposition of registers is the point of the lyric, since it presents a sexualized narrative in which, it seems, no sex actually takes place. The humor, such as it is, of this ballad is not immediately obvious to twenty-first-century readers; Belloc's voice and performance must have added charms not apparent in the text.[20]

The Poem Blunt Read To His Guests

Blunt's poetic contribution to the day participated in the same conversation. Perhaps because it was a dirty-old-man poem, openly and cheerfully amoristic—as naughty, in its way, as the box, though much less interesting artistically—none of the published accounts alluded to it. Blunt's diary says he "could think of nothing else to read them" but his translation of the Comte de Gobineau's "Leporello," which he had written only a couple of weeks earlier. He called it "Don Juan's Good-Night," and three stanzas give its flavor:

> Teach me, gentle Leporello,
> Since you are so wise a fellow,
>   How your master I may win.
> Leporello answers gaily
> Slip into his bed and way lay
>   Him; anon he shall come in.
>
>   .   .   .   .   .   .
>
> But remember, from next morning
> You must quite forget the adorning
>   Of to-night, or earn his curse.
> Gold is yours if you but ask it,
> Spain and Flanders in a basket.
>   I am keeper of his purse.
>
> To console you he a fortune
> Would not grudge. But to importune
>   His more tenderness? Nay, Nay.
> A return to even your beauty
> Were too costly a Duke's duty,
>   One his whole wealth could not pay.[21]

Blunt prefaced his reading of the poem "with the remark that he hoped they wouldn't be too shocked."[22] This was boy talk. Not only was the tone of the poem light and the subject matter low, but its "message" was anti-idealistic: the woman who sleeps with Don Juan may get money if she wants it, but no love. Blunt was deromanticizing the erotic as casually as he had deprofessionalized the poetic.

And yet in this forgotten contribution to the poets' dinner Blunt was actually in poetic conversation with members of a male-linked genealogy. His grandfather-in-law Byron had authored the mock epic *Don Juan*, and his friend Gobineau, with whom Blunt had dined in 1871, was another wealthy, anti-imperialist, literary diplomat and self-styled Byronic adventurer. (On the occasion of that earlier dinner, Blunt had given his host the newest edition of Byron's poems.) To translate Gobineau on Don Juan was to affirm that lineage.

Blunt's poem about Don Juan, Yeats's about Helen, Manning's about Persephone, and Aldington's about the "manifest harlot," together with the Gaudier-Brzeska carving and, in a lighter way, Belloc's lyric, create a discourse of female beauty, all posing the question how erotic womanhood is to be valued. This debate never took the form of direct argument on the day the authors spent together, but the poems were provisional positions on the topic offered by men to other men. No doubt the homosocial intimacy of the occasion inspired the writers and sculptor to assume explicitly masculine subjectivities and to consider how much the muse was worth and how she should be spoken of. She was the absent presence at the peacock dinner: but as a figure on a marble box, she connected the men with one another and made them a family.

Before the dinner, Blunt wrote Lady Gregory that he hoped she would "be of the poets' party," and afterward he wrote her that he wished she had been present. Would he have read "Don Juan's Good-Night" if she had been there? Its low subject, dismissal of love in preference to money, and crude, jaunty tone, would probably have disqualified it for reading when a "lady" was of the party.

The British Empire

When Yeats and Lady Gregory suggested the idea of a photograph of the poets with Blunt, "tell Lady Gregory," Pound had said to Yeats, "we hate the newspaper press as Blunt hates the British Empire." The idea of hostility was an important part of the persona Pound constructed for Blunt. In the presentation poem, Pound's Blunt had "made mock of the world, / Swung the grand style . . . Upheld Mazzini and detested institutions." He had, that is, used his moral energy, troped as physical ("Swung," "Upheld"), as a force opposing the views generally accepted by "the world." In his account of the dinner in the American little magazine *Poetry*, Pound continued this line of thought with a quotation from Blunt. Blunt, he wrote, "has never ceased to protest against the tyrannies and swindles of the Empire, 'a Semitic invention of Disraeli's.' "[23]

The phrase Pound quotes is one of the few informal conversational sound bites mentioned in any of the published accounts of the peacock dinner. This phrase stuck in his mind, possibly because it confirmed the kind of anti-imperialist Blunt that Pound already admired. Pound implicitly attributes the words to Blunt by putting them in quotation marks. Moreover, they conform precisely to what Blunt wrote about the British purchase of the Suez Canal shares in his *Secret History of the English Occupation of Egypt* (1907). There was not, Blunt wrote, "general approval" of the purchase, and

Disraeli was much blamed for involving the Government in a transaction which had almost necessarily political consequences . . . What may have been in Disraeli's mind politically about it I do not know, but I am very sure that Lord Derby, who was then at the Foreign Office, had no idea connected with it of political aggression. Lord Derby was a man whose view of foreign policy was essentially one of non-intervention, nor had Disraeli as yet succeeded in indoctrinating his party with his own imperialistic ideas. *The transaction, nevertheless, was one of evil augury for Egypt, and especially by reason of the part played in it by the Rothschilds. As will be seen later, the financial connection of this too powerful Hebrew house with Egypt was the determining cause, six years later, of England's military intervention.*[24] (emphasis added)

The evils of the Empire derive from Disraeli's "own imperialistic ideas," and they are aided and abetted by the "too powerful Hebrew house" of Rothschild. The empire is Disraeli's "Semitic invention."

Pound's phrase "the tyrannies and swindles of the Empire," followed by the quotation from Blunt, makes clear that he has absorbed the connection between Jews and empire. The vivid juxtaposition of a threatening racial group and the despised "British Empire" inspired the juxtaposition in Pound's sentence of "tyrannies" and "swindles": the empire "swindles" its subjects just as the Jews "swindle" their customers. With the phrase Pound quotes and whatever conversation inspired it, Blunt implicitly gave a kind of permission for anti-Semitism; at the very least, he revealed it to be part of the swaggering, macho, oppositional personality Pound had praised. The term "anti-Semitic" unquestionably applies to Blunt, and not only in his analysis of the "secret history" of British imperialism in Egypt. Blunt's unpublished ballad about the Irish martyr Roger Casement, written at the time of Casement's execution in August 1916, links Casement's death with the Jewish background of Sir Rufus Isaacs, the first Jewish Lord Chief Justice and the person who pronounced the death sentence at Casement's trial:

> And a cheer for Hebrew Isaacs
> Our great Chief Justice Lord,
> Who spoke your sentence trembling
> In fear of what you knew.
> One word would have sufficed you,
> But you nobly spared the word,
> "Marconi!" And he hanged you.
> All hail to our Chief Jew.[25]

Here Blunt implies that Casement could have accused the Lord Chief Justice of corruption in the recent "Marconi shares" controversy but was too noble to have done such a thing. The allusion connects the Casement poem with a subject much on Blunt's mind during the peacock dinner.

Even before the peacock dinner took place, it had already been associated indirectly with anti-Semitism. Blunt had decided to invite two neighbors—the adventurer Lord Osborne Beauclerk and the writer Hilaire Belloc—to join the poets. Beauclerk, a graduate of Eton who had hunted "wild sheep" in Persia and mined gold in Canada, was, wrote Blunt in 1908, "the most sympathetic young man I have met in years."[26] Belloc, the writer and journalist, visited Blunt frequently and had been invited with Beauclerk before.[27] Beauclerk was present for the dinner, but Belloc was only invited for tea because, Blunt wrote, he would dominate the conversation with talk of "Marconis and Jews."[28] In his weekly magazine the *Eye-Witness*, Belloc had fulminated against those involved, or said to be involved, in what came to be called the Marconi shares scandal (1912–1913). This political controversy arose over alleged insider trading by Jewish members of the government, chief among those Sir Rufus Isaacs. Sir Rufus's brother Godfrey was managing director of the Marconi Wireless Telegraph Company, which had been authorized to build six of the eighteen stations of the Imperial Wireless Scheme, and Cecil Chesterton (sub-editor of *Eye-Witness*) accused several members of the government of profiting from the anticipated contract before it was announced. A parliamentary inquiry determined that no one involved had been guilty of corruption, but regretted "their transactions in shares of the Marconi Company of America and the want of frankness displayed by them in their communications with the House."[29]

What Belloc may have uttered at the peacock dinner, other than the lyrics of the song about Mrs. Rhys, is not recorded in any published account or in any of the poets' letters or diaries: Aldington remarks only that Belloc had "a pint of claret in a large crystal goblet" while the others had tea.[30] To reconstruct the conversation that inspired Blunt's remark would be impossible, and we cannot know whether Blunt uttered it in Belloc's presence or not. But that it was uttered at all reveals that the association of empire and Jews, of anti-imperialism and anti-Semitism, formed part of the peacock dinner's table-talk as well as part of the political atmosphere of the day.

Pound's glancing allusion to the world against which Blunt protests reinforces the note of defiance expressed in his poem: "made mock of the world." In his account of the dinner in *Poetry*, Pound wrote that Blunt entertained the poets "with great charm, regaling us with the roast flesh of peacocks at Newbuildings, a sixteenth-century defensible grange in Sussex." It was a seventeenth-century house, but nonetheless, the notion of a "defensible grange" fits metaphorically Pound's sense of the single person or house pitted against the external enemies: "we hate the newspaper press as Blunt hates the British Empire." The notion better fits the tone of Pound's politics than Blunt's, because in spite of his profound and passionate anti-imperialism, Blunt did not altogether or not always make "mock of the world." His closest friend had been Lord Lytton; he dined with the likes of Balfour and Asquith, and kept up regularly with his cousin Winston Churchill. Yeats and Plarr were also anti-imperialists— Plarr was French, Irish, and Welsh—but not angrily so, at least not in 1914.[31]

In yet another account of the dinner, Pound wrote his mother that the peacock "went very well with the iron-studded barricades on the stairway and other medieval relics and Burne-Jones tapestry." Aldington remembered "a magnificent peacock's tail spread over the table as decoration."[32] But the dinner also took place in other, less picturesque histories, histories limned in the one conversational fragment about Disraeli, in Blunt's description of Belloc's interests at the time, the *Secret History of the English Occupation of Egypt*, and the poem about Casement.

7

"a really important event"

All were delighted with Blunt.
Yeats writing to Lady Gregory after the peacock dinner

If offensiveness is one measure of success, at least for avant-garde poets, then the peacock dinner was successful. At the end of January Yeats dined with Eva Fowler, a London salonnière, spiritualist, and good friend of Olivia Shakespear. "She tells me," Yeats wrote Lady Gregory, "that a man in the Foreign Office called Clark whom I have met at her house says he will 'never speak to any of those poets again.' This because of our paying honour to Blunt."[1]

The man "called Clark" was actually George Russell Clerk, CMG (1874–1951), later KCMG, a senior clerk in the Foreign Office at the time. Although he had served in various diplomatic posts in Addis Ababa and Turkey before 1914, and ended his career as Ambassador to France, he was not universally respected. Lord Vansittart called him "one of those coming men who never quite arrive," and Sir Warren Fisher of the Civil Service wrote of him, ". . . no one could possibly be such an ass as he looks."[2] His rather hyperbolic response to the peacock dinner may reveal more about his conventional sensibilities than about the extraordinary power of the dinner, but it must have delighted Yeats and Pound.

Offending the Foreign Office was a special talent of Blunt's, as offending his government and its foreign policy would become a specialty of Pound's also. Insofar as the dinner may have been inspired in opposition to the Royal Society of Literature and its "Academic Committee" with its "passion for the absolutely harmless," as Yeats called it, then the dinner had hit its mark.[3] By honoring Blunt, it was positioned, or seemed to be, not only as anti-imperialist but as deliberately, rudely, provocatively so. It had indeed provoked a member of the government to anger. When Clerk's comment was repeated to Lady Gregory, she wrote Blunt, "So that has struck home."[4]

Of course, this particular provocation was not widely known. It was expressed on a private occasion and mocked in a private letter. Lady Gregory, Blunt's old friend, must have been amused at Mr. Clerk's response, certainly the clearest and most definitive reaction to the dinner. But the peacock dinner was more than a provocation; after 14 January, it became an invisible presence in literary history. Its meaning and value were not altogether clear or stable in the weeks following the event, nor were they years later. Yet however unstable the significance attributed to the peacock dinner, it persisted as a source of literary inspiration years after the occasion. For its three central participants especially, it offered a ground from which to define their positions as poets and a site from which to intervene in literary tradition. What it inspired was a continuing debate or series of positions on the profession of poetry, positions articulated in poems and essays.

This debate was in a way begun by Pound's presentation poem for Blunt ("Because you have gone your individual gait"), but it was a debate in which Yeats was already engaged. The presentation poem links the three central poets through its key word "trade." More than the four poets at the edges of the photograph, the three standing in the middle interrogated the idea of poets as professional workers. Blunt's career posed that issue with special clarity because the many non-literary aspects of his life were so prominent. Blunt, wrote Pound, had "not made a trade of art"; that is, he had not written for money or professional advancement. In fact Blunt did not attend closely to those words as Pound read them; to the extent that he did, he was waiting for "a rhyme that did not seem to come." But if he had

considered the phrase, he might have agreed; had he not said something similar himself, many years earlier?

> I would not, if I could, be called a poet.
> I have no natural love of the "chaste muse."
> If aught be worth the doing I would do it;
> And others, if they will, may tell the news.[5]

Blunt formulates the issue in a metaphor that defines professional
authorship as inactivity. If being a poet involves chastity and merely
"tell[ing] the news," then Blunt chooses sex and making the news.
Yeats makes almost the same distinction in the *Oxford Book of Modern
Verse*: Blunt, Yeats thought originally, was a "fashionable amateur"
who had "sacrificed a capacity for literature and the visible arts to
personal adventure."[6]

"Adam's Curse" is one of many answers Yeats might have given to
Blunt's sonnet in order to claim that writing poetry is active work.
The complaint of the poem's opening is that conventional men who
do more visible kinds of labor think poets are lazy:

> '. . . Better go down upon your marrow-bones
> And scrub a kitchen pavement, or break stones
> Like an old pauper, in all kinds of weather;
> For to articulate sweet sounds together
> Is to work harder than all these, and yet
> Be thought an idler by the noisy set
> Of bankers, schoolmasters, and clergymen
> The martyrs call the world.'

The allusion to the pauper breaking stones "in all kinds of weather,"
like Yeats's later poems about beggars, identifies the poet with a social
outsider. The implication of the passage is not only that poets do
back-breaking work but that their "sweet sounds" are superior to the
noise made by "bankers, schoolmasters, and clergymen." Throughout
his career Yeats stresses that poets do hard, physical work, even if
theirs is a "sedentary trade." The word "labor" and its derivatives sig-
nal that train of thought, as in "what my laborious life imagined, even
/ The half-imagined, the half-written page," "this laborious stair and
this stark tower," and "Labor is blossoming . . ."

When he thinks of himself as part of a poets' collective, either a
survivor or an ancestor, Yeats uses the word "trade." In "The Grey
Rock," Yeats affectionately addresses all the dead Rhymers as *"Poets*

with whom I learned my trade, / Companions of the Cheshire Cheese,"
praising them because they

> *. . . never made a poorer song*
> *That you might have a heavier purse,*
> *Nor gave loud service to a cause*
> *That you might have a troop of friends.*
> *You kept the Muses' sterner laws . . .*

The "Muses' sterner laws" are the "laws" of poetry, not inscribed anywhere permanently, not material learned for an exam or an oath sworn in a formal ceremony. They are here stipulated by Yeats, who learned his "trade" with his friends in the upstairs room of a pub. Yeats's official farewell to fellow poets is, famously, "Irish poets, learn your trade; / Sing whatever is well made . . ." From his comments on Blunt as an "amateur," from his repeated use of the word "trade," from his emphasis on the "labor" of writing poetry, it is clear that Yeats throughout his career thought much on this matter, implying in his vocabulary and asserting directly the professionalism of poets.

The peacock dinner brings to light not only the centrality of ideas about poetic professionalism in the thought of the three major poets at the dinner, but the existence of a poetic *topos* rarely if ever noticed, the "profession of poetry" poem, in which a poet surveys the contemporary poetry scene and critiques it. Such are the poems that Pound wrote for Blunt and that Yeats wrote to the Rhymers and to future Irish poets, and such is Pound's *Hugh Selwyn Mauberley*, with its comprehensive and cranky vision of the poetry scene before the Great War. Such also, in prose, is Yeats's famous introduction to the *Oxford Book of Modern Verse*. This *topos* appears in satiric form in earlier poems such as Dryden's "Mac Flecknoe" and Pope's *Dunciad*. Byron's address to Southey in the "Dedication" to *Don Juan* is a "profession of poetry" poem: "Bob Southey! You're a poet—Poet-laureate, / And representative of all the race." It is Byron's *Mauberley*. As he writes, ". . . a poet nothing loses / In giving to his brethren their full meed / Of merit." All of these poems, from Pound and Yeats back to Dryden, show that however uncertain the professional status of poets may have been, and however unsystematized the profession, the subject of its status generated a continuing source of commentary by poets themselves.

The dinner is not explicitly named in Blunt's two-volume *Poetical Works* (1914), in Yeats's *Only Jealousy of Emer* (1919) or his *Oxford Book of Modern Verse* (1936), or Pound's *Hugh Selwyn Mauberley* (1920) or Canto LXXXI (1945), but it exists as a hidden source of inspiration for all of them. This series of texts shows a continuing debate expressed as assertions of authority to define the history of poetry. In these works, several of them major texts in modern literature in English, the alliances and rivalries of the peacock dinner are expressed as revisions and statements of ownership of literary history. The texts do not otherwise constitute a tradition, but all position themselves in relation to the peacock dinner; all are interventions whose meaning is understood completely only when they are seen as part of that distinct narrative. The later three works especially reconfigure the history of poetry and implicitly define the peacock dinner as a turning point in that history.

Spinning the Dinner

The textual debate did not occur immediately, in the first post-prandial correspondence, but nevertheless a kind of unease was present in it. In the weeks following the dinner, as the participants wrote letters to Blunt and one another, they defined and redefined the dinner's importance. No one seemed to feel that it was just an ordinary get-together. Everyone sensed there was something unusual or notable about it, but its significance was not obvious, because it was a somewhat anomalous event: it was not sponsored by any institution, it did not celebrate a birthday or the publication of a book, and there was no obvious cause for it. It had a formality and air of importance about it, but it needed to be publicized (so its organizers believed) in order for its full meaning to emerge; otherwise it would recede into obscurity, and only its participants remember it.

In the words of a later era, this was the kind of event that needed to be spun, and Pound spun it. Although he had objected to the presence of a photographer, according to Yeats's 12 January letter to Lady Gregory, Pound evidently had no objection to the wide dissemination of text. His own importance, after all, was keyed to the event, and his position in the poetry scene of the day would be enhanced by proximity to celebrities. He would be visible. Accounts of the peacock dinner were published in every journal to which Pound had access, from the mainstream to the avant-garde, and on both sides of the Atlantic. These five accounts, in almost identical words, were published in *The Times* (placed there by Yeats?), *The Egoist* (signed by Aldington), *Poetry* (signed by Pound), *Poetry and Drama* (Flint), and the *Boston Evening Transcript* (by J. Walter Smyth). The peacock dinner was hyped. As the publicist Pound knew better than anyone, it's not an intervention if nobody knows about it.

Nor did Pound object to the private dissemination of the photograph; it was the apparent vulgarity of publishing it in a newspaper that had bothered him. When he wrote Blunt after the dinner, he wanted extra copies: "Thank you very much for the photograph. I wonder could you send me the photographer's address as I know my people would like one and the other members of the committee will want theirs."[7] Handwritten on the address list (possibly by Miss Lawrence, Blunt's nurse) it says, *Mr. Pound. 3 + 1 rough one.*[8] The photograph was flattering to Pound, and like the newspaper accounts of the dinner, it went to both sides of the Atlantic. To Alice Corbin Henderson, the assistant editor to Harriet Monroe at *Poetry*, Pound wrote, "Do you want a photo of the Blunt presentation as an adornment to the office? It is good of everyone except Yeats."[9] That last point may have been one of the photo's secret advantages for both Pound and Blunt. Pound wrote Blunt that the picture of Yeats made him look "like a very moulting eagle indeed," and Blunt wrote Lady Gregory that all the poets looked good except Yeats, "who had kept his spectacles on. I think he has made a mistake in having his hair cut—it takes away something of his old romantic appearance."[10]

The residual discomfort of the men on the margins found expression in various ways. Frank Flint's position in the photo mirrored that of Victor Plarr's, though because his posture and height (he was six-feet-two) make him look more like Aldington than Plarr looks like Sturge Moore, he appears slightly less marginal.[11] But like most people deliberately placed on the margins, Flint was aware of his status. In his thank-you to Blunt for the photograph, his signature reads

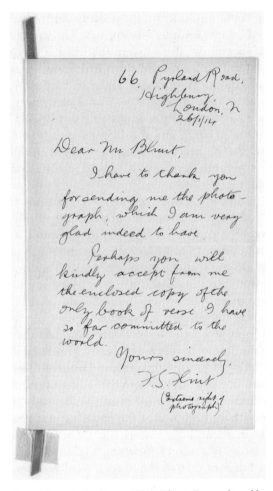

Figure 21. Letter from F. S. Flint to W. S. Blunt. Reproduced by permission of Oliver Flint, the Earl and Countess of Lytton, and the West Sussex Record Office.

this way: "Yours sincerely F. S. Flint (Extreme right of photograph)" (Figure 21).[12] Why does he say that? Presumably because he thinks he is so insignificant that Blunt will not remember which one he is. For that final phrase his handwriting is smaller, as if it were an afterthought or a footnote to his signature. Flint seems to have been troubled by the suspicion or the hunch that he was less memorable than the others; his phrase "extreme right" emphasizes his marginality.

Flint must have said something to Pound that revealed a less-than-grateful attitude about the dinner and expressed his aware-ness of the celebrity gap between the center and the margins. He must, in fact, have made a disrespectful comment about the dimmer wattage of the men on the *other* margin, Plarr and Sturge Moore. It's clear from a letter Pound wrote Flint in the summer that Flint knew perfectly well, as they all did, how the poets' wattage was calibrated: "My progenitors are coming from U.S.A. next week," Pound wrote; ". . . do look in, if you are out in this direction and let up that yawp about 'reporter fellow' etc. elected to the glorious fellowship of Plarr and Sturge Moore to lend lustre etc."[13] But Flint was less *in*significant and more noticed than he thought; Blunt indeed knew who he was and wanted to see him again, although there is no record that they ever met a second time. On 21 July 1914 Pound sent Flint a postcard that said, "Have just been down to old Blunt. He wants you to go down. Will you write and tell him what weekend will suit you. I said you would."[14] And in an undated let-ter from the same period, Pound wrote, "Blunt asked specifically about you and said he liked you and wanted you to come down."[15]

Sturge Moore, on the other side of the photo, did not want to be included in the first-person plural of Pound's presentation poem ("We who respect little . . ."). He evidently did not like the air of provocation about the dinner ("he says he respects a lot of things & Ezra has made him say he does not").[16] Yeats had (privately) described Sturge Moore as a "sheep in sheep's clothing," so it's likely that Yeats was amused at Moore's demurral.[17]

Lady Gregory's comment, as she thanked Blunt for her copy of the picture, offered a mild witticism reminding him of her contribu-tion: "I wish the peacock could have been photographed with the other celebrities!"[18]

Blunt's private preferences differed somewhat from the hierarchy implied in the picture. He wrote emphatically to Lady Gregory that he liked "all of them." And when the Masefields, both of them, vis-ited in April, Blunt wrote, "I like them extremely."[19] It seems unmis-takable from Blunt's diary entries of 25 and 26 March, when Pound and Aldington visited him again, that Blunt preferred Aldington to Pound. Aldington, he wrote, was "the more reasonable of [the] two as well as I think the cleverer." He thought Aldington's verses were "the best." And he was pleased by Aldington's appreciation "of country things . . . whereas Pound takes no notice at all of what he sees."

They are gay companions enough & Pound was a bit more than gay after a bottle of Madeira in the evening. I like them all the same—especially Aldington—and I am sure they have enjoyed themselves here.[20]

When Pound visited yet again in July, bringing his new bride with him, Blunt noted that Dorothy Pound had "deodorised" her husband, and, Blunt added, "he needed deodorising."[21]

Letters to Lady Gregory

Yeats had been involved in so many occasions like this one—the cat dinner for Thomas Hardy, for instance, and the presentation of the Polignac prize from the Royal Academy—that nothing much was at stake for him in the peacock dinner. He was one of the "celebrities" that Lady Gregory had referred to. He knew he owed Lady Gregory an account of the dinner, out of courtesy, because she had been instrumental in making the whole thing happen. Yeats sent Lady Gregory the kind of detailed and wonderfully gossipy account one wants one's friends to send. He didn't treat the occasion as a power-dinner but as an episode with funny little moments. The story of Plarr's *faux pas* was the best part of the account, but there were other good bits:

I promised to tell you about that day at New Buildings. I think all went well. We had lunch at 12.30 & there was a peacock which tasted just like Turkey I thought though Ezra said a more devine [sic] Turkey & after lunch we presented our stone box. Ezra read out his poem & Blunt spoke & proposed my health to which I responded with a speach. Blunt asked us to stay for Belloc who came about 3.30 & finding himself in a company who could not be shocked was I think a little bewildered.

Yeats then tells the story of Plarr's marriage to "his cook" and the too-eager acceptance of Blunt's invitation. He continues,

The motor cost me £5 but it was the only thing to be done to avoid inflicting the whole day on Blunt. As it was we did not get away until 5 & Blunt was tired but that was not our fault as we had to wait for Belloc, & then when we were going he told us tea was ready. Blunt has written to Ezra since & I think all the poets except myself have had copies of the photograph of the group—as I have come out badly they say he probably did not send me one. Sturge Moore is a little unhappy about Ezra's verses as he says he respects a lot of things & Ezra has made him say he does not.

Yours

WB Yeats

All were delighted with Blunt.[22]

Wisely Yeats added that final sentence, because it was quotable and flattering, and naturally Gregory quoted it back to Blunt. The event was spun in circles; indeed, it was made possible through the triangular friendship of Blunt, Gregory, and Yeats. Both men acknowledged her role in the dinner and each man praised the other while implicitly praising her.

To Wilfrid Scawen Blunt, the honored man in the center, the cause of the peacock dinner remained ever baffling, because he couldn't figure out why men whose poetry was so different from his would admire what he wrote. He hid his confusion from Lady Gregory and gave her a somewhat censored version of the day: he didn't mention reading "Don Juan's Goodnight," nor Pound's mistaking Mazzini for Urabi, nor his dislike of the naked woman on the Gaudier-Brzeska box, nor his inability to understand any of the poems they gave him. His letter, as was appropriate, expressed gratitude. Thoughtfully, he wrote Lady Gregory the very next day, knowing she would be waiting for his account:

I write to report that all went off most successfully yesterday—I found all the young men charming and think they enjoyed their meal, most of them, Miss Lawrence tells me, eating two helpings of the peacock, which figured in full plumage on the table, and some of them going on afterward to beef. The marble box was presented, & Ezra Pound read an address in verse which the poets had signed and I made a little speech in thanks and Yeats made a speech in reply and there was some good talk about literature which they all seemed to know far better than I do, and then Belloc came in—much depressed, poor man, about his wife's condition which is almost hopeless. The sun came out and we were photographed in the open air in a group, successfully I believe—& they stayed on to tea & went back at 5:30 in their motor to London. Yeats did his part of cicerone admirably & I think all were pleased. I know I found all of them interesting and hope they will come down again separately that I may make their acquaintance better, for you know how difficult it is to talk to half a dozen people you do not know, all together—I only wish you had been with us.[23]

THE NILE FLIGHTS.

(FROM OUR CORRESPONDENT.)

CAIRO, JAN. 19.

The airman McClean left Assuan about 10
this morning for the South. The Frenchman
Pourpe left Khartum at 6.30 a.m. and arrived
at Atbara at 10.40 this morning. He leaves
to-morrow for Abu Hamed.

MR. W. S. BLUNT.

At Newbuildings Place, Sussex, on Sunday, a committee of poets consisting of W. B. Yeats, Sturge
Moore, John Masefield, Victor Plarr, Frederic Manning, Ezra Pound, F. S. Flint, and Richard Aldington,
presented to Mr. Wilfrid Scawen Blunt, in token of
homage for his poetry, a carved reliquary of Pentelican marble, the work of the sculptor Gaudier
Brzeska. It bears a recumbent female figure and
an inscription. The committee had intended to give
a dinner in Mr. Blunt's honour, but he preferred to
receive them at Newbuildings.
The following verses of address were read :—

" To Wilfrid Blunt.
" Because you have gone your individual gait,
" Written fine verses, made mock of the world,
" Swung the grand style, not made a trade of art,
" Upheld Mazzini and detested institutions ;
" We, who are little given to respect,
" Respect you, and having no better way to show it
" Bring you this stone to be some record of it."

Mr. BLUNT said in his reply that he was to some
extent an impostor. He had been all sorts of other
things, but never a poet. He was not brought up
that way at all. He was never at a public school,
nor at a college. He had written a certain amount of
verse, but only when he was rather down on his luck
and had made mistakes either in love or politics or
some branch of active life. He found that it relieved
his feelings. He never thought in the least of getting
it published ; he did not even show it to his friends.
His first little anonymous work was published when
he was 35 or 36—and it was not much of a thing
even then. He did not publish a single verse over
his own name till he was about 43. His life had
been an active one in various connexions, and people
wrote to him sometimes, " We have great admiration
for you." But it was never about his poetry. It
had been either because he had taken up the cause of
the Indian or the Egyptian, or more generally because
he bred horses, that he was generally known. In
one of the very first things he wrote he was ill-advised
enough to say that he would not be called a poet, and
that had stuck to him ever since. However, he had
come round rather from that now. Within the last
year or two he had washed his hands of politics and
all forms of public life, and had withdrawn to a great
extent from horse-breeding, and, having nothing to
do, he had taken up with verse-writing to console him
for a new disappointment. He had been writing a
certain amount in the last year, and was very pleased
now to be considered a poet.
There was then some general discussion of rhyme,
blank verse, and assonance as Mr. Blunt's speech
became less formal and was mingled with replies from
individual members of the committee.

BOXING IN FRANCE.

NICE, JAN. 19.*

In a boxing match between Carpentier and O'Keefe
here to-night Carpentier was declared the winner in
the second round, O'Keefe being knocked out by a
right hook on the jaw.

Figure 22. Account of the dinner for Blunt published in *The Times*, 20
January 1914.

That was for Lady Gregory. To his friend Sydney Cockerell, the director of the Fitzwilliam Museum, Blunt wrote more critically: "[S]everal of the young men are futurists and believe that verse should be written without metre rhyme or scansion, a region where I am unable to follow. I can't make out what brought them down to *me* or who suggested the idea. Yeats was the only one I had ever met, nor had I so much as heard of the others except Masefield . . ."[24]

Privately, Blunt was at first a bit distressed; the modern poems in the box made him feel like an old man:

Somehow or another the poets' visit has left me out of conceit with poetry. The modern poetry represented by these young men is too entirely unlike anything I can recognise as good verse that I feel there is something absurd in their expressing admiration for mine . . . they do not follow at all in my footsteps and it is difficult to recognize, in what they themselves write, anything but word puzzles . . . I feel myself like a stranger in their land & too old to learn a new language.[25]

However, the appearance in *The Times* of the article about the dinner took Blunt completely by surprise and gave him a new confidence in his poetry. Reading about himself in the newspaper, he discovered that he was a more important literary figure than he had hitherto supposed:

There is a very prominent account in *The Times* this morning of the poets presentation to me, which makes it look like a really important event & so it seems to be regarded. All this is very curious considering that I have not published a line of verse for the last dozen years nor has my name been mentioned anywhere in connection with poetry. I do not mean that I consider it altogether undeserved because I *do* believe that my verse is good or I should burn it. I also have always held that good poetry will sooner or later find its level and that if it remains unknown it is because it deserves its obscurity . . . It encourages me now to go on writing and probably will make it easier for me to deal with Macmillan about publishing.[26]

The article in *The Times*—only four paragraphs—was enough to provoke Mr. Clerk of the Foreign Office to forswear all future intercourse with "any of those poets," but it persuaded Blunt that the dinner in his honor had been "a really important event." If someone at *The Times* agreed to print it, and to print it on page five, then "so it seems to be regarded" (Figure 22).

The Poetical Works of Wilfrid Scawen Blunt

Although the idea of prodding Blunt to publication had never been in Pound's mind or Yeats's when they wrote Lady Gregory about inviting Blunt to dinner, it was in her mind, and because of Lady Gregory the dinner got entangled both with the peacock and the collected works. That "new edition," *The Poetical Works of Wilfrid Scawen Blunt* (in two volumes; 1914), was the indirect result of the peacock dinner: if Blunt was a poet worth honoring, then, he came to believe, he probably deserved a complete edition. The dinner had given him literary authority: only one week after the peacock dinner, as he and Dorothy worked over the materials to send Macmillan, he wrote in his diary, ". . . it seems really as if my position as a poet was at last to become recognized."[27] The *Poetical Works* is the first of several literary works in which the peacock dinner is invisibly present. As a volume implicitly, and in its preface explicitly, the book embodies the alliances and rivalries present in the interesting triangle of Blunt, Lady Gregory, and Yeats.

That triangle might also be characterized as a circulation of literary and erotic impulses, a flow of professional power and authority that was erotically tinged. The triangle is constructed in large part by Blunt, whose rivalry with Yeats is expressed in his repeated denigration of Yeats in his diaries. In letters to Lady Gregory, however, he is respectful and polite when speaking of Yeats—as he often does. Behind this is a hint of concern about just how closely Lady Gregory and Yeats are working together. Blunt is always asserting the priority of his own acquaintance with Lady Gregory: I knew her when, he appears to be saying. Lady Gregory contributes also to the construction of this triangle: she takes pleasure in serving as intermediary between Blunt and the great literary world, not only initiating contact with Macmillan but keeping Yeats in the loop also, and blessing Blunt's poetry by communicating Yeats's approval. She is always there, keeping up with the stages of publication and asking about the book's progress, but behind her there is always Yeats. In one letter, suggesting an alternative in case Macmillan doesn't work out, Lady Gregory suggests publishing a fancy edition with Bullen, as Yeats has done; and Blunt writes back, "Yeats has a far larger public to appeal to than I have, and I think a publication of that sort would leave me practically where I am."[28] Blunt feels Yeats's presence with her so strongly that in the letter in which he announces publication of the book to Lady Gregory he asks, "Where is Yeats? In America or where?"[29]

In the first mention of the dinner in his diary, on Sunday, 28 December, the dinner and the possible publication of his poems are mentioned together, both subjects introduced by Lady Gregory during her visit to Newbuildings, with Yeats a presence in the background. She brings the invitation "with which she had been charged by a group of young poets," and she agrees to help Dorothy Carleton "in her literary executorship of my Will" but is "anxious that I should forestall it in some degree by publishing now a complete Edition of my verses." His literary executor was his "niece"/ partner Dorothy Carleton, but she did not have Lady Gregory's literary talent and experience, and would, if there were no collected edition before Blunt died, depend on Lady Gregory to do that work. In the next day's diary entry, he remembers what a "silent part" she played in her marriage with Sir William, and how her "connection with me was her first emancipation"—literary as well as erotic, Blunt presumably means, but he doesn't specify. One sentence later he writes, "she has been the real inspirer of the Irish literary movement, having created Yeats out of almost nothing . . ." Yeats enters Blunt's private discussion of Lady Gregory as the third point in the triangle, replacing the dead Sir William: "it was not till years after his death that she began to assert herself publicly," Blunt writes.[30] Blunt "emancipates" Lady Gregory— from Sir William primarily—and then, thinking of her current important position in the world of culture, and her connection with Yeats, attributes Yeats's importance to her—and perhaps, by transitivity, to himself.

Lady Gregory is also the intermediary between Blunt and Yeats on the subject of the date and timing of the peacock dinner. It is she who suggests the peacock; it is to her Blunt writes "I understand that the 18th is to be the day & have had the peacock slain in preparation," and he assumes she will be one of the guests: "I hope you are to be of the poets' party to give me a countenance at it. I should feel it lacked reality without you."[31] At the dinner itself, completing the triangle, and inserting himself in another aspect of Lady Gregory's intimacy with Blunt, Yeats mentions the publication of Blunt's poems. As Blunt wrote Lady Gregory after the dinner, "Yeats was very kind in asking about this matter of Macmillan, but of course there [was] no time to go into it with him yesterday."[32]

The three members of this triangle meet in print in the preface to the *Poetical Works*. In its second paragraph, Blunt explains why he has decided to "yield to an impulse . . . that of arranging for the publication of a final and complete edition of my verse . . ." His first reason repeats what he had written in his diary on 27 December of the previous year, that he should publish now rather than burden Lady Gregory with the editing of his complete works. He wishes, the preface says, to publish the poems "while I still can, instead of leaving that care, should it be needed, to the chance kindness of others after my death."

His second reason comes directly out of the peacock dinner:

I am the more impelled to this because it seems that latterly my work, nearly all of it out of print, has begun to have a certain *bric-à-brac* value with readers, as that of a mid-Victorian poet a little in advance of his epoch . . .[33]

This is a paraphrase of what Yeats said in his response to Blunt's response to Pound's poem: "We are now at the end of Victorian romance . . . Just as the Victorian tide recedes, your work becomes younger and more fascinating to us." There is the peacock dinner, invisibly present within its first literary result, Blunt's "complete edition," published in October 1914; the copy signed to Lady Gregory is dated 24 October 1914.

And finally, in the reception of the *Poetical Works*, the triangle makes another appearance. On 27 December 1914—exactly one year after Lady Gregory's visit to Blunt to convey the invitation and to discuss the publication—she writes him about his book:

I was pleased to see a quite appreciative notice of the poems in *The Times* Literary Supplement. I thought they were going to Boycott them, but they will be in such good humour now at annexing Egypt they will forgive you everything . . . Yeats has been reading the Wisdom of Merlyn with great delight (I am not sure if I wrote you this before) He thinks the first three quarters almost as fine as anything you have written; the metre wonderful— means to steal it some time. He is only sorry you didn't take out the last page and a half or so, says it is rather in the Tennysonian tradition, that the rest of the poem belongs to all time and is too fine to be dated, and this reminds him of the philosophy of the sixties. I dont mind telling his criticism because of his enthusiasm. The extraordinary wisdom, and the fullness of life struck him so much. He is back here now, for Xmas.[34]

With this letter Lady Gregory blesses Blunt with Yeats's praise, thereby elevating him with the approval of a celebrity poet, and also reminding him of her proximity to Yeats: "He is back here now . . . ." Blunt's response turns this three-point flow of commentary into a triangle:

What you say about my poetry encourages me & I am glad to have Yeats opinion, though I value it less than I do yours. The press has been on the whole very friendly to me and though I never expect to be popular I think I have now an acquired position of some sort in the poetic world—and there I must rest.[35]

One year earlier Blunt had been writing in his diary that Lady Gregory had "created Yeats out of almost nothing." Now once more the thought of Yeats irritates: Blunt cannot restrain himself from expressing his rivalry, but he does it politely by turning it into a compliment to Lady Gregory: "I value it less than I do yours."

Throughout 1914, Blunt is constantly thanking Lady Gregory for her help and support of him and his work. In his letter about the dinner itself, he writes, "I feel that I owe this most agreeable little fete to you."[36] On 9 February, writing about Macmillan's generous financial terms, Blunt says, ". . . if Macmillan has been so amiable about it, it has been entirely due to you." And then, writing about future visits by some of the young poets, he says, "All this has given me quite a renewal of my poetic youth. I am the better for it, and I feel that I owe it to you." When he sends Lady Gregory an inscribed copy of the book, he writes her, "I feel that I owe you a debt of gratitude in connection with it, which this copy feebly repays."[37]

The Only Jealousy of Blunt

Yeats thinks "the metre wonderful—means to steal it some time," Lady Gregory wrote Blunt. Was Yeats remembering Blunt's comment about *Fand*—Yeats "was good enough to offer to turn it into blank verse"—and trying to be flattering? Blunt's post-prandial jest had not entirely hidden his irritation. According to Blunt's diary, Yeats had already flattered Blunt in 1909, telling Blunt "he had been converted to my use of the Alexandrine metre for plays in verse," and an early version of *The Green Helmet*—when it was *The Golden*

Helmet—mixed alexandrines and fourteeners, though not very successfully (the final version is written entirely in fourteeners).[38] "When Yeats wrote his play ten years after the performance of *Fand*," writes the editor of the Cornell edition of *The Only Jealousy of Emer*, "he may have recalled some of the dramatic possibilities and problems raised by Blunt's play," but here again, the peacock dinner exists as an invisible presence.[39] The toasts at the dinner explicitly discussed the two poets' disagreement about meter, and in December 1914, Yeats was reading Blunt's *Poetical Works*, which included *Fand*, and discussing Blunt's use of meter with Lady Gregory. Only sixteen months later, in April 1916, Yeats wrote Lady Gregory that he wanted to write "a play on The Only Jealousy of Emer," but the Rising distracted him and formed the subject of his next Noh play, *The Dreaming of the Bones*.[40]

Like Blunt's *Poetical Works* then, Yeats's play *The Only Jealousy of Emer* is a response to one of the speeches at the peacock dinner. Here Yeats turns Blunt's play "into blank verse." Yeats never thought of Blunt as a sexual rival, though he did flirt briefly, but not very seriously, with Blunt's final beloved, Dorothy Carleton, when she visited Coole in 1906, "proposing to mesmerize her and draw her horoscope . . ." However, he appears to have been arguing Blunt's case to Dorothy, who had not yet been definitively adopted: "He is very handsome—and has written a volume of most magnificent Sonnets."[41]

The territory in which Yeats engaged with Blunt was the telling of the Cuchulain story about Emer. Here indeed Yeats may have been inspired by Blunt, if only to "correct" Blunt's meter and to revise his version of the story. In fact what Yeats got from Blunt (and Blunt's peacock dinner speech must have reminded Yeats of this territory) was the idea of using the Emer story to explore the topic of how to manage competing erotic loyalties. Blunt's sexual escapades in general, if not his romance with Lady Gregory, must certainly have been known to Yeats, and he evidently discussed this rich topic with his wife George. In a letter of 1931 Yeats—staying at Coole during the last year of Lady Gregory's life—wrote George about Gregory's maid Ellen, who apparently went out late every night to meet a suitor: "The trouble about her seems to be that she is in no need of the advice Wilfred Blunt used to give his women friends 'get engaged but never get married'."[42]

Yeats's play is a revision of Blunt's not only because of the meter but because of the way erotic interests are managed. As Blunt's cousin George Wyndham pointed out about Blunt's *Fand*, "it should be called a tragedy, because it ends in the hero going back to his wife."[43] In Blunt's play, the four main characters—Fand, the beautiful, seductive, supernatural beloved; Cuchulain; Eithne, his mistress; and Emer, his wife—all have agency. (The role of the mistress is less important here than in Yeats's play.) Emer seems to be drawn fairly clearly from Blunt's "long-suffering" wife Lady Anne: as King Conhor says, "She has a mighty heart, / And has forgiven him much, and once he loved her well." Blunt's Cuchulain seems a self-portrait, especially as Conhor describes his marriage:

> He was a man, inconstant. Spite of his great name,
> He stooped to things inglorious. Foolish loves he had
> With foolish, pretty women, whom his fame drove mad,
> And who must tempt him from her. She was high-born, proud.
> She scorned to be their rival. Silently, calm-browed,
> She stepped back from his life.[44]

When Cuchulain is "entranced," Fand offers to cure him if Emer will lend him to her for forty days, allegedly to fight her battles, but also, of course, to be her lover: "Your purpose is too dim, / Your face too full of meaning," Emer notes. However, she agrees to the bargain.

Fand keeps her bargain, but Cuchulain isn't happy with it: "Where is Fand?" he cries when she has magically disappeared in a storm. Mistress Eithne and wife Emer are present, and he is angry at both of them. The only way to get him quiet is to put a "robe of full forgetfulness" around him. As Emer says wishfully at the end, "O to begin again / With a clean memory, purged alike of love and hate!" *Fand* (completed in 1904) reflected, to some extent, the way Blunt managed his erotic life through July 1906. At that time Lady Anne stopped forgiving him "much," and moved out of Newbuildings forever, and he could live more openly with the final Eithne of his life, Dorothy Carleton.

The Instability of the Erotic

Yeats's version of the Cuchulain/Emer story was different from Blunt's; his revision reflected the erotic tensions of his new-married state and in a way anticipated aspects of his future. As is well known, from the summer of 1916 through the summer of 1917 Yeats considered marriage with Maud Gonne (then aged 49) and then with her daughter Iseult (20), before proposing to and being accepted by Georgie Hyde Lees in September 1917. In the same way as Sir William Gregory first, and Yeats later, seemed to be ghostly presences in the relationship of Lady Gregory and Blunt, so, immediately before and always after Yeats's proposal, Maud Gonne, Iseult, and George existed in a triadic relationship in Yeats's imagination, like pieces in a mobile, kept in a kind of balance, but one that was always shifting. In the weeks between the accepted proposal and actual marriage, Yeats wrote five letters to his fiancée. He had insisted that she meet Maud Gonne and Iseult, and afterwards he wrote Georgie:

A letter has come from Maud Gonne praising you. She calls you 'charming'—graceful and beautiful; and adds 'I think she has an intense spiritual life of her own and on [?] this side you must be careful not to disappoint her . . . Iseult likes her very much & Iseult is difficult & does not take to everybody. She is sure that you & I will be very happy . . .'[45]

But "as soon as the day was fixed," Yeats became "convinced that he would forever love Iseult." A visit with Iseult calmed him down.[46]

Three years later, Yeats was summoned to Ireland from Oxford by Maud Gonne to help when Iseult's new husband Francis Stuart was treating her abusively. From Ireland Yeats wrote George, "I feel it was right to come and I thank you for letting me do so—all that happens but shows me some new side of yr. goodness." She wrote him back,

My thought is so much more for you than for her, because the spectator suffers more poignantly than the victim . . . As for my "goodness in letting you come"—that was really nothing but the foreseeing that you would have found it difficult to forgive me if I had dissuaded you.[47]

Yeats responded to this tolerance as if his emotions were stabilized: "The truth is that so much has happened since that time in Normandy that though I admire Iseults subtle thought I have no contact with her mind."[48]

But they were not stabilized. Fifteen years later, the same pattern persisted. When Yeats's biographer Richard Ellmann interviewed Iseult Gonne in 1946, she told him about a conversation she had had with Yeats in 1935: Yeats said to her, "everything was terrible. He and his wife had gradually been alienated—he said she was a mother rather than a wife—that she had humiliated him in public." And then, to Ellmann, Iseult added "But George must have put up with a lot." Yeats said to Iseult, "If only you and I had married," to which she responded, "Why we wouldn't have stayed together a year."[49]

This is the pattern of Yeats's *Only Jealousy of Emer*, which he began writing on his honeymoon. Cuchulain has been seduced and enchanted by the fairy Fand, and lies passive and silent throughout the brief play. His wife Emer and his mistress Eithne Inguba sit by his bed. He is like one "taken" by the fairies; what is on the bed is a being substituted by the fairies. The only way to get the "real" Cuchulain back, it seems, is for Emer to "renounce Cuchulain's love for ever." At first she resists, but because she loves him and does not want him to die, she acquiesces, and as she says those words, Cuchulain is returned to himself; he "wakes." As he does, Eithne Inguba cries out, "Come to me, my beloved. It is I. / I, Eithne Inguba!" and Cuchulain's first waking words, his last words in the play, are for her: "Your arms, your arms! O Eithne Inguba, / I have been in some strange place and am afraid."

Thus the Maud Gonne figure, Fand, the powerful magical seductress, is less important in Yeats's play than she is in Blunt's, but the wife and mistress exist in a struggle for him: only by giving him up, by sacrificing her own interest in him, can the wife get him back. As George wrote Yeats, "As for my 'goodness in letting you come'—that was really nothing but the foreseeing that you would have found it difficult to forgive me if I had dissuaded you." Yeats's Emer understands the sacrifice she has made, whereas Blunt's Emer must hope that the cloak of forgetfulness will do its magic. But whatever the differences, for Yeats, the issue of managing competing erotic ties was Blunt territory, because of Blunt's great experience in that field, both in life and in theater.

8

A Live Tradition

To have gathered from the air a live tradition
or from a fine old eye the unconquered flame . . .

Ezra Pound, Canto LXXXI

The tallest, most famous poets in the photograph contended
obliquely and politely for a powerful woman and a Cuchulain
story, but the shortest one was not in contention for anything. As
Yeats had written to Lady Gregory, "On the way home the poets
kept Plarr out of all the conversation—they would not give him the
clue to anything—he had become an ordinary person, an enemy . . ."
Pound's comment to Yeats the next day was more significant: "Plarr
has made his last public appearance."

Plarr's appearance in "Siena Mi Fè; Disfecemi Maremma," the
seventh section of Pound's poem *Hugh Selwyn Mauberly* (1920), is
not exactly public, and he isn't named, but it is indisputably, recognizably Plarr. Who else could be the "last scion of the / Senatorial
families of Strasbourg," telling stories of the Marquis de Galliffet's
charge in the Franco-Prussian war and of Dowson and Johnson,
surrounded by "pickled fetuses and bottled bones," as Plarr was,
in the library of the Royal College of Surgeons? There are not
two people in whom all those eccentric characteristics coexist, and
they are all aspects of Plarr that Pound mentions explicitly in other
poems and in reviews.

The peacock dinner effected a dramatic though not a permanent
change in Pound's attitude to Plarr. In his 1912 "Status Rerum" in
Poetry, Pound mentioned Plarr favorably as one of those "who are

little known to the general public, but who contribute liberally to the 'charm' or the 'atmosphere' of London." Blunt, "the grandest of old men," is the first of these, and the final one is

Victor Plarr, one of the 'old' Rhymers' Club . . . a friend of Dowson and of Lionel Johnson. His volume, *In the Dorian Mood*, has been half forgotten, but not his verses *Epitaphium Citharistriae*.[1]

When, however, Pound came to review Plarr's book about Dowson two years later, the year after the peacock dinner, he was less flattering. Again he uses the phrase "half-forgotten" for *In the Dorian Mood*, an ambiguous phrase to say the least. The review begins promisingly—"This is a most charming monograph"—and praises the opening chapters as "the best account of Ernest Dowson that has been written." And the review ends with a mildly positive statement that might sell a few copies of the book: ". . . no one who loves his Dowson will go without this memoir." But the middle of the review is somewhat negative.[2]

Pound's basic criticism is that Plarr's book attempts to make the notoriously, infamously decadent Dowson "respectable." It's certainly the case that the book takes precisely that tack: of Dowson's letters, which are included in the volume, Plarr writes at the beginning,

In them no ugly slur of passion, no ill savours, are to be found. Instead, we are refreshed by fragrance . . . and by an unfailing touch of good breeding, a gracious and insistent air of modesty—by something diffident, boyishly shy, often beautiful and noble.

As a young man, Dowson had a "charming face unscathed by any serious sorrows or dissipations." Contrary to Dowson's reputation for drunkenness, Plarr remembers "only a trifling aberration from the path of temperance."[3] Even some rather jolly times were "far, very far, from the depth of lurid dissipation that is being allowed to cover the poet's good fame."[4] And then there's the fascinating subject of Dowson's romance with Adelaide Foltinowicz, the "Cynara" of Marion Plarr's novel. But of this Plarr says—and this is his entire coverage of the subject—"And then the love affair! We will cut a long story short by saying simply—it failed."[5]

It would take a lot of patience to accept the stylistic affectations quietly, but it's the bourgeoisification of Dowson that gets to Pound most intensely. Instead of complaining directly, he writes,

Certain people would rather think of Dowson in cabmen's shelters, or squabbling with drunken fishermen in Dieppe and the Breton towns. Certain people will rather remember the beautiful story of the French magistrate who had condemned Dowson for assaulting the local baker. Someone rushed into the court protesting that Dowson was a distinguished writer. "What, what, Monsieur Dowson, a distinguished English litterateur! Release M. Dowson—at once! Imprison the baker."[6]

"Certain people" got those vignettes and that story from Yeats, who was to publish them in "The Tragic Generation," a section of his memoir *The Trembling of the Veil* (1922).[7] By a kind of *occupatio*, Pound inserts into the review precisely the kind of anecdote Plarr was at pains to omit. And then Pound says more directly,

Some will resent what they will call Mr. Plarr's attempt to make Dowson more acceptable to people who live in three-story houses instead of in chambers and attics. They will say that even the gospels would lose a great deal of their force were their hero not represented with a taste for bohemian company.

"Some" here includes of course the reviewer himself, who calls the book "charming" a second time, less persuasively, and sneaks in a characterization of Plarr that he was later to use, in part, in his description of M. Verog: "a survivor of the senatorial families of Strasburg whose tradition is, '*On porte sa bourgeoisie comme un marquisat*' " ("We carry our bourgeois status as if it were a marquisate").

The tone of Pound's review anticipates the disdain implied in Yeats's letter to Lady Gregory after the peacock dinner; the portrait of Plarr in *Hugh Selwyn Mauberley* articulates it more directly and makes it more permanent. It's in a long poem, a pronouncement on the pre-war poetry scene, not an obscure review; this is a major "profession of poetry" poem. The title of the section about Plarr ("Siena Mi Fè; Disfecemi Maremma"), as all commentators on the poem have noted, comes from Dante's La Pia's sad, purgatorial résumé, a source Eliot was using in revised form in *The Waste Land*'s "Fire Sermon" not long after Pound used it: "Highbury bore me. Richmond and Kew / Undid me." In the Plarr section of *Hugh Selwyn Mauberley* the line suggests an ironic connection with Plarr's life: Strasbourg made him, London unmade him. That, at least, is the way Pound saw it. For the "last scion of the / Senatorial families of Strasbourg" to be found "among the pickled foetuses and bottled bones"—all this in the first

stanza—may be seen as an unmaking. Of course as librarian of the
Royal College of Surgeons, Plarr would necessarily be found among
medical specimens, but the phrases obviously sound undignified, disgusting, and silly. There's also of course the implication that Plarr
himself is not much more alive than the bottled specimens. Although
few critics have commented on the patent insult to Plarr, the mock
grandiosity of "the last scion" etc. is clear.

And it's also clear that the speaker, who "found" the last scion
there among the foetuses, is bored by Plarr:

> For two hours he talked of Galliffet;
> Of Dowson; of the Rhymers' Club;
> Told me how Johnson (Lionel) died
> By falling from a high stool in a pub . . .

What this scion "talked of" for two hours goes on for two more stanzas; he's a bore. "For two hours" is the point; that's an awfully long
monologue. But as Yeats wrote to Lady Gregory, ". . . having a story
to tell & the cook have undone him. He has developed his small talk
in telling how Dowson & Johnson drank themselves to death."

At the end, Pound identifies Plarr in all but name:

> So spoke the author of "The Dorian Mood",
>
> M. Verog, out of step with the decade,
> Detached from his contemporaries,
> Neglected by the young,
> Because of these reveries.

Plarr was indeed "neglected by the young," if that includes Pound,
Aldington, and Flint, all the way back to London from West
Sussex: "On the way home the poets kept Plarr out of all the conversation—they would not give him the clue to anything . . ." And then
of course there is his "half-forgotten" book.

Like the first section of *Hugh Selwyn Mauberley*, the Verog poem is in
quatrains. The first section's quatrains rhyme ABAB, and there is some
musicality, driven especially by the lengthened sound of the B-rhymes:

> His true Penelope was Flaubert,
> He fished by obstinate isles;
> Observed the elegance of Circe's hair
> Rather than the mottoes on sun-dials.

The Verog section's quatrains, however, rhyme ABCB, and they are not only unmusical, they are deliberately, emphatically flat and anti-musical. This is the kind of prosey flatness Eliot perfected in lines like, "And I say, 'Cousin Harriet, here is the *Boston Evening Transcript*'." Pound's flatness here imitates the boredom he experiences in the company of M. Verog and also ironizes the whole context.

> Among the pickled foetuses and bottled bones,
> Engaged in perfecting the catalogue,
> I found the last scion of the
> Senatorial families of Strasbourg, Monsieur Verog.

That enjambment—"last scion of the / Senatorial families" is the most insulting enjambment ever devised. It suggests that the poet is indifferent to the meaning of the line and ends it arbitrarily between article and noun when it seems to be long enough; ends it out of weariness and a complete lack of curiosity about who the "scion" is: that can wait till the next line. Using the formal phrase "Senatorial families of Strasbourg" gives it a mock pomposity, as if we all have heard of this subculture and will of course be impressed by such a category, the "Senatorial families." This last scion is as much a pickled specimen as the ones in the jars. And he is "perfecting the catalogue," devoting his attention to work that is less than fascinating.

M. Verog tells all the stories about Dowson that were left out of his introduction to the letters—"Dowson found harlots cheaper than hotels"—but his stories, too, are like pickled fetuses and bottled bones. Who wants this old Rhymers stuff? Well, Pound did, for a while. But it was after the peacock dinner that Pound began to consider Plarr "out of step with the decade, / Detached from his contemporaries." That was his "last public appearance" with luminaries such as Yeats and Pound.

The "M. Verog" section of *Hugh Selwyn Mauberley*, Pound's salvo at Plarr, is well known. What is not known at all, I believe, is Plarr's poetic salvo at Pound: he, too, wrote a "profession of poetry" poem, damning contemporary American poetry. In August 2011, Maggs Rare Books in London advertised a first edition of Pound's 1908 book *A Quinzaine for this Yule*, "printed for Elkin Mathews by W. Pollock and Co." This copy seems to have been the personal

copy of Victor Plarr, and a holograph poem appears on the terminal
blank page:

> Oh, in our dwindling age, 'tis ours to meet
> Rubbish Unspeakable at every turn.
> Claudian the Teutons had perforce to greet,
> And we dare not America now to spurn.
> The Quack survives when Arts of Learning die,
> And every critic learns to cringe & lie!
> I have not long to live, but let me damn
> Asses while I, once Victor Plarr, still am![8]

According to the description of the book, the poem is signed "Nov
21 '09," a date after Plarr had met Pound. In a letter dated "[after 27
May 1909]," Pound wrote his father, "I find one Victor Plarr of the
old Rhymers club most congenial. He is in on Sunday supper-&-
evenings."[9] These eighteenth-century-style quatrains were written
eleven years before *Mauberley*, and the privacy of the publishing venue
(Plarr's own copy of Pound's book) suggests it is unlikely that Pound
ever knew about the poem. The poem states fairly explicitly Plarr's
dislike of Pound's poetry and also implies tensions in the friendship
even at this early stage, only six months after they had met. It's interesting to know that each man attacked the other in verse, however
privately in Plarr's case.

Yeats's letter to Lady Gregory after the peacock dinner makes it
possible to interpret "Siena Mi Fè" in a new way, not only as a rejection of the literary past represented by Victor Plarr's stories about
the Nineties but as a rejection that began to take shape on that very
occasion. As Pound's review of Plarr's book on Dowson and as Yeats's
autobiography make clear, both poets loved Dowson's decadence; it
was Plarr's stories about him—and Plarr's later censorship of those
stories—that they found tiresome.

By the time Pound wrote the later Cantos, however, he had mellowed, if that word can ever be used of Pound, and Plarr in his three
cameos is more sympathetically rendered. In Canto XVI, one of the
"Hell" Cantos, Pound gives what he characterizes in the margin as
"*Plarr's narration*," describing the heroic "triple charge" of General
de Galliffet against the Prussians at the battle of Sedan in 1870. It
was Plarr's side, the French, for whom that battle was "Hell." This
passage revises the "Siena Mi Fè . . ." line "For two hours he talked
of Galliffet"; Plarr's long-winded account has now found a more

sympathetic place in Pound's memory. And the beautiful elegiac passage of Canto LXXIV is one of many in which Pound mourns the people he truly misses, among them, surprisingly, Plarr:

> Lordly men are to earth o'er given
> these the companions:
> Fordie that wrote of giants
> and William who dreamed of nobility
> and Jim the comedian singing:
> "Blarrney castle me darlin'
> you're nothing now but a StOWne"
> and Plarr talking of mathematics
> or Jepson lover of jade
> Maurie who wrote historical novels
> and Newbolt who looked twice bathed
> are to earth o'er given.

In this collective context, Plarr adds color and eccentricity to the rich variety of writers Pound remembers; and Plarr is not, for once, talking of Dowson or of Galliffet.

"... this is my table of values"

Like Pound's *Hugh Selwyn Mauberley*, Yeats's *Oxford Book of Modern Verse* (1936) put into print his understanding of the recent history of poetry in English. In it, Yeats pronounces on the profession of poetry as he has known it during his entire career. Yeats had been invited by Oxford in 1934 to choose the poems for an anthology of modern poetry, and he accepted almost immediately.[10] The anthology became, for Yeats, part of the deliberate packaging of his ideas that he made in many different ways in the late 1930s. "Under Ben Bulben" was originally titled "His Convictions," and Yeats wrote Lady Elizabeth Pelham several weeks before his death, "When I try to put all into a phrase I say, 'Man can embody the truth but he cannot know it.'" Of the Oxford anthology, Yeats wrote Laura Riding, "My anthology has ... a first domestic object, to get under one cover poems I want to read to myself, to a friend, or to my children ... If I give my anthology to a man, or as is more likely a woman, I must be able to say this is my table of values." The phrase "get under one cover," like "put all into a phrase" or "His Convictions," suggests that

Yeats was thinking of the *Oxford Book of Modern Verse* as a compact, unitary package of all his poetic "values." It is an intervention in the history of poetry. Yeats's introduction to the volume, like Pound's *Mauberley*, is an autobiography with a focus on the development of his poetic taste. And for Yeats as for Pound, the deaths of the Nineties poets form a crucial marker in that development and in the history of modern poetry. It was here that Yeats, after an affectionate account of his friends Dowson, Johnson, and the rest, wrote his famous lines about the Nineties poets:

Some of these Hamlets went mad, some drank, drinking not as happy men drink but in solitude, all had courage, all had suffered public opprobrium— generally for their virtues or for sins they did not commit—all had good manners . . . all had gaiety, some had wit . . . Some turned Catholic . . . that too was a tradition . . . Lionel Johnson was the first to convert . . . Then in 1900 everybody got down off his stilts; henceforth nobody drank absinthe with his black coffee; nobody went mad; nobody committed suicide; nobody joined the Catholic church; or if they did I have forgotten.[11]

This is as concise and powerful an articulation as Pound's of the heady combination of substances and religiosity that animated the decadents:

> For two hours he talked of Galliffet;
> Of Dowson; of the Rhymers' Club;
> Told me how Johnson (Lionel) died
> By falling from a high stool in a pub . . .
>
> But showed no trace of alcohol
> At the autopsy, privately performed—
> Tissue preserved—the pure mind
> Arose toward Newman as the whiskey warmed.

In Pound's account the peacock dinner is invisibly present through Plarr; in Yeats's anthology, Plarr is the only guest at the dinner not accounted for.

During the time Yeats was assembling the Oxford anthology, the entire cast of characters from the peacock dinner—with the exception of Plarr—appears in his correspondence, and in positions similar to those in the picture. That is, the three men in the center are the most important, and the four on the margins are—marginal.[12] To work from the edges to the center: in Yeats's hundreds of letters about the anthology between 1934 and 1936, the name Victor Plarr never once occurs. The names Aldington and Flint occur only once, to be rejected, in a letter of 24 October 1935 to Yeats's editor at Oxford, Charles Williams. Yeats here discusses (and rejects) suggestions that Williams has apparently made in a previous letter:

Aldington . . . is a friend of mine, but I have always known that if I did an Anthology I would have to reject his work . . . There is nothing in Flint, an old acquaintance of mine, except gilded stucco.[13]

Well, so much for them! Aldington's rejection does not even merit an excuse.

Thomas Sturge Moore, Yeats's book designer and old friend of many years, could not be rejected, and Yeats liked his poetry and claimed to have been influenced by it. The volume includes six of his poems, one of them "The Dying Swan," the poem Moore placed in the marble Gaudier-Brzeska box. When, at the end of his response to Blunt at the peacock dinner, Yeats began to characterize the work of the various poets present, he said, "Sturge Moore . . . does not dramatise himself but centaurs and great beings of that kind," and he says more or less the same twenty-one years later in the introduction to the anthology: "Sturge Moore [wrote] of centaurs, amazons, gazelles copied from a Persian picture . . ."[14] Yeats echoes, or believes he echoes, "The Dying Swan" at the end of "The Tower," and it has been suggested that Sturge Moore's poem "The Gazelles" influenced the use of that word in the elegy for Eva Gore-Booth and Constance Markiewicz; and that his poem "Leda" influenced Yeats's "Leda and the Swan," so it was precisely those great creaturely beings in Moore that Yeats appropriated from him.[15]

Blunt's position in the volume reflects the position in the history of modern poetry that Yeats attributed to him in his speech at the dinner: he is the first "modern" poet, and his is the first poetry included in the *Oxford Book of Modern Verse*, which is organized chronologically. (The volume opens, notoriously, with the prose of Walter Pater's description of the *Mona Lisa* printed as if it were free verse, so Blunt is actually the first poet in the anthology.)

Yeats writes of Blunt in the introduction,

Wilfred [sic] Blunt one knew through the report of friends as a fashionable amateur who had sacrificed a capacity for literature and the visible arts to personal adventure. Some ten years had to pass before anybody understood that certain sonnets, lyrics, stanzas of his were permanent in our literature.[16]

What precisely those ten years are is not clear; they might be the ten years between the publication of Blunt's *In Vinculis* (1889) and the time Yeats met him through Lady Gregory, presumably the "friend" whose report Yeats had heard. In the *Oxford Book of Modern Verse,* Yeats does not explain his placement at the beginning of the volume in the terms he used at the peacock dinner, where he explained that when Blunt published his poems "Victorian romance" was "completely at an end," and Blunt wrote as if "in some real situation of life."

The poems Yeats anthologizes are the sonnets to Esther he and Pound had both praised in the past, a sonnet from *In Vinculis*, a short lyric, and the passages from "The Wisdom of Merlyn" that he had praised in 1914, according to Lady Gregory's 27 December 1914 letter to Blunt. So the place of Blunt in the *Oxford Book of Modern Verse* confirmed, in the permanence of print, precisely the beliefs about Blunt's poems that Yeats had been expressing in private over the past twenty-one years.

The mild irritation with Pound that Yeats had begun to express at the end of his peacock dinner speech ("Ezra Pound has a desire personally to insult the world. He has a volume of manuscript at present in which his insults to the world are so deadly that it is rather a complicated publishing problem") was articulated at greater length in the 1930s. Yeats was annoyed at the cost of permissions for Pound's poems and told him so directly:

Dear Ezra,

There is only man in the English language as expensive as you and I am going to reduce him to one poem. I have only a limited amount of money for permissions and have to pay both English and American copyright out of this sum. I can spend twenty pounds on poems from you. What can I have for that? I should like to use Canto XVII and anything else from my selection you can throw in. I have personally never got more than two guineas for a poem on either side of the water. It is clear that I shall have to raise my charge. I know you have no dislike for anthologies as you have published a couple yourself . . .[17]

In the event Yeats did include Canto XVII and two other poems, but Pound cannot have been pleased with what Yeats said about him in the introduction. Pound gets three entire pages of the introduction, more than most of the other poets, but Yeats's comments on the Cantos are ambivalent at best:

> The relation of all the elements to one another, repeated or unrepeated, is to become apparent when the whole is finished . . . Like other readers I discover at present merely exquisite or grotesque fragments. His belief in his own conception is so great that since the appearance of the first Canto I have tried to suspend judgement.[18]

Sneakily Yeats includes in the introduction, as if it were a part of his commentary, the entire text of "The Return," the poem placed in the marble box in 1914. He gets it free, as if in a kind of swipe at Pound.

Of course, there was another poet at the peacock dinner, not one of the seven in the picture: Hilaire Belloc. He too is represented in the *Oxford Book of Modern Verse* with "Tarantella" ("Do you remember an Inn, / Miranda? / Do you remember an Inn?"), but in a letter written months before the anthology was published, Yeats remembers, without naming it precisely, the occasion of the peacock dinner. It was at the time he was finishing work on the anthology that Yeats wrote requesting a copy of the "delightful song about a delightful Mrs. Rees" that Belloc had sung at the peacock dinner. The association of Belloc with Blunt and Newbuildings Place was still vivid in Yeats's mind ("When I met you at Wilfred [*sic*] Blunt's before the war, or during the war, you sang a delightful song about a delightful Mrs. Rees").

"that a Blunt should open"

Like Blunt in Galway Gaol in 1887, Pound in 1945 at the U.S. Army Disciplinary Training Center in Pisa used his unscheduled hours to write poetry. He "found on the jo-house seat" *The Pocket Book of Modern Verse*, edited by M. E. Speare (1940). Pound's thoughts may have returned to the peacock dinner because he saw Blunt's double sonnet "To Esther" in the anthology, or because the dinner formed part of the pre-war London material that he was remembering. Whatever the cause, the famous lines in Canto LXXXI appear to begin with a precise visual memory of seeing Blunt for the first time. Remembering the dinner over thirty years later, Pound says nothing of Blunt's politics or the macho swagger his occasional poem had praised; nor does he mention any of the other poets, nor the house or the peacock. What he recalls is an encounter charged with emotion:

> To have, with decency, knocked
> That a Blunt should open
>   To have gathered from the air a live tradition
> or from a fine old eye the unconquered flame
> This is not vanity.

Three points of memory in these lines indicate the way poetic culture exists in the person of the poet and is transmitted through proximity. The simple beginning of the visit, knocking on the door, initiates an exchange: the younger poets have sought Blunt out, and he welcomes them himself. Because of Blunt's age and complaints about ill health, the poets no doubt expected a servant to open the door, so the sight of Blunt himself there must have been a surprise. Pound's memory constructs in a particular way a moment in the history of poetry; he makes the simple act of opening the door into a gesture of cultural generosity as well as hospitality. Opening the door, Blunt makes himself, his house, and his poetic tradition accessible to the six visitors. To have breathed the same air as Blunt for five hours is to have had access to "a live tradition." Precisely what tradition Pound doesn't say: the tradition of anti-imperialist poets? Romantic poets? Or simply the tradition of writing poetry, "live" when seven poets debate the practice of their craft? Whatever it was, Pound got it by being in the same interior space as Blunt.

The "fine old eye" is of course Blunt's; he was the only person present who could have been called "old." It also testifies to the location of culture in the poet's body: looking at the eye grants access to "the unconquered flame." The "live tradition" is associated with the air that is breathed; the "unconquered flame" suggests a visual form of spiritual and poetic power, the bright eye. The door, the air, and the light in the eye, in diminishing materiality and increasing intimacy, show imagistically how the transmission took place (Figure 23).

No doubt the experience was made possible by Blunt's hospitality: the opening of the door begins the occasion with a show of generosity and interest, a desire on Blunt's part to greet his guests, to meet them face to face at once, and to be the person to let them into

Figure 23. The front door of Newbuildings Place with the original knocker. Reproduced by permission of the Earl and Countess of Lytton.

his house. The "air" is the welcoming air of Newbuildings as well as the poets' breaths, their words in communal, professional exchange.

This vision of the peacock dinner is indeed a re-imagining of the event without any of its conflicts, those known and those not known to Pound. There is no differentiation of the visitors, in fact no pronoun whatsoever. There may be an implied first person pronoun, singular or plural, in "To have, with decency, knocked," but it's never stated; and the only person mentioned is Blunt himself. The invidious divisions of the dinner are not even thought of here, are not remembered. If "What thou lovest well remains, / the rest is dross," as that same Canto says, then the art of poetry and the communal conversation about it is what Pound loves well, and "the rest is dross."

These five lines constitute a revision of *Hugh Selwyn Mauberley*, in which Pound sees himself, or his persona Mauberley, as having failed to "resuscitate the dead art / Of poetry," as having been "Wrong from the start—." The literary world of that poem is populated by the variously sterile M. Verog, Brennbaum, Mr Nixon, the Lady Valentine, and other uninspiring figures; there is no "live tradition." "The age," "his time," and "'the march of events'" are all unpropitious. But in Canto LXXXI, the art of poetry is not "dead"; Pound has "gathered from the air a live tradition," and he remembers that occasion under the most unpropitious of circumstances. The profession of poetry is a live tradition, its survival embodied in and assured by the peacock dinner. "What thou lovest well is thy true heritage / What thou lov'st well shall not be reft from thee."

Epilogue

The Long Peacock Dinner

Figure 24. Blunt's grave at Newbuildings Place. Reproduced by permission of the Earl and Countess of Lytton.

If Wilfrid Blunt had read his own *Times* obituary, he would have written a letter of protest to the paper. "Everywhere he found oppressed Nationalists," it read, "whose cause he straightway championed with a fervor which recked little of facts." He had no conception, it added, of the "slow processes of political evolution in the case of backward peoples."[1] It would have taken a long letter to set the record straight. Ahead of his time in his ideas about empire and "oppressed Nationalists," Blunt had written *Secret History of the English Occupation of Egypt* and *The Land War in Ireland* precisely to get the facts out there.

One part of his obituary he might have liked. It read,

Hardly less important than his own poetry was Blunt's influence on the younger generation. Early in 1914 he received a remarkable tribute from a committee of younger poets, including W. B. Yeats and John Masefield, who presented to him, in token of homage for his poetry, a carved reliquary of Pentelican marble, the work of the sculptor, Gaudier Brzeska.

But here, too, the obituary was wrong. As Blunt himself realized when he read the poems, he had had no literary influence whatsoever on the visiting poets: "The modern poetry represented by these young men is too entirely unlike anything I can recognize as good verse that I feel there is something absurd in their expressing admiration for mine . . . they do not follow at all in my footsteps . . ."[2] There was no trace of Blunt's poetic style in any of the poems placed in the carved reliquary of Pentelican marble, in spite of Yeats's eloquent remark that "As the tide of romance recedes I am driven back simply on myself and my thoughts in actual life, and my work becomes more and more like your earlier work . . ."

The peacock dinner was not about the minutiae of style or the trappings of "Victorian romance." It was about the way literary intimacies create means of transmitting the professional culture of poetry, the "apostolic succession," as Pound called it in 1913. The "succession" embodied in the dinner itself also formed part of a longer sequence. In its short form, the peacock dinner looks tidily self-contained, lasting almost five hours beginning at 12:30 p.m. on Sunday the 18th of January 1914. But understood generously, like the "long nineteenth century" that lasts till 1914, it can be seen to extend over a greater period of time. The dinner took place in many histories, erotic, literary, and political, and its meanings are embedded in the personal lives of its participants. Its final appearance can be fixed to 1949, when Pound's *Pisan Cantos*, with its evocative lines about the peacock dinner, was awarded the Bollingen Prize for Poetry. The origins of the long peacock dinner are harder to locate: they could conceivably be found in the summer of 1882, when, in Blunt's words about Lady Gregory, "by a spontaneous impulse we found comfort in each other's arms." The six visiting poets never knew that hidden antecedent of the dinner, Blunt and Gregory's romance, for him another fling, for her an erotic and a professional awakening.[3]

It was the Byronic Blunt, with his macho persona, his iconoclasm, and his panache, who had provoked Pound's curiosity, the Blunt who modeled his own tabloid life on that of his grandfather-in-law. An even longer peacock dinner can be understood, then, to originate in 1823 (Byron's voyage to Greece) or even 1815 (his marriage to Anne Isabella Milbanke), and it reveals another and longer pattern of poets' intimacies. As a terminus to this narrative, the awarding of the Bollingen Prize to the *Pisan Cantos* defines a sequence of poetic relationships that should be viewed in reverse chronological order.[4] From early 1949, when Robert Lowell pressed the committee to select Pound, looking back to 1823, when Byron left Italy for Greece, we can see a series of politically active, philandering poets seeking apprenticeships with older, kindred poets. The long peacock dinner reveals one tradition of masculine poetic professionalism in diachronic form, existing over time as descendants and ancestors, a lineage constructed by successive poets as they find and claim their masculine precursors.

The point from which this lineage is made visible occurs in the spring of 1949, when a controversy was deliberately provoked over Pound's receipt of the prize. In a series of articles and letters, the *Saturday Review of Literature* called attention to the fact that a man who had been tried for treason, who only three years previously had broadcast speeches urging Americans to support Fascist governments, had been given an award by the very government to which he had been a traitor.[5] Along with many beautiful passages, the Cantos contained offensive anti-Semitic lines about "yidds" and Jewish bankers. Congressman Jacob Javits (Republican of New York) called for an investigation, and by August the Library of Congress had canceled "all arrangements of the giving of prizes and the making of awards," and the Bollingen Prize moved to Yale.[6]

The committee of poets who had made the selection (Conrad Aiken, W. H. Auden, Louise Bogan, Katherine Garrison Chapin, T. S. Eliot, Paul Green, Robert Lowell, Katherine Anne Porter, Karl Shapiro, Theodore Spencer, Allen Tate, Willard Thorp, and Robert Penn Warren) had not failed to confront the complexities of their decision. Its members had been troubled by the anti-Semitism and took several votes, but the *Pisan Cantos* won by a large majority.[7] Pound's strongest supporter on the committee was Lowell, who had urged that the prize be given to Pound in spite of objections: "I really think we should go ahead and instigate the consequences," he wrote.

"It's a very important decision . . . I think it will look better and better as the years go by. We really are right."[8]

Lowell and Pound were already friends. Both men were living in Washington, D.C., Pound because he was incarcerated in St. Elizabeth's psychiatric hospital, housed there since the insanity plea offered by his lawyer to the charge of treason in 1946 saved him from the sentence of life imprisonment; Lowell because he had been appointed poetry consultant to the Library of Congress. Lowell visited Pound in St Elizabeth's, and the two poets talked shop: Eliot, Milton, Synge, "Bill Williams." Most days Pound repeated the stories he had told Lowell before, but one day—7 September 1948—he made it new. "Had a good afternoon with Pound," Lowell wrote Elizabeth Bishop. "New this time: stories about the seven male poets of England (who were they?) going to call on Wilfrid S. Blunt and his 20 year old mistress."[9]

Of course, Dorothy Carleton was not styled a "mistress" by Blunt—she had been "adopted" as his "niece"—and she was actually 39 when Pound met her, ten years older than he, but she was youthful and lovely, with the Pre-Raphaelite looks that Blunt favored. Contrasted to the 73-year-old Blunt, Dorothy (whom Pound met on one of his later visits) must have seemed 20.[10]

Lowell's letter to Bishop offers the last recorded mention of the peacock dinner by someone who was there.[11] Had Lowell been able to follow his youthful dream of living with Pound, he might have known who those "seven male poets" were. Back in May 1936, when he was a 19-year-old freshman at Harvard, Lowell had written the 50-year-old Pound, "You will probably think that I am very impudent and presumptuous, but I want to come to Italy and work under you and forge my way into reality." Writing from his dorm, Lowell confessed that he had outgrown his interests in butterflies, snakes, turtles, and Napoleon, and now poetry was the thing. At Harvard he "yearned after iron" but was "choked with cobwebs." He was in earnest: "I pray you to take me!" he begged, and added, "You shan't be sorry."[12]

A second letter, quoting and praising Pound's poetry alongside Shakespeare's, yielded no result.

Pound never welcomed Lowell to Italy, but Allen Tate welcomed him to Tennessee the following year, and Lowell pitched his Sears

Roebuck tent on Tate's lawn. Eleven years later, however, Pound in St. Elizabeth's was a captive audience, and meeting him there, Lowell had something like the arrangement he had sought earlier, intimate conversations about Life and Art with an established poet.

In seeking and later championing Pound, Lowell was doing what Pound himself had done in seeking Yeats ("sitting on the same hearth rug") and in seeking Blunt. It was Pound who had put together the "committee of poets" to honor an iconoclastic older poet who had opposed his own government's policies. And just as the prize given to Pound had upset members of Congress, so the honor given to Blunt had annoyed Mr. Clerk of the Foreign Office. And as Lowell had sought in Pound, and Pound in Blunt, proximity, friendship, and the transmission of poetic culture, so Blunt had sought Byron, finding him in places where Byron had stayed and in marriage to his grand-daughter. As the youngest in this series, Lowell is the one who makes these separate links look like a chain. The lineage is not like a genetic ancestry, because it is only a single link, and not the entire chain, that is known to each of the poets involved. Lowell manifests no interest in or even knowledge of Blunt, nor does Pound ever refer to Blunt's relationship with Byron.

Each man in this sequence admired the transgressive masculinity of his immediate predecessor, a masculinity expressed not only in poetry but in philandering and in political interventions of various kinds. Of course Pound's support of Mussolini is hardly the moral equivalent of Lowell's conscientious objection to World War II, Blunt's work for Egypt and Ireland, or Byron's republican sympathies with Greece, but all are alike in parading their politics on a large, public stage, expressing political angers and enthusiasms in direct confrontation with a government. The lineage is not a poetic tradi-tion, because no two of these poets' poems sound alike: what the later three men adopt and recreate is the oppositional persona originated by Byron. Blunt, Pound, and Lowell were also all jailed by their own governments and wrote some of their best poems out of that experience, Blunt's *In Vinculis*, Pound's *Pisan Cantos*, and Lowell's "Memories of West Street and Lepke." It could be said of all of them, as Oscar Wilde wrote in a review, "Prison has had an admirable effect on Mr. Wilfrid Blunt as a poet."[13]

The peacock dinner, then, should not be seen as a discrete event, an eccentric gathering of random poets for a unique and peculiar testimonial occasion, but as one point in a long continuum, a series of interlocking personal connections—an "apostolic succession" of poets—over several generations. Its friendships, romances, and rivalries show the way the profession of poetry, lacking systematic schools and licenses, lacking a single dominant institutional structure or any permanent institutions at all, functions through intimacies, visits, cohabitations, and provisional groupings like that of the seven men who assembled to eat the peacock.

The photograph hides altogether the network of women who connected the men, but it keeps alive in literary history the faces and sometimes the names of Plarr, Flint, and Sturge Moore, the minor poets on the edges. In its way, it immortalizes Flint as the "POET AND MAN OF LETTERS" he called himself in the 1911 English Census. No one now, and possibly no one in 1914, would doubt that Yeats and Pound were by far the superior poets in the group, the ones whose poetry would be read and admired a century later. But had only Pound and Yeats gone to Blunt's for dinner, the compliment to Blunt would have been less and the occasion a minor one; a testimonial by two people for a third, even if the two are Yeats and Pound, doesn't carry much weight. The dissenting voices of the poets on the sides (Sturge Moore's insistence that he "respects a lot of things," Flint's resentment at being the "reporter fellow") form other parts of the dinner's hidden history. The photograph also shows Pound in close proximity to two poets he had been eager to meet. He left America for such moments, and the picture that he had originally objected to was mailed to Chicago to grace the offices of *Poetry* magazine. The photograph freezes the moment when the seven male poets, professional poets in seven different ways, stood in their symmetrical arrangement, together and apart.

Notes

PROLOGUE: SEVEN POETS AND A PEACOCK

1. "As it was we did not get away till 5 . . ." (WBY to AG, 31 January 1914, Berg Collection). However, Blunt wrote Lady Gregory that they stayed till 5:30 (WSB to AG, 19 January 1914, Berg Collection).

2. Meynell, ed., *Friends of a Lifetime*, 186.

3. Accounts were published in *The Times* (no author named), *Poetry* (Pound), *The Egoist* (Aldington), *Poetry and Drama* (Flint), and the *Boston Evening Transcript* (J. Walter Smyth). Pound wrote to Blunt that Cournos wanted to publish an account in an American paper (EP to WSB, 20 January 1914, West Sussex Record Office), but the information about the dinner (the same as in all the other versions) was written by the *Transcript's* regular London literary correspondent.

4. Lytton, *Wilfrid Scawen Blunt*, 235.

5. See, for instance, Nilsen, "The Coming Cubists Explain Their Picture Puzzles. Picasso and Cézanne Tell Us What They Mean," 34.

6. Blunt, *My Diaries, Part Two*, 383.

7. Meynell, ed., *Friends of a Lifetime*, 186.

8. Pound, "How I Began," 707.

9. Shattuck, *The Banquet Years*, 66.

10. Frelinghuysen, *Louis Comfort Tiffany and Laurelton Hall*, 195–9.

11. 176e. Plato, *The Symposium*, trans. W. R. M. Lamb, 97.

12. Socrates agrees to the subject of love, which is proposed by Eryximachus, because "I do not see how I could myself decline, when I set up to understand nothing but love-matters" (177 d/e). The word for "love-matters" is ἐρωτικά, which transliterates "erotica"; that is the same subject in which Blunt had expertise, as all the visiting poets knew, and the poem Blunt read to them was about Don Juan. Needless to say, the ἐρωτικά of Socrates and the erotica of Blunt represent different specialties; the love that Diotima explained to Socrates is a love "ever-existent," that "neither waxes nor wanes" (211a). The chief characteristic of Blunt's love was that it did wax and wane, so notoriously as to make him interesting on that account.

13. Frelinghuysen, *Louis Comfort Tiffany and Laurelton Hall*, 196.

14. Frelinghuysen, *Louis Comfort Tiffany and Laurelton Hall*, 198.

15. Katharine Tynan was a close friend of Yeats, and it was most likely through reading her *Reminiscences* that he was reminded of Wilfrid Blunt

in November 1913. Charlotte Mew's poem "The Fête" was published by Pound in *The Egoist*, where it was printed in 1914 in the same issue as one of the chapters of *Portrait of the Artist as a Young Man*. Blunt's good friend and literary executor Sydney Cockerell was responsible for procuring a Civil List pension for Mew. Pound was an admirer of Mina Loy's poetry and wrote an essay on Loy and Marianne Moore: ". . . these girls have written a distinctly national product . . . they are . . . interesting and readable . . ." Hilda Doolittle received her *nom de plume* H.D. from Pound, her quondam fiancé. Moore admired Yeats and wrote a poem to him, "To William Butler Yeats on Tagore." Anna Wickham met Pound in Paris in 1922 and wrote a poem to him, "Song to Amidon." Elizabeth Daryush was the daughter of the Poet Laureate at the time of the peacock dinner, Robert Bridges, who turned down the invitation because of Blunt's politics. Yeats included Sylvia Townsend Warner in his notorious *Oxford Book of Modern Verse* (Rice, *A New Matrix for Modernism*, 66; Pound, "Marianne Moore and Mina Loy," *Ezra Pound: Selected Prose 1909–1965*, 424–5; Vaughan Jones, *Anna Wickham*, 163, 319).

16. Amy Lowell gave a second, competitive dinner in London for the Imagists after the one organized by Pound, but the guests were not limited by gender; see Brooker, *Bohemia in London*, 114-16. The genre of the male dinner has been countered most famously by Judy Chicago's brilliant installation *The Dinner Party*, with its place settings for thirty-nine women famous in history and myth, and the names of 999 more inscribed in the floor. *The Dinner Party* is installed in the Brooklyn Museum.

17. Beerbohm, *Seven Men and Two Others*, 47–94.

18. Yeats, "A Letter to Lady Gregory," *Explorations*, 254, 255.

19. Foster, *W. B. Yeats, Vol. II*, 39.

20. Rainey, *Institutions of Modernism*, 17–27.

21. Elizabeth Day, "January 1914: Suffragettes, Blizzards, Exploration—But No Hint of War," <http://www.theguardian.com/world/2014/jan/04/january-1914-no-hint-war>.

22. Meynell, ed., *Friends of a Lifetime*, 189.

23. Pound, *The Letters of Ezra Pound 1907–1941*, ed. Paige, 46.

24. Zilboorg, *Richard Aldington and H.D.*, 25.

25. Copp, ed., *Imagist Dialogues*, 230.

26. WBY to G. H. Mair, undated letter [1914–1915], Berg Collection.

27. Silber and Finn, *Gaudier-Brzeska*, 48.

28. Pound, *The Letters of Ezra Pound 1907–1941*, ed. Paige, 61.

29. Meynell, ed., *Friends of a Lifetime*, 186.

I. MALE POETS IN PROXIMITY

1. "Mr Hardy on Literature," *The Times*, 4 June 1912, 7. The question of whether Yeats was a member of the IRB is discussed by Foster (*W. B. Yeats, Vol. I*, 112–13).

2. Newbolt, ed., *The Later Life and Letters of Sir Henry Newbolt*, 166–8.
3. Hardy, *The Later Years of Thomas Hardy*, 152.
4. For one of the first and most significant discussions of modern literary professionalism, see Chapter 5, "Literature and Professionalism," in Louis Menand's *Discovering Modernism: T. S. Eliot and His Context*. See especially Menand's comments on "the tendency toward group publication in the early modernist period," a practice that "does seem in certain significant respects to reflect the general practice of associationism" (120).
5. The Poetry Society, <http://www.poetrysociety.org.uk/content/aboutus/>.
6. WBY to AG, 12 January 1914, Berg Collection.
7. Perkin, *The Rise of Professional Society*, 85.
8. Pound, "Patria Mia," *Ezra Pound: Selected Prose 1909–1965*, 127.
9. Pound, "Patria Mia," *Ezra Pound: Selected Prose 1909–1965*, 135–6.
10. Perkin, *The Rise of Professional Society*, 85.
11. "Biography: A Brief Life of Count Stenbock," <http://www.mmhistory.org.uk/cce/Jo/biography4.htm>.
12. Yeats, *OBMV*, xi–xii.
13. Brooker, *Bohemia in London*, 14; Carr, *The Verse Revolutionaries*, 1.
14. Edward Marsh, *A Number of People*, 320–1.
15. Perkin, *The Rise of Professional Society*, 85ff.
16. Parini, *Robert Frost*, 123–4; Poirier, "Robert Frost, The Art of Poetry No 2," 5.
17. Parini, *Robert Frost*, 153.
18. Street, *The Dymock Poets*, 91–2.
19. Farjeon, *Edward Thomas*, 92.
20. Farjeon, *Edward Thomas*, 93.
21. Farjeon, *Edward Thomas*, 94–5.
22. On male homosocial literary collaboration, see Kostenbaum, *Double Talk*.
23. Carpenter, 80. For the most detailed version of this story, see James Longenbach, "Ezra Pound at Home," 152–3.
24. Carpenter, *A Serious Character*, 93.
25. de Rachewiltz et al., eds, *Ezra Pound to His Parents*, 120, 181.
26. Carpenter, *A Serious Character*, 105; the date was 16 February 1909.
27. Pound and Litz, eds, *Ezra Pound and Dorothy Shakespear*, 3.
28. de Rachewiltz et al., eds, *Ezra Pound to His Parents*, 170.
29. Pound, *The Cantos*, 533–4.
30. WBY to AG, 9 November 1913, Letter 2287, *CL InteLex*.
31. Tynan, *Reminiscences*, 299.
32. James Longenbach thinks the Blunt dinner may have been inspired by the wish to counter the cultural force of the Royal Society. See Longenbach, *Stone Cottage*, 67.
33. Pound and Litz, eds., *Ezra Pound and Dorothy Shakespear*, 280.
34. Bridge, ed., *W. B. Yeats and T. Sturge Moore*, 18–21.
35. Pound, "Status Rerum," 127.

36. Pound, "A Retrospect," in *Literary Essays of Ezra Pound*, ed. Eliot, 3, 5, 6.
37. Blunt, *Poetical Works, Vol. I*, 28.
38. Longford, *Pilgrimage of Passion*, 25. See also Longford, 55: "They were to stay at Ouchy in the same little old-fashioned Anchor Inn that Byron and Shelley had patronized on their visit to Chillon fifty years before. Indeed Blunt was assigned Byron's traditional room, still provided with the same European furniture that had been new in his day. Blunt was reading Rousseau's *Confessions* just as Byron had read them."
39. Tetreault, "Heirs to His Virtues," 64.
40. See, for instance, McDayter, *Byromania and the Birth of Celebrity Culture*, and Mole, *Byron's Romantic Celebrity*. According to the *OED*, the earliest recorded use of the word "celebrity" in this sense was 1849.
41. Eisler, *Byron*, 60.
42. Blessington, *The Idler in Italy*, 162.
43. The original copy of this letter is in the Berg Collection.
44. Eliot and Haughton, eds, *The Letters of T. S. Eliot: Vol. 1: 1898–1922*, 220.
45. Rhys, *Everyman Remembers*, 244.
46. Homberger, "A Glimpse of Pound in 1912 by Arundel del Re," 88. See Carpenter, *A Serious Character*, 134, for a complete analysis of this episode.
47. Rhys, *Everyman Remembers*, 243.
48. Longford, *Pilgrimage of Passion*, 394; de Rachewiltz et al., eds, *Ezra Pound to His Parents*, 318.
49. Blunt, *Diaries*, 19 April 1914, Fitzwilliam Museum, MS 418/1975.
50. Saddlemyer, *Becoming George*, 261.
51. Saddlemyer, *Becoming George*, 261.
52. Pound, "Homage to Wilfrid Blunt," 222–3.
53. Longford, *Pilgrimage of Passion*, 4.
54. Rainey, *Institutions of Modernism*, 16ff.
55. Gwynn, *Sturge Moore and the Life of Art*, 37.
56. Doyle, *Richard Aldington*, 1–12.
57. EP to AG, 4 January 1914, West Sussex Record Office.
58. "Plarr's Lives of the Fellows" of the Royal College of Surgeons of England is now online at: <http://livesonline.rcseng.ac.uk/>.
59. Carr, *The Verse Revolutionaries*, 156.
60. "Mr. F. S. Flint," *The Times* (29 February 1960), 14.
61. 1911 England Census, <http://www.ukcensusonline.com/census/1911.php>.
62. Flint responded to the dry, statistical census form with imagination: for his baby daughter Ianthe, then ten months old, he wrote under the category Personal Occupation the words "Feeding and Squalling."
63. Coleman, *The Last Exquisite*, 113.
64. de Rachewiltz et al., eds, *Ezra Pound to His Parents*, 318.
65. Finneran, *The Correspondence of Robert Bridges and W. B. Yeats*, 28.
66. N.A., *Society for Pure English*, Tract No. 1, 6. For biographical background on Bridges, see Phillips, *Robert Bridges*; and for discussion of his poetics, see Martin, *The Rise and Fall of Meter*.
67. AG to John Quinn, 1 January 1914, Berg Collection.

2. LADY GREGORY'S IDEAS

1. Walkowitz, *Nights Out*, 3.
2. Victorian London—Publications—Etiquette and Advice Manuals—Dinners and Diners, by Lieut.-Col. Newnham-Davis, 1899—Chapter 22—Dieudonné's (Ryder Street), <http://www.victorianlondon.org/publications2/dinners-22.htm>.
3. Poirier, "Robert Frost, The Art of Poetry No 2," 15–16, <http://www.theparisreview.org/interviews/4678/the-art-of-poetry-no-2-robert-frost>.
4. For excellent accounts of both events, see Brooker, *Bohemia in London*, 119.
5. Brooker, *Bohemia in London*, 115.
6. Beerbohm, "Felix Argallo and Walter Ledgett," in *Seven Men and Two Others*, 167.
7. Brooker, *Bohemia in London*, 114.
8. WSB to AG, 13 December 1913, Berg Collection.
9. AG to WBY, 28 November 1913, Berg Collection.
10. WSB to AG, 19 January 1914, Berg Collection.
11. Blunt, *Diaries*, 28 December 1913, Fitzwilliam Museum, MS 416/1975.
12. WSB to AG, 7 January 1914, Berg Collection.
13. AG to WSB, "Thursday," Berg Collection. The date must be 2, 9, or 16 January, 1914. Of her sister's husband, AG writes, "He was old and not very interesting, but after all, as an old cousin of mine used to say 'when a woman loses her husband, she loses her crown.'"
14. EP to AG, 4 January 1914, West Sussex Record Office.
15. WSB to AG, 9 January 1914, Berg Collection.
16. Carpenter, *A Serious Character*, 230; see also Longford, *Pilgrimage of Passion*, 398.
17. Longenbach, *Stone Cottage*, 51.
18. "The Peacock Room: A Closer Look," Freer / Sackler, <http://www.asia.si.edu/exhibitions/online/peacock/4.htm>.
19. Merrill, *The Peacock Room*, 244–5.
20. Merrill, *The Peacock Room*, 239–40.
21. Gregory, *Seventy Years*, 479.
22. de Rachewiltz et al., eds, *Ezra Pound to His Parents*, 318.
23. Carpenter, *A Serious Character*, 229.
24. "Presentation to Lord Harrington," *The Times*, 10 January 1914, 10.
25. "Poets' Tribute to Thomas Hardy," *The Times*, 31 October 1915, 15. Hardy's 80th birthday was actually 3 June 1920, and the event itself was recognized by many similar tributes.
26. Silber and Finn, *Gaudier-Brzeska*, 42ff.
27. Pound, "Homage to Wilfrid Blunt," 222.
28. Getsy, "Give and Take," 43.
29. Getsy, "Give and Take," 43, 46.

30. Getsy, "Give and Take," 47.
31. Silber and Finn, *Gaudier-Brzeska*, 44.
32. WBY to AG, 12 January 1914, Berg Collection. I have silently emended places where Yeats repeated words and tested spellings.
33. "Yone Noguchi (1875–1947)," <http://www.botchanmedia.com/high-slide/examples/Bio-short.htm>.
34. Pound, "Homage to Wilfrid Blunt," 222–3.
35. AG to WBY, 28 November 1913, Berg Collection.
36. AG to Sydney Pawling (carbon), 5 January 1914, Berg Collection.
37. WSB to AG, 7 January 1914, Berg Collection.
38. WBY to AG, 1 February 1914, Berg Collection.
39. For a detailed discussion of this dispute, see McDiarmid, "The Abbey, Its 'Helpers,' and the Field of Cultural Production in 1913," in *Irish Theatre in America: Essays on Irish Theatrical Diaspora,* ed. Harrington.
40. I found it in Walter, "The Book in London," *Boston Evening Transcript,* 14 February 1914, 35.

3. VICTORIAN ADULTERY

1. WBY, "Estrangement," *Autobiographies,* 323.
2. Colum, *Life and the Dream,* 179; Longford, *Pilgrimage of Passion,* 295; Lutyens, *A Blessed Girl,* 216.
3. Gregory, *Seventy Years,* 35.
4. Gregory, "Foreword," in Blunt, *Diaries,* xii.
5. Marsh, *A Number of People,* 146.
6. Longford, "Wilfrid Scawen Blunt," 64.
7. Longford, "Lady Gregory and Wilfrid Scawen Blunt," 86.
8. Perry, *Belgrave Square,* 240.
9. "Cad" is from Andrew Saint, "'Between Farce and Misery,'" <http://www.guardian.co.uk/books/2002/jul/13/biography.highereducation1>; "insatiable womaniser" is from Girouard, *The Return to Camelot,* 204.
10. Lytton, *Wilfrid Scawen Blunt,* 285.
11. Eisler, *Byron,* 477, 479.
12. WSB's lovers who were cousins or family connections: Madeline Wyndham, married to Blunt's cousin Percy Wyndham; Mary Elcho, her daughter; and Dorothy Carleton, Madeline Wyndham's niece. See Dakers, *Clouds,* 89, to find them all in one sentence.
13. Girouard, *The Return to Camelot,* 198.
14. Girouard, *The Return to Camelot,* 204.
15. Lutyens, *A Blessed Girl,* 225. WSB also presented Mary Elcho with "an acrostic love-sonnet" before they became lovers. In her case, however, "this broke down her reserve" (Longford, *Pilgrimage of Passion,* 310).
16. Blunt, *Diaries,* 24 August 1892, Fitzwilliam Museum, MS 32/1975.

17. Walter Pater, end of "The Renaissance," 1868, 153. N.B. his note: "This brief 'Conclusion' was omitted in the second edition of this book, as I conceived it might possibly mislead some of those young men into whose hands it might fall. On the whole, I have thought it best to reprint it here, with some slight changes which bring it closer to my original meaning."

18. Blunt, *Diaries*, 15 July 1896, Fitzwilliam Museum, MS 35/1975.

19. Blunt, *Diaries*, 17 July 1894, Fitzwilliam Museum, MS 33/1975.

20. Blunt, *Diaries*, 2 June 1894, Fitzwilliam Museum, MS 33/1975.

21. Blunt, *Diaries*, 25 December 1898, Fitzwilliam Museum, MS 37/1975.

22. Longford, *Pilgrimage of Passion*, 191.

23. Blunt, *My Diaries, Part Two*, 100.

24. Pethica, "'A Woman's Sonnets.' Lady Gregory, with a Commentary," in *Lady Gregory, Fifty Years After*, ed. Saddlemyer and Smythe, 108.

25. Anne Blunt, *Journals and Correspondence 1878–1917*, 177–8.

26. Longford, *Pilgrimage of Passion*, 194–6. "For there is no reason to suppose that Anne did not know about that adulterous night at Crabbet on 7 August, as she had known of so many others" (Longford, 196–7). The date is taken from Winstone, *Lady Anne Blunt*, 203.

27. Blunt Papers, 10 August 1883, Fitzwilliam Museum, MS 244/1975.

28. Blunt Papers, 10 August 1883, Fitzwilliam Museum, MS 244/1975.

29. In the context of Lady Anne's "two pages of lined foolscap," it is worth noting the effusions of Emma Hardy, she who was exiled with her cats from the dinner for Thomas Hardy. After her death, Hardy found— and destroyed—her "manuscript diary" titled "What I Think of My Husband" (Knoepflmacher, 117).

30. Lutyens, *A Blessed Girl*, 217.

31. Lutyens, *A Blessed Girl*, 223.

32. Lutyens, *A Blessed Girl*, 274.

33. Noel Anthony Scawen Lytton, 4th Earl of Lytton, does not put much credence in Lady Emily's version of her dalliance with Blunt. He cites benign, avuncular letters from Blunt such as one that begins, "Dear Emily, So long as you will promise to take care of yourself and get rid of your cough, I will do everything you ask" (44). See Lytton, *Wilfrid Scawen Blunt*, 40–55. Whoever was the anonymous "correspondent" who is quoted in Lady Emily's obituary did not accept her story either. The first of his paragraphs says, "From 17 to 21 Emily Lytton was the friend of the magnificent 'oriental' Englishman, Wilfrid Scawen Blunt. At 21 (when he was 57) she was among the women who fascinated him; when he had been dead for more than 30 years the spell and the danger of him lingered in her so vividly that, in her first book (*A Blessed Girl*), written when she was 80, she proclaimed his dishonourable intentions with charm and some unfairness" ("Lady Emily Lutyens," *The Times*, 4 January 1964, 10). This point of view—that Lady Emily "misunderstood" Blunt's intentions—is contradicted by the letter he wrote to his daughter Judith, saying that "what he had had in

mind would have done Emily all the good in the world" and she "wasn't pretty enough to get much of a husband, and wasn't likely to get such a chance again" (Winstone, *Lady Anne Blunt*, 271).

34. Findlay Dunachie, review of *The Architect and His Wife*, <http://www. samizdata.net/2005/08/an-odd-but-loving-couple/>.

35. Lutyens, *A Blessed Girl*, 287.

36. Lutyens, *A Blessed Girl*, 23.

37. Lutyens, *Krishnamurti*, 82: "*A Blessed Girl* when it was published in October '53 was a great success. It had splendid reviews and sold some 10,000 copies."

38. Anne Blunt, *Journals and Correspondence 1878–1917*, 1883–7, 177.

39. Longford, *Pilgrimage of Passion*, 191.

40. Gregory, Sonnet III, Pethica, ed. "'A Woman's Sonnets.' Lady Gregory, with a Comentary," in Saddlemyer and Smythe, eds, *Lady Gregory, Fifty Years After*, 104.

41. Blunt and Lady Gregory used the spelling *Arabi*, but contemporary transliteration spells the name *Urabi*.

42. Blunt, *Diaries*, 29 December 1913, Fitzwilliam Museum, MS 416/1975.

43. See, for instance, Blunt's letters of 19 January and 9 February 1914 to Lady Gregory, Berg Collection.

44. Gregory, Seventy Years, 4–5.

45. Hill, *Lady Gregory*, 56.

46. Gregory, *Seventy Years*, 34.

47. Cannadine, *The Decline and Fall of the British Aristocracy*, 382.

48. Longford, *Pilgrimage of Passion*, 172.

49. Gregory, *Diaries*, 2 December 1881, Berg Collection.

50. Gregory, *Seventy Years*, 37.

51. Gregory, *Seventy Years*, 37–8.

52. Gregory, *Seventy Years*, 40, 41.

53. Longford, *Pilgrimage of Passion*, 175.

54. Longford, *Pilgrimage of Passion*, 184ff.

55. Longford, "Lady Gregory and Wilfrid Blunt," 90.

56. Blunt, *Alms to Oblivion*, Part VI, "Gods and False Gods," Chapter 6, "The Future of Islam," 55–7, Fitzwilliam Museum, MS 324/1975.

57. All quotations from "Arabi and His Household" are from *The Times* (23 October 1882), 4.

58. For Blunt's own account of his devotion to saving Urabi's life, see *The Wind and the Whirlwind*.

59. AG to WSB, 24 July 1882, Berg Collection.

60. WSB to AG, 26 August 1882, Berg Collection.

61. WSB to AG, 29 August 1882, Berg Collection.

62. AG to WSB, 15 September 1882, Berg Collection.

63. AG to WSB, 17 September 1882, Berg Collection.

64. Gregory, *Seventy Years*, 46.

65. Gregory, *Seventy Years*, 46.

4. A WOMAN'S SONNETS

1. Houston, "Affecting Authenticity," 103.
2. Houston, "Affecting Authenticity," 103.
3. Blunt, *Alms to Oblivion*, Part VI, "Gods and False Gods," Chapter 6: "The Future of Islam," 55–7, Fitzwilliam Museum, MS 324/1975.
4. Longford, *Pilgrimage of Passion*, 194.
5. AG to WSB, 14 October 1891, Berg Collection.
6. Blunt, *Alms to Oblivion*, Part VI, "Gods and False Gods," Chapter 6: "The Future of Islam," 55–7, Fitzwilliam Museum, MS 324/1975.
7. Pethica, "'A Woman's Sonnets.' Lady Gregory, with a Commentary," in Saddlemyer and Smythe, eds, *Lady Gregory, Fifty Years After*, 102.
8. Blunt, *Diaries*, 29 December 1913, Fitzwilliam Museum, MS 416/1975.
9. The story of Blunt's arrest and trial is told in Longford, *Pilgrimage of Passion*, 239–69, and (with less detail) in Lytton, *Wilfrid Scawen Blunt*, 204ff. See also Mitchell, "The Imprisonment of Wilfrid Scawen Blunt in Galway," *passim*.
10. Dakers, *Clouds*, 128.
11. Longford, *Pilgrimage of Passion*, 252; AG to WSB, 29 October 1887, Berg Collection.
12. Mitchell, "The Imprisonment of Wilfrid Scawen Blunt in Galway," 90.
13. Longford, *Pilgrimage of Passion*, 252.
14. WSB to AG, 27 August 1888, Berg Collection.
15. WSB to AG, 4 June 1888, Berg Collection.
16. AG to WSB, 5 June 1888, Berg Collection.
17. Gregory, *Diary*, 11 May 1888, Berg Collection.
18. Mitchell, "The Imprisonment of Wilfrid Scawen Blunt in Galway," 100.
19. Longford, *Pilgrimage of Passion*, 279.
20. Tynan, *Reminiscences*, 120–1.
21. AG to WSB, 5 June 1888, Berg Collection.
22. Mitchell, "The Imprisonment of Wilfrid Scawen Blunt in Galway," 92.
23. Gregory, *Seventy Years*, 13–14.
24. Writers of the Nation, *The Spirit of the Nation*, 25, 34.
25. Mitchell, "The Imprisonment of Wilfrid Scawen Blunt in Galway," 91.
26. AG to WSB, 2 March 1888, Berg Collection.
27. Mitchell, "The Imprisonment of Wilfrid Scawen Blunt in Galway," 91–2.
28. Gregory, "The Felons of Our Land," in *Lady Gregory: Selected Writings*, McDiarmid and Waters, eds, 206.
29. I owe to James L. Pethica the information that these lines were inscribed by Blunt in Lady Gregory's copy of his book *The Wind and the Whirlwind* (London, 1883). See James L. Pethica, "A Dialogue of Self and Service: Lady Gregory's Emergence as an Irish Writer and Partnership with W. B. Yeats," D. Phil. Thesis (Oxford University, 1987), 106.
30. For the text of *Gaol Gate*, see Gregory: *Selected Writings*, McDiarmid and Waters, eds, 356–62. For more examples of Lady Gregory's fixation on the erotic charge of the man "within the gate" and the woman "without," see McDiarmid, "The Demotic Lady Gregory."

31. WSB to AG, 27 August 1888, Berg Collection.
32. Blunt, *Poetical Works, Vol. I*, 150.
33. The Kelmscott edition may be found online at: <https://archive.org/details/TheLove-lyricsSongsOfProteusByWilfridScawenBluntWithThe>.
34. AG to WSB, 5 June 1888, Berg Collection. For Sir William's relationship to his tenants, see Jenkins, *Sir William Gregory of Coole*, 266–99.
35. Gregory, "Dies Irae," 376.
36. In his story "Silence," Colm Tóibín imagines the episode behind Henry James's 1894 diary entry about Lady Gregory. James records a story she told him about a man's reaction to the information that his bride had a previous lover, and Tóibín suggests that the story is Lady Gregory's oblique way of telling James about her own affair with Blunt (3–20).
37. Jenkins, *Sir William Gregory of Coole*, 270.
38. Pethica, ed., *Lady Gregory's Diaries 1892–1902*, 118.
39. Pethica, ed., *Lady Gregory's Diaries 1892–1902*, 183.

5. ALLIANCES AND RIVALRIES

1. Blunt, *My Diaries, Part One*, 291.
2. Blunt, *My Diaries, Part Two*, 28.
3. Blunt, *My Diaries, Part Two*, 53.
4. Blunt, *My Diaries, Part Two*, 100.
5. Murray, *Euripides*, 5.
6. Winstone, *Lady Anne Blunt*, 119.
7. Blunt, *My Diaries, Part Two*, 310.
8. Blunt, *Diaries*, 11 January 1914, Fitzwilliam Museum, MS 417/1975.
9. Foster, *W. B. Yeats, Vol. I*, 509.
10. Longford, *Pilgrimage of Passion*, 396.
11. WSB to AG, 19 January 1914, Berg Collection.
12. Marwil, *Frederic Manning*, 151.
13. Sturge Moore was never one of the Rhymers, although comments on this photograph often identify him as such.
14. Babington Smith, *John Masefield*, 123.
15. Babington Smith, *John Masefield*, 73.
16. Carr, *The Verse Revolutionaries*, 425.
17. Longford, *Pilgrimage of Passion*, 25.
18. Longford, *Pilgrimage of Passion*, 106, 164, 324, 428.
19. See Jeffares, White, and Bridgewater, eds, *Letters to W. B. Yeats and Ezra Pound from Iseult Gonne*, 136–8.
20. Foster, *W. B. Yeats, Vol. II*, 112.
21. WBY to Edith Shackleton Heald, 14 November 1937, Letter 7116, *CL InteLex*.
22. Doyle, *Richard Aldington*, 13.
23. Winstone, *Lady Anne Blunt*, 91, 257. Many of her lovely water-colors may be seen in this biography.

24. Lady Anne's obituary also adds that she was "a first class chess player" and a "remarkable long distance runner" ("Byron's Granddaughter. The Late Baroness Wentworth," *The Times* [29 December 1917], 8).

25. Middleton, "T. Sturge Moore," 336.

26. Bridge, ed., *W. B. Yeats and T. Sturge Moore: Their Correspondence 1901–1937*, 20, 21.

27. Carr, *The Verse Revolutionaries*, 221.

28. Carr, *The Verse Revolutionaries*, 422.

29. Carr, *The Verse Revolutionaries*, 422.

30. WBY to AG, postmarked 1 February 1914, Berg Collection. Yeatsian spelling variations have been silently emended.

31. "Isle of Wight L-Archives," <http://archiver.rootsweb.ancestry.com/th/read/ISLE-OF-WIGHT/ 2001-04/0987360265>. Some of the information on this site is incorrect, such as Marion Plarr's birthdate. However, the dates for Helen Plarr appear to be consistent with other information about the family.

32. The England 1891 Census lists all names of those in the house of Stewart Headlam, "Clerk in Holy Orders"; Yeats, *Autobiographies*, 225.

33. Victor Plarr, ed., *Ernest Dowson, 1888–1897*, 69.

34. But Plarr himself "was no bohemian; his French culture was quite distinct from the 'decadent' and symbolist affections of Symons . . . Plarr's sympathies were fundamentally rational and Republican" (Fletcher, *Collected Poems of Victor Plarr*, xiv).

35. The poet Ernest Dowson, whose letters Plarr was later to edit, was visiting the Plarr family the day the Census was taken. He is listed as "dock master," a phrase the original transcriber misread as "dressmaker." Fletcher says that Plarr was living in Blackheath in 1890 (xii).

36. Marion [Plarr] Barwell, *India Without Sentiment*, 41.

37. Marion Plarr, *Cynara*, 31.

38. Lady Anne Blunt and her daughter Judith both wrote books about breeding Arab horses.

39. The poets had more children than the daughters mentioned here; I focus on one daughter per poet to indicate how the argument about gender plays out in the next generation.

40. As a child Marion Plarr acted in the Granville-Barker production of Yeats's play *Where There is Nothing* (1902). She was born in 1893 and must have been attractive and talented, because as a young girl she acted in a number of other plays. At the age of 11, she was singled out for praise in a review of Maeterlinck's *Aglavaine et Selysette* (produced at the Court Theatre) for her performance as Yssaline (Reginald Farber, "Much Cry and Little Wool," *The Speaker* [26 November 1904], 209). She married Noel Frederick Barwell, the last British barrister of the Calcutta High Court, and died in India. The most recent sighting of Marion Plarr Barwell may be found at <http://www.thehindu.com/todays-paper/

tp-national/wouldn't-have-been-an-author-had-I-not-met-barwell-sankar/article5721044.ece>, where (on 24 February 2014, more than a hundred years after the peacock dinner) she is called "remarkable" by the Bengal writer, Sankar.

41. Longford, *Pilgrimage of Passion*, 396.
42. Blunt, *Diaries*, 20 January 1914, Fitzwilliam Museum, MS 417/1975.
43. "Mr. W. S. Blunt," *The Times* (20 January 1914), 5.
44. WBY to AG, 15 January 1914, Berg Collection.
45. de Rachewiltz et al., eds, *Ezra Pound to His Parents: Letters 1895–1929*, 125.
46. de Rachewiltz et al., eds, *Ezra Pound to His Parents: Letters 1895–1929*, 110.
47. Rainey, *Institutions of Modernism*, 40.
48. WBY to Herbert Grierson, 21 February 1926, Letter 4839, *CL InteLex*.
49. All quotations from the speeches of Blunt and Yeats are taken from the Flint Papers, Harry Ransom Center, The University of Texas at Austin.
50. Blunt, *My Diaries, Part One*, 144.
51. Blunt, *My Diaries, Part One*, 83.
52. Blunt, *My Diaries, Part Two*, 204.
53. The association of meter with national identity is the subject of Martin, *The Rise and Fall of Meter*.
54. Longford, *Pilgrimage of Passion*, 252.
55. Padraic Colum, ed., *An Anthology of Irish Verse*, 297, 139.
56. "W. S. Blunt. Poet, Traveller, and Agitator. A Picturesque Personality," *The Times*, 12 September 1922, 15.
57. WBY to WSB, 7 May 1905, Letter 151, *CL InteLex*.
58. Longford, *Pilgrimage of Passion*, 338, 362, 368.
59. Blunt, *My Diaries, Part Two*, 28.
60. Blunt, *My Diaries, Part Two*, 115.
61. Blunt, *My Diaries, Part Two*, 169.
62. Kelly and Schuchard, eds, *The Collected Letters of W. B. Yeats*, 202.
63. Foster, *W. B. Yeats, Vol. II*, 107.
64. Blunt, *Poetical Works, Vol. II*, 306.
65. Yeats, *The Only Jealousy of Emer and Fighting the Waves*, ed. Winnett, 279.
66. Foster, *W. B. Yeats, Vol. I*, 336.
67. Longenbach, *Stone Cottage*, 71.
68. Pound, "Ferrex on Petulance," 9–10.

6. THE NAKED MUSE

1. WBY to Walter Beals, 15 July 1933, Letter 5916, *CL InteLex*.
2. Blunt, *Diaries*, 19 January 1914, Fitzwilliam Museum, MS 417/1975.
3. "In the Via Sestina," "The Swan," and "The Return" were published in Pound's edited anthology *Des Imagistes* (1914); "Ad Cinerarium" was published in Dowson et al., *The Second Book of the Rhymers' Club* (1892); "Koré" was

published in Manning's *Poems* (1910); "Truth" was published in Masefield's *The Story of a Round-house and Other Poems* (1912); "The Dying Swan" was published in Moore's *The Vinedresser, and Other Poems* (1899); and Yeats's "Where Helen Lived" was published in the volume *Responsibilities* (1914).

4. Reproduced by kind permission of the Estate of Richard Aldington.

5. Carr, *The Verse Revolutionaries*, 262.

6. See Carr's discussion of the possible influence of Frazer's *The Golden Bough* on this poem, *The Verse Revolutionaries* (262–4).

7. "Koré" was originally dedicated to "Mrs. W. N. MacMillan," an American woman from St Louis who in 1904 traveled to Abyssinia with her husband and with Sir John Harrington, then continuing alone along the upper Nile with only "my doctor, my maid, and my body guard" (*New York Times*, 18 July 1904); see Manning, *Poems*, 38–9.

8. Yeats, *OBMV*, xxvi.

9. Froula, *A Guide to Ezra Pound's Selected Poems*, 43.

10. Mandelbaum, ed., *Selected Writings of Edward Sapir in Language, Culture, and Personality*, 496.

11. Pound, *Des Imagistes*, 35.

12. EP to FSF, n.d. [January 1914], Flint Papers, Harry Ransom Center, The University of Texas at Austin.

13. Carr, *The Verse Revolutionaries*, 543–4.

14. WBY to Hilaire Belloc, 20 June 1936, Letter 6584, *CL InteLex*.

15. Lady Gregory and Yeats visited Blunt at Newbuildings for a few days beginning 15 May 1915, but from Blunt's description (in his unpublished diaries) it seems unlikely there was any singing on that occasion. He writes, "*May 16 Sunday.* Mark Napier and Belloc came to dinner but they did not amalgamate well with the other two. Belloc and Yeats showed themselves shy of each other as rival literary lions, though Mark and Lady Gregory were more or less old friends from Arabi times. So we did not get as much confidential news from Belloc as usual." Thanks to James Kelly for transcribing this passage. Blunt, *Diaries*, 16 May 1915, Fitzwilliam Museum, MS 15/1975.

16. de Rachewiltz et al., eds, *Ezra Pound to His Parents*, 168.

17. WBY to DW, 30 June 1936, Letter 6596, *CL InteLex*.

18. An original copy of the Broadside may be found in the James J. Burns Library, Boston College.

19. Belloc, *Collected Verse*, 103.

20. At this time Belloc's beloved wife Elodie was dying; she got sick on 23 December and died on 3 February (Speaight, *The Life of Hilaire Belloc*, 342).

21. Blunt, *Poetical Works, Vol. I*, 380–1.

22. Longford, *Pilgrimage of Passion*, 396.

23. Pound, "Homage to Wilfrid Blunt," 220. The word "swindles" turns up sixteen times in Pound's "Radio Speeches of World War II"; see

<http://www.whale.to/b/pound.html>. In, for instance, the broadcast of 2 October 1941, see the phrases "Anglo-Jew Empire" and "this so bloody series of swindles."

24. Blunt, *Secret History of the English Occupation of Egypt*, 26.
25. Blunt, "The Ballad of Sir Roger Casement," holograph ms. 5463, McGarrity Papers, National Library of Ireland.
26. Blunt, *My Diaries, Part Two*, 224.
27. Blunt, My *Diaries, Part Two*, 370.
28. Longford, *Pilgrimage of Passion*, 394.
29. Donaldson, *The Marconi Scandal*, 227.
30. Aldington, *Life for Life's Sake*, 168.
31. For Plarr's anti-imperialism, see Part one of his daughter's affectionate memoir, *India Without Sentiment* by Marion Barwell.
32. Aldington, *Life for Life's Sake*, 168.

7. "A REALLY IMPORTANT EVENT"

1. WBY to AG, postmarked 1 February 1914, Berg Collection.
2. "George Clerk," <http://en.wikipedia.org/wiki/George_Clerk_(diplomat)>.
3. Pound and Litz, eds, *Ezra Pound and Dorothy Shakespear*, 283.
4. AG to WSB, 5 February 1914, Berg Collection.
5. Blunt, *Poetical Works, Vol. I*, 86.
6. Yeats, *OBMV*, vi.
7. EP to WSB, 20 January 1914, West Sussex Record Office.
8. Blunt Papers, West Sussex Record Office.
9. Pound, *The Letters of Ezra Pound to Alice Corbin Henderson*, ed. Nadel, 67.
10. EP to WSB, 21 January 1914, West Sussex Record Office; WSB to AG, 28 January 1914, Berg Collection.
11. Copp, ed., *The Fourth Imagist*, 18.
12. FSF to WSB, 26 January 1914, WSRO Blunt Mss Box 21, West Sussex Record Office.
13. EP to FSF, n.d. [early summer 1914], F. S. Flint Papers, Harry Ransom Center, The University of Texas at Austin.
14. EP to FSF, 21 July 1914, postcard, F. S. Flint Papers, Harry Ransom Center, The University of Texas at Austin.
15. EP to FSF, undated, F. S. Flint Papers, Harry Ransom Center, The University of Texas at Austin.
16. WBY to AG, postmarked 1 February 1914, Berg Collection.
17. ". . . he is called 'The Sheep in sheep's clothing . . .'" AG to WSB, 5 February 1914, Berg Collection.
18. AG to WSB, 21 January 1914, West Sussex Record Office.
19. Longford, *Pilgrimage of Passion*, 397; Blunt, *Diaries*, 19 April 1914, Fitzwilliam Museum, MS 418/1975.

20. Blunt, *Diaries*, 25 March and 26 March 1914, Fitzwilliam Museum, MS 417/1975.
21. Longford, *Pilgrimage of Passion*, 398.
22. WBY to AG, postmarked 1 February 1914, Berg Collection. The text of this letter has been silently emended to omit the variant spellings Yeats offers for several names.
23. WSB to AG, 19 January 1914, Berg Collection.
24. Meynell, ed., *Friends of a Lifetime*, 186.
25. Blunt, *Diaries*, 19 January 1914, Fitzwilliam Museum, MS 417/1975.
26. Blunt, *Diaries*, 20 January 1914, Fitzwilliam Museum, MS 417/1975.
27. Blunt, *Diaries*, 25 January 1914, Fitzwilliam Museum, MS 417/1975.
28. WSB to AG, 7 January 1914, Berg Collection.
29. WSB to AG, 24 October 1914, Berg Collection.
30. Blunt, *Diaries*, 28 December 1913, Fitzwilliam Museum, MS 416/1975.
31. WSB to AG, 7 January 1914, Berg Collection.
32. WSB to AG, 19 January 1914, Berg Collection.
33. Blunt, *Poetical Works, Vol. I*, v.
34. AG to WSB, 27 December 1914, Berg Collection.
35. WSB to AG, 31 December 1914, Berg Collection.
36. WSB to AG, 19 January 1914, Berg Collection.
37. WSB to AG, 19 January 1914; 9 February 1914; and 24 October 1914, Berg Collection.
38. Blunt, *My Diaries, Part Two*, 252.
39. Yeats, *The Only Jealousy of Emer and Fighting the Waves*, ed. Winnett, xxxiii.
40. Yeats, *The Letters of W. B. Yeats*, ed. Wade, 612.
41. Longford, *Pilgrimage of Passion*, 365–6.
42. Saddlemyer, ed., *W. B. Yeats and George Yeats*, 256–7.
43. Blunt, *My Diaries, Part Two*, 105.
44. Blunt, *Poetical Works, Vol. II*, 305–6.
45. Saddlemyer, ed., *W. B. Yeats and George Yeats*, 10.
46. Saddlemyer, *Becoming George*, 98.
47. Saddlemyer, ed., *W. B. Yeats and George Yeats*, 40, 44.
48. Saddlemyer, ed., *W. B. Yeats and George Yeats*, 45.
49. Saddlemyer, *Becoming George*, 473–4.

8. A LIVE TRADITION

1. Pound, "Status Rerum," 127.
2. Pound, review of *Ernest Dowson* by Plarr, 43, 45.
3. Victor Plarr, ed., *Ernest Dowson 1888–1897*, 9, 14, 16.
4. Victor Plarr, ed., *Ernest Dowson 1888–1897*, 16.
5. Victor Plarr, ed., *Ernest Dowson 1888–1897*, 103.
6. Pound, Review of *Ernest Dowson* by Victor Plarr, 43.

7. Yeats, *Autobiographies*, 251.
8. The description is no longer on line. The book is owned by the library of the University of Delaware.
9. de Rachewiltz et al., eds, *Ezra Pound to His Parents*, 171.
10. Rubin, "Some Heroic Discipline," 14.
11. Yeats, *OBMV*, xi–xii.
12. WBY includes poems by Bridges (who declined the invitation) and Masefield (whose poem was in the marble box but who didn't attend), but not Manning (whose "Koré" was in the marble box but who didn't attend).
13. WBY to EP, 12 November 1935, Letter 6440, *CL InteLex*.
14. Yeats, *OBVM*, xvi.
15. Rubin, "Some Heroic Discipline," 163–4.
16. Yeats, *OBMV*, v–vi.
17. WBY, Letter 6440. *The Collected Letters of W. B. Yeats.* Electronic edition, ed. John Kelly, et al., <http://www.nlx.com/collections/130>.
18. Yeats, *OBMV*, xxiv–xxv.

EPILOGUE: THE LONG PEACOCK DINNER

1. "W. S. Blunt. Poet, Traveller, and Agitator. A Picturesque Personality," *The Times*, 12 September 1922, 15.
2. Blunt, *Diaries*, 19 January 1914, Fitzwilliam Museum, MS 417/1975.
3. It was not Lady Gregory's only affair; she had a brief affair with the wealthy American lawyer and patron of the arts John Quinn, but it was not an adulterous affair. Lady Gregory was then a widow, and Quinn was unmarried.
4. In 1948, the Bollingen Foundation (founded by Paul Mellon) gave funds to the Library of Congress for the awarding of a prize to honor the best new book of poems each year. The prize was given for the first time in 1949 to Pound's *Pisan Cantos*. See "The Bollingen Prize for Poetry at Yale," <http://brbl-archive.library.yale.edu/programs/bollingen/>.
5. Leick, "Ezra Pound v. *The Saturday Review of Literature*," 19–37.
6. Leick, "Ezra Pound v. *The Saturday Review of Literature*," 31.
7. Leick, "Ezra Pound v. *The Saturday Review of Literature*," 21–5.
8. Leick, "Ezra Pound v. *The Saturday Review of Literature*," 23–4.
9. Travisano and Hamilton, eds, *Words in Air*, 58.
10. Dorothy Carleton was not at Newbuildings for the peacock dinner; she was in London that week. Blunt's diary says "Dorothy has gone to London for a week, and Miss Hawsin has come to keep me company" (*Diaries*, 16 January 1914, Fitzwilliam Museum, MS 417/1975). Pound

met her in March when he and Aldington went down to Newbuildings Place to visit WSB again.

11. In 1948, Pound and Aldington were the only ones of the poets still alive, but Lord Osborne Beauclerk, Blunt's neighbor who had also attended the dinner, was still alive. See <http://thepeerage.com/>: Osbourne de Vere Beauclerk, 12th Duke of St Albans M, #11696, b. 16 October 1874, d. 2 March 1964.

12. Hamilton, ed., *The Letters of Robert Lowell*, 3, 4.

13. Wilde, "Poetry and Prison," *Pall Mall Gazette* XLIX:7425 (3 January 1889), 3.

Bibliography

MANUSCRIPT SOURCES

The Henry W. and Albert A. Berg Collection of English and American Literature, The New York Public Library, Astor, Lenox, and Tilden Foundations
Lady Gregory Papers.
William Butler Yeats Papers.

John J. Burns Library, Boston College
Hilaire Belloc Papers, MS.2005.002.

Fitzwilliam Museum, University of Cambridge
Blunt Papers, MSS 1–38, 13–1975.

Harry Ransom Center, The University of Texas at Austin
F. S. Flint Papers.

National Library of Ireland
McGarrity Papers: Blunt, Wilfrid Scawen, "The Ballad of Sir Roger Casement," Holograph ms. 5463.

University of Delaware Library
Ezra Pound, *A Quinzaine for this Yule*, with inscription by Victor Plarr.

West Sussex Record Office
WSRO Blunt Manuscripts Box 21.

NEWSPAPERS

The Times (London)
"Arabi and his Household," 23 October 1882, 4.
"Byron's Granddaughter. The Late Baroness Wentworth," 29 December, 1917, 8.
"Lady Emily Lutyens," 4 January, 1964, 10.

"Mr F. S. Flint," 20 February, 1964, 14.
"Mr Hardy on Literature," 4 June, 1912, 7.
"Mr W. S. Blunt," 20 January, 1914, 5.
"Presentation to Lord Harrington," 10 January, 1914, 10.
"Poets' Tribute to Thomas Hardy," 31 October, 1919, 15.
"W. S. Blunt. Poet, Traveller, and Agitator, A Picturesque Personality," 12 September, 1922, 15.

UNPUBLISHED ACADEMIC WORK

Lees, Maureen, "Secret Histories: Lady Gregory's Egyptian Intrigues," M.A. thesis, Villanova University, May 1996.
Pethica, James L. "A Dialogue of Self and Service: Lady Gregory's Emergence as an Irish Writer and Partnership with W. B. Yeats," D. Phil. Thesis, Oxford University, 1987.
Rubin, Robert Alden, "Some Heroic Discipline: William Butler Yeats and the Oxford Book of Modern Verse," Ph.D. thesis, University of North Carolina, Chapel Hill, 2011.

BOOKS AND ARTICLES

Primary Sources

Aldington, Richard, "Presentation to Mr. W. S. Blunt," *The Egoist* 1, 3 (February 1914): 56–7.
——, *Life for Life's Sake: A Book of Reminiscences* (New York: Viking, 1941).
——, *The Complete Poems* (London: Allan Wingate, 1948).
Allt, Peter and Russell K. Alsbach, *The Variorum Edition of the Poems of W. B. Yeats* (New York: Macmillan, 1977).
Barwell, Marion (*see under* Plarr, Marion).
Belloc, Hilaire, *Collected Verse* (Harmondsworth: Penguin, 1958).
Blunt, Lady Anne, *Journals and Correspondence 1878–1917* (Cheltenham, Glos.: Alexander Heriot, 1986).
Blunt, Wilfrid Scawen, *The Wind and the Whirlwind* (London: Kegan Paul Trench, 1883).
——, *The Land War in Ireland; Being a Personal Narrative of Events* (London: Stephen Swift, 1912).
——, *The Poetical Works, Vol. I* (London: Macmillan, 1914).
——, *The Poetical Works, Vol. II* (London: Macmillan, 1914).
——, *My Diaries: Being a Personal Narrative of Events, Part One: 1888–1900* (New York: Knopf, 1921).
——, *My Diaries: Being a Personal Narrative of Events, Part Two: 1900–1914* (New York: Knopf, 1921).
——, *Secret History of the English Occupation of Egypt* (New York: Knopf, 1922).

Bridge, Ursula, ed., *W. B. Yeats and T. Sturge Moore: Their Correspondence 1901–1937* (London: Routledge & Kegan Paul, 1953).

Copp, Michael, ed., *The Fourth Imagist: Selected Poems of F. S. Flint* (Madison, NJ: Fairleigh Dickinson University Press, 2007).

——, *Imagist Dialogues: Letters Between Aldington, Flint, and Others* (Cambridge: Lutterworth Press, 2009).

de Rachewiltz, Mary A. *Ezra Pound, Father and Teacher: Discretions* (New York: New Directions, 2005).

——, David Moody, and Joanna Moody, eds, *Ezra Pound to His Parents: Letters 1895–1929* (Oxford: Oxford University Press, 2010).

Dowson, Ernest, Ellis, Edwin, Greene, G. A., et al., *The Second Book of the Rhymers' Club* (London: Elkin Mathews and John Lane, 1894).

Eliot, Valerie and Hugh Haughton, eds, *The Letters of T. S. Eliot, Vol. 1: 1898–1922* (London: Faber and Faber, 2011).

Finneran, Richard J., ed., *The Correspondence of Robert Bridges and W. B. Yeats* (London: Macmillan, 1977).

Fletcher, Ian, ed., *Collected Poems of Victor Plarr* (London: E. & J. Stevens, 1974).

Flint, F. S., "Imagisme," *Poetry* 1, 6 (March 1913): 198–200.

——, "Wilfrid Scawen Blunt," *Poetry and Drama* (March 1914): 5.

Gregory, Augusta, "Dies Irae," *The Sketch* (25 March 1896): 376.

——, *Seventy Years: Being the Autobiography of Lady Gregory*, ed. Colin Smythe (New York: Macmillan, 1974).

——, *Lady Gregory: Selected Writings*, Lucy McDiarmid and Maureen Waters, eds (London: Penguin, 1995).

Hamilton, Saskia, ed., *The Letters of Robert Lowell* (New York: Farrar, Straus, & Giroux, 2005).

Jeffares, A. N., Anna White, and Christina Bridgewater, eds, *Letters to W. B. Yeats and Ezra Pound from Iseult Gonne: A Girl That Knew All Dante Once* (New York: Palgrave Macmillan, 2004).

Kelly, John and Ronald Schuchard, eds, *The Collected Letters of W. B. Yeats, Vol. III: 1901–1904* (Oxford: Clarendon Press, 1994).

Lutyens, Lady Emily, *A Blessed Girl: Memoirs of a Victorian Girlhood Chronicled in an Exchange of Letters 1887–1896* (New York and Philadelphia: Lippincott, 1954).

Manning, Frederic, *Poems* (London: Murray, 1910).

Masefield, John, *The Story of a Round-House and Other Poems* (New York: Macmillan, 1912).

Meynell, Violet, ed., *Friends of a Lifetime: Letters to Sydney Carlyle Cockerell* (London: Jonathan Cape, 1940).

Moore, Thomas Sturge, *The Vinedresser, and Other Poems* (London: At the Sign of the Unicorn, 1899).

Murray, Gilbert, *Euripides, Translated into English Rhyming Verse* (New York: Longmans Green; London: George Allen, 1912).

Nadel, Ira B., ed., *The Letters of Ezra Pound to Alice Corbin Henderson* (Austin: The University of Texas Press, 1993).

Newbolt, Margaret, ed., *The Later Life and Letters of Sir Henry Newbolt* (London: Faber and Faber, 1942).

Paige, D. D., ed., *The Letters of Ezra Pound 1907–1941* (New York: Harcourt Brace, 1950).

Pethica, James, ed., "'A Woman's Sonnets.' Lady Gregory, with a Commentary," in Ann Saddlemyer and Colin Smythe, eds, *Lady Gregory, Fifty Years After* (Gerrards Cross, Bucks: Colin Smythe, 1987), 98–122.

——, *Lady Gregory's Diaries: 1892–1902* (Gerrards Cross, Bucks: Colin Smythe, 1996).

Plarr, Marion, *Cynara: The Story of Ernest and Adelaide* (London: Grant Richards, 1933).

——, (as Barwell, Marion), *India Without Sentiment: An Autobiography* (Calcutta: New Age Publishers, 1960).

Plarr, Victor, ed., *Ernest Dowson, 1888–1897: Reminiscences, Unpublished Letters and Marginalia* (London: Elkin Mathews, 1914).

Plato, *Symposium*, trans. W. R. M. Lamb (Cambridge, Massachusetts and London: Harvard University Press, 1925, rpt. 1996).

Pound, Ezra, "Status Rerum," *Poetry Magazine* 1, 4 (January 1913): 123–7.

——, "A Few Don'ts for an Imagiste," *Poetry: A Magazine of Verse* 1, 6 (March 1913): 200–6.

——, "How I Began," *T. P.'s Weekly* 21 (6 June 1913): 707.

——, ed., *Des Imagistes: An Anthology* (New York: Albert and Charles Boni, 1914).

——, "Ferrex on Petulance," *The Egoist* 1, 1 (1 January 1914): 9–10.

——, "Porrex on Ferrex," *The Egoist* 1, 1 (1 January 1914): 10.

——, "Homage to Wilfrid Blunt," *Poetry: A Magazine of Verse* 3, 6 (March 1914): 220–3.

——, Review of *Ernest Dowson*, by Victor Plarr, *Poetry: A Magazine of Verse* 6, 1 (April 1915): 43–5.

——, *Selected Poems* (New York: New Directions, 1957).

——, *Literary Essays of Ezra Pound*, ed. T. S. Eliot (New York: New Directions 1968, rpt).

——, *The Cantos* (New York: New Directions, 1972).

——, *Ezra Pound: Prose 1909–1965*, ed. Wiliam Cookson (New York: New Directions, 1973).

Pound, Omar and A. Walton Litz, eds, *Ezra Pound and Dorothy Shakespear: Their Letters: 1909–1914* (New York: New Directions, 1984).

Saddlemyer, Ann, ed., *W. B. Yeats and George Yeats: The Letters* (Oxford: Oxford University Press, 2011).

Smith, J. Walter, "The Book in London: A Tribute to the Literary Work of Wilfrid Blunt," *Boston Evening Transcript* (14 February 1914): 7.

Travisano, Thomas and Saskia Hamilton, eds, *Words in Air: The Complete Correspondence Between Elizabeth Bishop and Robert Lowell* (New York: Farrar, Straus, & Giroux, 2010).

Wade, Allan, ed., *The Letters of W. B. Yeats* (London: Rupert Hart-Davis, 1954).

Wilde, Oscar, "Poetry and Prison," *Pall Mall Gazette*, 3 January 1889.

Winnett, Steven, ed., *The Only Jealousy of Emer and Fighting the Waves. Manuscript Materials. By W. B. Yeats* (Ithaca: Cornell University Press, 2004).

Writers of the Nation, *The Spirit of the Nation* (Dublin: Duffy, 1845).

Yeats, W. B., *The Oxford Book of Modern Verse 1892–1935* (New York: Oxford University Press, 1936).

——, *The Variorum Edition of the Poems of W. B. Yeats*, ed. Peter Alit and Russell K. Aispach (New York: Macmillan, 1957).

——, *Explorations* (New York: Macmillan, 1962).

——, *Autobiographies* (New York: Macmillan, 1965; New York: Scribner, 1999).

——, *The Collected Letters of W. B. Yeats*. Electronic edition, ed. John Kelly et al., <http://www.nlx.com/collections/130>. Intelex Corporation, 2014.

Zilboorg, Caroline, *Richard Aldington and H.D.: Their Lives in Letters 1918–1961* (Manchester and New York: Manchester University Press, 2003).

Secondary Sources

Beerbohm, Max, *Seven Men and Two Others* (Oxford: Oxford University Press, rpt 1980).

Blessington, Marguerite, Countess of, *The Idler in Italy* (Paris: Baudry's European Library, 1839).

Brooker, Peter, *Bohemia in London: The Social Scene of Early Modernism* (Basingstoke and New York: Palgrave Macmillan, 2007).

Cannadine, David, *The Decline and Fall of the British Aristocracy* (New York: Random House, 1990).

Carpenter, Humphrey, *A Serious Character: The Life of Ezra Pound* (New York: Bantam Doubleday, 1988).

Carr, Helen, *The Verse Revolutionaries: Ezra Pound, H.D. and the Imagists* (London: Jonathan Cape, 2009).

Coleman, Verna, *The Last Exquisite: A Portrait of Frederic Manning* (Melbourne: Melbourne University Press, 1990).

Colum, Mary, *Life and the Dream* (New York: Doubleday, 1947).

Colum, Padraic, ed., *An Anthology of Irish Verse* (New York: Liveright, 1948).

Dakers, Caroline, *Clouds: The Biography of a Country House* (New Haven and London: Yale University Press, 1993).

Day, Elizabeth, "January 1914: Suffragettes, Blizzards, Exploration—But No Hint of War," *The Guardian/The Observer*, 4 January 2014: <http://www.theguardian.com/world/2014/jan/04/january-1914-no-hint-war>.

Donaldson, Frances, *The Marconi Scandal* (London: Rupert Hart-Davis, 1962).

Doyle, Charles, *Richard Aldington: A Biography* (London: Macmillan, 1989).

Eisler, Benita, *Byron: Child of Passion, Fool of Fame* (New York: Vintage Books, 1999).

Farjeon, Eleanor, *Edward Thomas: The Last Four Years* (Oxford: Oxford University Press, 1958).

Finch, Edith, *Wilfrid Scawen Blunt 1840–1922* (London: Jonathan Cape, 1938).

Foster, R. F., *W. B. Yeats: A Life. Vol. I: The Apprentice Mage 1865–1914* (New York: Oxford University Press, 1997).

——, *W. B. Yeats: A Life. Vol. II: The Arch-Poet 1915–1939* (New York: Oxford University Press, 2003).

Frelinghuysen, Alice Cooney, *Louis Comfort Tiffany and Laurelton Hall: An Artist's Country Estate* (New York: Metropolitan Museum of Art and Yale University Press, 2006).

Froula, Christine, *A Guide to Ezra Pound's Selected Poems* (New York: New Directions, 1982).

Getsy, David, "Give and Take: Henri Gaudier-Brzeska's Coffer for Wilfrid Scawen Blunt and Ezra Pound's Homosocial Modernism in 1914," *Sculpture Journal* 16, 2 (Fall 2007): 43.

Girouard, Mark, *The Return to Camelot: Chivalry and the English Gentleman* (New Haven and London: Yale University Press, 1981).

Going, William T., "A Peacock Dinner: The Homage of Pound and Yeats to Wilfred [*sic*] Scawen Blunt," *Journal of Modern Literature* 1, 3 (March 1971): 303–10.

Gwynn, Frederic, *Sturge Moore and the Life of Art* (Lawrence, Kansas: University of Kansas Press, 1951).

Hallett Hughes, Penelope, *The Immortal Dinner: A Famous Evening of Genius & Laughter in Literary London, 1817* (Chicago, IL: New Amsterdam Books, 2002).

Hardy, Florence Emily, *The Later Years of Thomas Hardy, 1892–1928* (London: Macmillan, 1930).

Hassall, Christopher, *A Biography of Edward Marsh* (New York: Harcourt Brace, 1959).

Hill, Judith, *Lady Gregory: An Irish Life* (Cork: Collins Press, 2011).

Homberger, Eric, "A Glimpse of Pound in 1912 by Arundel del Re," *Paideuma* 3 (1974): 86–8.

Houston, Natalie M., "Affecting Authenticity: *Sonnets from the Portuguese* and *Modern Love*," *Studies in the Literary Imagination* 35, 2 (Fall 2002): 99–121.

Jenkins, Brian, *Sir William Gregory of Coole* (Gerrards Cross, Bucks: Colin Smythe, 1986).

Kenner, Hugh, *The Pound Era* (Berkeley, CA: University of California Press, 1971).

Knoepflmacher, U.C., "Hardy Ruins: Female Spaces and Male Designs," in *The Sense of Sex: Feminist Perspectives on Hardy*, ed. Margaret R. Higgonet (Champaign, Illinois: University of Illinois Press, 1992), 107–131.

Kohfeldt, Mary Lou, *Lady Gregory: The Woman Behind the Irish Renaissance* (New York: Atheneum, 1985).

Kostenbaum, Wayne, *Double Talk: The Erotics of Male Literary Collaboration* (New York and London: Routledge, 1989).

Lambert, Angela, *Unquiet Souls: The Indian Summer of the British Aristocracy* (London: Macmillan 1984).

Leick, Karen, "Ezra Pound v. *The Saturday Review of Literature*," *Journal of Modern Literature* 25, 2 (2001–2002): 19–37.

Longenbach, James, *Stone Cottage: Pound, Yeats, and Modernism* (New York: Oxford University Press, 1988).

——, "Ezra Pound at Home," *Southwest Review* 94, 2 (2009): 147–59.

Longford, Elizabeth, *A Pilgrimage of Passion: The Life of Wilfrid Scawen Blunt* (New York: Knopf, 1980).

——"Wilfrid Scawen Blunt," in *The Craft of Literary Biography*, ed. J. Myers (London: Macmillan, 1985), 55–68.

——, "Lady Gregory and Wilfrid Scawen Blunt," in *Lady Gregory: Fifty Years After*, Ann Saddlemyer and Colin Smythe, eds (Gerrards Cross, Bucks: Colin Smythe, 1987), 85–97.

Lutyens, Mary, *Krishnamurti: The Years of Fulfillment* (New York: Avon, 1984).

——, *Edwin Lutyens* (London: Black Swan, rev. 1991).

Lytton, Noel Anthony Scawen, Fourth Earl of, *Wilfrid Scawen Blunt: A Memoir by his Grandson* (London: MacDonald, 1961).

McDayter, Ghislaine, *Byromania and the Birth of Celebrity Culture* (Albany: State University of New York Press, 2009).

McDiarmid, Lucy, "The Demotic Lady Gregory," in Maria DiBattista and Lucy McDiiarmid, eds, *High and Low Moderns: Literature and Culture 1889–1939* (New York: Oxford University Press, 1996), 212–34.

——, "Lady Gregory, Wilfrid Blunt, and London Table Talk," *Irish University Review* 43, 1 (Spring/Summer 2004): 67–80.

——, "A Box for Wilfrid Blunt," *PMLA* (special issue on poetry), 120, 1 (January 2005): 163–80.

——, "The Abbey, Its 'Helpers,' and the Field of Cultural Production in 1913," in John P. Harrington, ed., *Irish Theatre in America: Essays on Irish Theatrical Diaspora* (Syracuse: Syracuse University Press, 2009), 93–102.

——, "Resentment on the Menu: Poets of the Peacock Dinner," Commentary, *TLS* (17 January 2014): 14–15.

Mandelbaum, David G., ed., *Selected Writings of Edward Sapir in Language, Culture, and Personality* (Berkeley, CA: University of California Press, 1985).

Marsh, Alec, *Ezra Pound* (London: Reaktion Books, 2011).

Marsh, Sir Edward, *A Number of People: A Book of Reminiscences* (London: Heinemann, 1939).

Martin, Meredith, *The Rise and Fall of Meter: Poetry and English National Culture, 1860–1930* (Princeton, NJ and Oxford: Princeton University Press, 2012).

Marwil, Jonathan, *Frederic Manning: An Unfinished Life* (Durham, NC: Duke University Press, 1988).

Menand, Louis, *Discovering Modernism: T. S. Eliot and His Context* (New York and Oxford: Oxford University Press, 1987).

Merrill, Linda, *The Peacock Room: A Cultural Biography* (Washington, D.C.: Freer Gallery of Art in association with Yale University Press, 1998).

Middleton, David W., "T. Sturge Moore," in Donald E. Stanford, ed., *British Poets, 1880–1914*, Vol. 19 of *Dictionary of Literary Biography* (Detroit: Gale, 1983), 333–53.

Mitchell, James, "The Imprisonment of Wilfrid Scawen Blunt in Galway: Cause and Consequence," *Journal of the Galway Archaeological and Historical Society* 46 (1994): 65–110.

Mole, Tom, *Byron's Romantic Celebrity* (Basingstoke: Palgrave Macmillan, 2007).

Moody, A. David, *Ezra Pound: Poet—A Portrait of the Man and His Work. Vol. I: The Young Genius 1895–1920* (New York and Oxford: Oxford University Press, 2007).

N. A., *Society for Pure English, Tract No. 1* (Oxford: Oxford University Press, 1919).

Nilsen, Lauryvik J., "The Coming Cubists Explain Their Picture Puzzles. Picasso and Cézanne Tell Us What They Mean," *Boston Evening Transcript* (12 April 1913): part 3, 2.

Parini, Jay, *Robert Frost: A Life* (New York: Henry Holt, 1999).

Pater, Walter, *The Renaissance. Studies in Art and Poetry*, ed. Adam Philips (Oxford: Oxford University Press, 1986).

Perkin, Harold James, *The Rise of Professional Society: England Since 1880* (London: Routledge, 1989).

Perry, Anne, *Belgrave Square* (New York: Ballantine Books, 2011).

Phillips, Catherine, *Robert Bridges: A Biography* (New York: Oxford University Press, 1992).

Rabaté, Jean-Michel, *1913: The Cradle of Modernism* (London: Blackwell, 2007).

Rainey, Lawrence, *Institutions of Modernism: Literary Elites and Political Culture* (New Haven and London: Yale University Press, 1998).

Rhys, Ernest, *Everyman Remembers* (New York: J. J. Little & Ives, 1931).

Rice, Nelljean, *A New Matrix for Modernism: A Study of the Lives and Poetry of Charlotte Mew & Anna Wickham* (London: Routledge, 2003).

Ridley, Jane, *The Architect and His Wife: A Life of Edwin Lutyens* (London: Chatto & Windus, 2002).

Saddlemyer, Ann, *Becoming George: The Life of Mrs. W. B. Yeats* (Oxford: Oxford University Press, 2002).

——, and Colin Smythe, eds, *Lady Gregory: Fifty Years After* (Gerrards Cross, Bucks: Colin Smythe, 1987).

Schuchard, Ronald, *The Last Minstrels: Yeats and the Revival of the Bardic Arts* (Oxford: Oxford University Press, 2008).

Shattuck, Roger, *The Banquet Years: The Origins of the Avant-Garde in France, 1885 to World War 1* (New York: Random House, 1955).

Sheeran, Patrick F., "The Absence of Galway City from the Literature of the Revival," in D. Ó Cearbhaill, *Galway: Town and Gown, 1484–1984*, (Dublin: Gill and Macmillan, 1984), 223–44.

——, "Wilfrid Scawen Blunt: A Tourist of the Revolutions," in Wolfgang Zach and Heinz Kosok, eds, *Literary Interrelations: Ireland, England and the World* (Tübingen: Gunter Narr Verlag, 1987), 153–60.

Silber, Evelyn and David Finn, *Gaudier-Brzeska: Life and Art* (London and New York: Thames and Hudson, 1996).

Smith, Constance Babington, *John Masefield: A Life* (Stroud, Glos: The History Press, 2008 rpt).

Smith, Denis Edwin, *From Symposium to Eucharist: The Banquet in the Early Christian World* (Minneapolis: Augsburg Fortress, 2003).

Speaight, Robert, *The Life of Hilaire Belloc* (New York: Farrar, Straus, & Cudahy, 1957).

Speare, M. E., *The Pocket Book of Verse* (New York: The Pocket Library, 1958, third edn).

Street, Sean, *The Dymock Poets* (Mid Glamorgan: Poetry Wales Press, 1994).

Sullivan, J. P., ed., *Ezra Pound: A Critical Anthology* (London: Penguin, 1970).

Tell, Darcy, ed., "The Armory Show at 100," *Archives of American Art Journal* 51, 3–4 (2013): 1–80.

Tetreault, James, "Heirs to His Virtues: Byron, Blunt, Gobineau," *Byron Journal* 16 (1988): 57–70.

Tóibín, Colm, "Silence," in *The Empty Family* (New York: Scribner, 2011), 1–20.

Tynan, Katharine, *Reminiscences* (London: Smith, Elder, 1913).

Van den Beukel, Karlien, "Arthur Symons's Night Life," in Valeria Tinkler-Villani, ed., *Babylon or New Jerusalem? Perceptions of the City in Literature* (Amsterdam: Rodopi, 2005), 136–54.

Vaughan Jones, Jennifer, *Anna Wickham: A Poet's Daring Life* (Lanham, MD: Madison Books, 2003).

Walkowitz, Judith, *Nights Out: Life in Cosmopolitan London* (New Haven and London: Yale University Press, 2012).

Whelpton, Vivien, *Richard Aldington: Poet, Soldier and Lover, 1911–1929* (Cambridge: Lutterworth Press, 2014).

Wilde, Oscar, "Poetry and Prison," *Pall Mall Gazette* XLIX:7425 (3 January 1889), 3.

Winstone, H. V. F., *Lady Anne Blunt: A Biography* (London: Barzan, 2003).

WEB SITES AND ELECTRONIC RESOURCES

1891 England Census, <http://www.ukcensusonline.com/census/1981.php>.

"Biography: A brief Life of Count Stenbock," <http://www.mmhistory. org.uk/cce/Jo/biography.htm>.

"The Bollingen Prize for Poetry at Yale," <http://brbl-archive.library.yale. edu/programs/bollingen>.

Day, Elizabeth, "January 1914: Suffragettes, Blizzards, Exploration—But No Hint of War," <http://www.theguardian.comworld/2014/jan/04/ january-1914-no-hint-war>.

Dunachie, Findlay, Review of *The Architect and His Wife: A Life of Edwin Lutyens*, < http://www.samizdata.net/author/findlay/>.

"Ezra Pound Speaking," <http://www.whale.to/b/pound.html>.

"George Clerk," <http://en.wikipedia.org/wiki/George_Clerk_(diplomat)>.

Hall, Donald, "Ezra Pound, The Art of Poetry No. 5," *Paris Review* 28 (Summer–Fall 1960), <http://www.theparisreview.org/interviews/4598/ the-art-of-poetry-no-5-ezra-pound>.

"India Today," <http://indiatoday.intoday.in/content_mail.php?option= com_content&name=print&id=14532>.

"Isle of Wight L-Archive," <http://archiver.rootsweb.ancestry.com/th/ read/ISLE-OF-WIGHT/2001-04/0987360265>.

"The Love-Lyrics & Songs of Proteus by Wilfrid Scawen Blunt," <http://archive.org/details/TheLove-lyricsSongsofProteusByWilfirds ScawenBluntWithThe>.

"The Peacock Room: A Closer Look," Freer Gallery of Art and Arthur M. Sschler Gallery, <http://www.asia.si.edu/exhibitions/online/peacock/4.htm>.

"Plarr's Lives of the Fellows," <http://livesonline.rcseng.ac.uk/>.

The Poetry Society, <http://www.poetrysociety.org.uk/content/aboutus/>.

Poirier, Richard, "Robert Frost, The Art of Poetr No. 2," *Paris Review* 24 (Summer–Fall 1960), <http://www.theparisreview.org/ interviews/2678/the-art-of-poetry-no-2-robert-frost>.

Pound, Ezra, "Radio Speeches of World War II," <http:www.whale.to/b/ pound.thml?.

Saint, Andrew, "'Between Farce and Misery,' Review of *The Architect and His Wife: A Life of Edwin Lutyens*," <http:www.guardian.co.uk/ books2002/jul/13/biographyhighereducation1>.

"Victorian London—Publications—Etiquette and Advice Manuals— Dinners and Diners, by Lieut.-Col. Newnham-Davis, 1899—Chapter 22—Dieudonné's (Ryder Street)," <http://www.victorianlondon.org/ publications2/dinners-22.htm>.

Yeats, W. B., *The Collected Letters of W. B. Yeats*, ed. John Kelly (Oxford: Oxford University Press [InteLex Electronic Edition], 2002), <http://www.nlx.com/collections/130>.

"Yone Noguchi (1875–1947)," <http://www.botchanmedia.com/highslide/ examples/Bioshort.htm>.

Index